Irwin H. Hoover.

Forty-Two Years
in the White House

By IRWIN HOOD (IKE) HOOVER, Chief Usher

With Illustrations

Boston and New York
HOUGHTON MIFFLIN COMPANY
The Riverside Press Cambridge

FIRST PRINTING, AUGUST, 1934
SECOND PRINTING, SEPTEMBER, 1934
THIRD PRINTING, SEPTEMBER, 1934

The Riverside Press
CAMBRIDGE · MASSACHUSETTS
PRINTED IN THE U.S.A.

PUBLISHERS' NOTE

IRWIN HOOD HOOVER, known to the world as 'Ike,' was born in Washington, D.C., on October 24, 1871, the son of a grocer. As an employee of the Edison Company, he was sent to the White House on May 6, 1891, to install the first electric lights for the Benjamin Harrisons. He stayed on as permanent electrician, was soon promoted to the ushers' force, and under the Taft Administration was appointed Chief Usher. He held this position until his death on September 14, 1933.

During these forty-two years of service, Ike Hoover had intimate daily contact with ten Presidents, their wives, and their families. As Chief Usher he was the executive head of the household, in charge of all social affairs and entrusted with confidential matters of every description. It was also his duty to welcome guests of the President, to arrange the details of their visits, and — a difficult task — to make them feel at home in the White House.

Mr. Hoover planned to retire in 1935 and publish his reminiscences. At the time of his death he had carried his story through the Taft Administration; the rest of the material, far more copious and detailed, remained in the form of isolated chapters and rough notes. In presenting this material, the publishers have simply arranged it in convenient form, supplied appropriate headings — taken when possible from the text itself — deleted repetitions and irrelevant matter, and changed the original wording only when necessary for the sake of clarity.

CONTENTS

PART I

THE GLORIES OF THE OLD GUARD

PART II

A SPOTLIGHT ON YESTERDAY'S HEROES

PART III

COMPARISONS AND VERDICTS

ILLUSTRATIONS

[xii]

FORTY-TWO YEARS IN THE WHITE HOUSE

.·.

PART I
THE GLORIES OF THE OLD GUARD

Forty-Two Years
in the White House

1

EDISON LIGHTS AND THE HARRISONS

I ACQUIRE A JOB AND A NICKNAME

BENJAMIN HARRISON became President on March 4, 1889. At that time electric lighting was still in the experimental stage. I believe the only public building in Washington that was equipped with it was the old Bureau of Engraving and Printing. A few business houses used electric lights in their windows for advertising purposes, but they were practically unknown to private residences. Congress, however, saw fit to equip the White House and the old State, War, and Navy Building with this novel luxury and appropriated money accordingly. The job of installing was turned over to Admiral Baird, an engineer officer in the Navy. The Admiral, with his meager knowledge of electric light installation, proceeded as best he could with the help at his disposal. The installation included not only the necessary wiring, and so forth, but a generating plant as well. There was no incandescent service from the one small company then operating in the neighborhood of the White House. The old arc lamps on the street were the nearest thing to it. Machines, material, and supplies for the installation had been purchased from the old Edison Electric Company.

The work was started in the State, War, and Navy Building where the generating plant was to be located — and where it still is today. There must have been trouble as the work proceeded, for the Admiral in charge requested the Edison Company to send him two men familiar with electrical apparatus. I was selected as one of the two who were sent in response to this call.

Upon reporting we were asked our names. When I answered, 'I. H. Hoover,' the question was shot back at me: 'Does the "I" stand for "Ike"?' Naturally I answered, 'No,' and told the Admiral that it stood for 'Irwin.' Regardless of this he said, after some pause, 'Ike, you go over to the White House. I will see you later.' He told the other fellow to remain at the State, War, and Navy Building. Thus I became 'Ike' Hoover, and thus began a service of forty-two years, dating from May 6, 1891.

During the course of actual installation, not only were electric lights placed throughout the White House, but also the first electric bells as well. The old mechanical bell for the domestics was operated by wires and pulls from every part of the house, each servant answering to a certain combination of rings. I removed it and held on to it personally for forty years. It was eventually turned over to Mr. Henry Ford for his exhibit of American heirlooms at Dearborn, Michigan. The outside pulls of the old front-door bell remained in place until the house was remodeled by President Roosevelt in 1903. It was the last bit of the old-time call system to go.

THE OLD WHITE HOUSE

According to orders I reported to the White House mechanical department and began looking things over. It was my first visit to that historic building. I had lived in Washington practically all of my twenty years, but had never been within its portals. So one can imagine the thrill I felt! While waiting for definite orders, I looked about in what was then the basement. The floor was covered with damp and slimy brick; dust webs were everywhere. An old wooden heating trough hung the entire length of the ceiling of the long corridor. Everything was black and dirty. Rooms that are now parlors were then used for storage of wood and coal. In the kitchen of the original house, now an engine-room, could be seen the old open fireplaces once used for broiling the chickens and baking the hoecakes for the early Fathers of our country, the old cranes and spits still in place. Out of the door to the rear there yet remained the old wine-vault, the meathouse, and the smokehouse. So vivid were these reminders you could still almost smell the wine odors and the aroma from the hams and bacon that must have been so deliciously and painstakingly prepared here.

Even the outside appearance of the place was so different from the present day. There was no east wing or terrace, as it is called, the original one having disappeared about the time of the fire of 1814. The west wing was hidden almost wholly by the old conservatory that had been built on its top. The dear old conservatory where the couples would roam during parties and be lost among the tall palms and ferns! Here, too, would be stationed the Marine Band with their scarlet coats standing out against the green foliage. Here were all the funny kinds of plants and the tropical fruit trees whose dwarf fruit we were all so proud of. There were bananas, oranges, lemons, figs, and nuts of various kinds; the artillery plant, whose blossoms would burst and send forth a sort of vapor like a cannon-blast; the fly-catching plant, whose tender leaves would curl up when tickled in the center. Westward to the street, in the space now occupied by the Executive Offices, came the various greenhouses: the rose house, the carnation house, the croton house, the orchid house, the camellia house, the propagating house, etc., all to serve the whims of the occupants. These formed a lasting picture of the times and have always been associated in my memory with my first day at the White House.

I BECOME, LIKE THE ELECTRIC LIGHTS, A PERMANENT FIXTURE

In due time I got down to the job of wiring and installing the electric appliances. The wonderful old chandeliers, built for gas, were converted into combination fixtures and the candle wall brackets were replaced by electric fixtures in the fashion of the time. While working through the house, necessarily going into every room, we often ran across the Harrison family.

The Harrisons were all much interested in this new and unusual device that was being installed; so much so, that we got quite well acquainted with them. They gave us much encouragement, and it was a genuine pleasure to be thus surrounded while doing what was, at best, a hard job. By the fifteenth of September, a little over four months after we began, the job was finished, the current turned on, and the White House illuminated with electric lights for the whole world to behold.

I had been notified in advance that I should not be needed after the fifteenth, and had planned to take a little holiday before returning to my old job. To my surprise, in the next day's mail came a letter from the officer in charge of Public Buildings and Grounds inviting me to take on a permanent position as Electrician at the White House to look after the system I had just helped to install. Upon presenting myself, I was a little dismayed to hear that my salary would be a good deal less than what I had received as a temporary employee. But after taking everything into consideration, I accepted the offer and went to work once more.

WHEN EVERYBODY KNEW EVERYBODY ELSE

Of necessity the hours were long, for the Harrison family were actually afraid to turn the lights on and off for fear of getting a shock. They really did not use the lights in their private chambers for a long time. I would turn on the lights in the halls and parlors in the evening and they would burn until I returned the next morning to extinguish them. The family were even timid about pushing the electric bell buttons to call the servants! There was a family conference almost every time this had to be done.

There were not nearly so many employees about the place as there are today. The whole Executive office staff, which was then domiciled in the White House proper, consisted of but ten people, and four of these were doorkeepers and messengers. There was but one bathroom in the entire house, and perhaps not more than half a dozen domestic help. Everybody got to know everybody else well. It was all just like one family.

I remained in the mechanical end of the establishment until 1904, when I was promoted 'upstairs,' as the saying went, and appointed to the ushers' force. Since I had previously been drafted from time to time to serve as an usher, I was no stranger to the job. The new duties brought me even closer to the families and their guests, so that when the Tafts came I was appointed Chief Usher, and have so remained for the twenty-five years since.

A HOMELIKE ADMINISTRATION

The one term of President Harrison was a most simple and homelike affair all the way through. The Harrisons' Hoosier ideas of simplicity, as practiced in their Indianapolis home, were continued at the White House. An eight o'clock breakfast, a one o'clock lunch, and an early dinner were the order of the day. 'Early to bed and early to rise' was truly a motto of this plain, unassuming régime.

Immediately after breakfast all the family would retire to the upper floor and be closeted in one of the rooms for a half-hour of prayer. The entire atmosphere of the household was surcharged with religious feeling during this time. Until this ceremony had been completed, one could not go about one's daily duties without a feeling that prayer was being disturbed. After prayers the President retired immediately to his office, never arriving there later than nine o'clock. Mrs. Harrison proceeded to make her regular inspection of the household and to confer with the steward, who, by the way, played a very important part during this Administration.

The family group was always large. More often than not, both a son and a daughter would have their families in the White House. Then there were nieces and nephews — and even their husbands and wives — staying great lengths of time. In fact the accommodations were very often too small to house the members of the family properly, and doubling up in sleeping quarters was the rule.

The McKees formed a most interesting part of the history of this Administration. The boy, known at the time as 'Baby McKee,' received great publicity in the newspapers and elsewhere because of his supposed intimacy with his grandfather. This was greatly exaggerated, for it was really seldom that one ever saw the President and his grandson together. There was never any actual foundation for the popular belief that the two were inseparable. The President was, judging from everyday observation, a very indifferent and distant person. He was never unkind, but always appeared to be satisfied with himself and willing to be let alone.

President Harrison was an unusually systematic individual. His days varied but little and he never seemed to let his duties worry him in the slightest degree. Very seldom did he work after lunch. It was always an afternoon of leisure — either a long stroll off to the suburbs with his wife's niece,

Bain News Service

BENJAMIN HARRISON

Bain News Service

CAROLINE SCOTT HARRISON

Mrs. Dimmick, or some other young member of the household, or an afternoon in the billiard-room with these same companions. The fact that this room was located in the then very dirty and unsightly basement did not prevent the family from spending many happy hours there. The ladies as well as the men took part in the games and, to all appearances, became quite as expert. The billiard-room was short-lived, however, having been installed during the Arthur Administration and abandoned at the coming of Roosevelt, who did not find the game strenuous enough for him.

GROWING WITH THE CITY

It was during these years that the old house really took on its modern aspect. Prior to the coming of the Harrisons, it had undergone only the routine repairs, except for the addition, about 1825, of the North Portico, which really turned the house entirely around, in so far as entrances were concerned. As originally planned, the south was to be the front, but the growth of the city toward the northwest made an entrance on the north side desirable. So this has grown to be the main entrance, and the south, or original front, has really become the back of the house.

At this time the old basement was in a pitiable condition. Here was the kitchen — and such a kitchen it was! The wonder is how it ever survived all these years. The rest of the floor was used for housing machinery, for storing coal, for sleeping quarters for the colored help, etc. Such was the conglomeration just below where great affairs of state and society were being enacted.

With the coming of the Harrison Administration began the first agitation for a new White House — or Executive Mansion, as it was then called. Many schemes were suggested both for changing the old structure and for erecting a new one, either on the same ground or on some other plot of land, notably at the head of Sixteenth Street.

The Sixteenth Street idea went so far that plans were made and even á model constructed of what was known as 'Mrs. Harrison's place.' This was a very complete job, but the entire idea eventually failed, more for the lack of someone boldly to champion the cause than for any other particular reason. Then again the newspapers universally disapproved of the abolition of what they termed an old landmark. In fact, sentiment was responsible almost entirely for the abandonment of a scheme that at one time seemed on the point of execution.

With the idea of a new house gone, Mrs. Harrison set to work to improve the old place so as to make it habitable. Private bathrooms were installed; the bedroom floor was divided into suites; the kitchen was completely torn out and modernized. Electric lights and bells were installed for the first time. All the old floors — dirty, mouldy bricks — were torn up and replaced with cement and wood; the engine-room was reconstructed; a new area built around the entire house; the old conservatory rebuilt and many new greenhouses added. All the rooms were frescoed and painted, new furnishings were purchased, and in fact everything was done that was possible without destroying the plan of the old place. The change was so great that when the Clevelands came back a few years later, they hardly recognized the house which they had left only four years before.

A SAD FAREWELL

The Harrison Administration was plain and unsensational. All business was transacted during office hours and there were none of the history-making luncheons and dinners that were so numerous in after years.

The Tracy fire, where the wife and daughter of the Secretary of the Navy were burned to death — their funeral held in the famous East Room — was the beginning of a chain

of sad events that seemed to cast a continuous gloom over
everything. The death of Mrs. Harrison's father was followed by the death of the wives of his two secretaries, Mrs.
Halford and Mrs. Pruden, and finally by the death of the
President's own wife just as the election was coming on.

The preparations for leaving were undertaken with a
feeling of relief such as characterized the departure of but
few administrations. The days from November to March
were spent by the family in packing belongings, of which
there was an exceptionally large quantity, and apparently
wishing for the day of departure to arrive. As the day drew
near this feeling seemed to grow stronger, and we were all
relieved when, on the evening of March 3, the Clevelands
arrived for the farewell and introductory dinner. Mrs.
McKee presided in the absence of Mrs. Harrison, who had
gone to her reward, good woman that she was. The reward
must have been in keeping with the spotless life she had led.

In after years the return of this family for social visits
seemed very strange. Mrs. Dimmick came back as Mrs.
Harrison, the wife of the ex-President, with a little baby;
and Mrs. McKee came with her children, Benjamin and
Mary, both grown up.

So closed an administration that goes down in history as
having accomplished nothing startling, yet which left its
imprint everywhere around the White House.

2

YEARS OF GRACE — RETURN OF THE CLEVELANDS

THEY KNEW WHAT THEY WANTED

THE Clevelands returned to the White House after four years of absence with knowledge of how things should be and with the lesson of experience already learned. Knowing just what they wanted, the Clevelands set about to enjoy in their second term some things they evidently had missed in their first.

During the early part of the first Cleveland régime, while the President was still single, his sister, Miss Rose Cleveland, fulfilled the duties of 'First Lady of the Land.' But with his marriage a new light in the firmament made its appearance. The two years or thereabouts in which Mrs. Cleveland presided over the place during this first term but acted as an initiation, giving her, on her second arrival, a feeling of security and confidence. She entered immediately upon the discharge of the necessary duties with her characteristic vim and dash. The much improved condition of the establishment made the task a simpler one than she had expected, but with new attendants in many parts of the house she set about righting things as she saw them. One of her first acts was to discharge practically all of the domestic help; had a cyclone struck this portion of the establishment, it could not have been swept cleaner. The mechanical part of the staff was not so much affected.

More changes were made during the first two or three days of this Administration than at any other time which the oldest employee can remember. With this upheaval past

and the decks cleared for action, things returned to normal
and the family set about enjoying life — that is, so far as
they could when the head of the family had constant demands on his time from every direction.

THE HARDEST WORKER OF THEM ALL

President Cleveland, naturally a hard-working individual,
on many accounts seemed to be the most laborious of all
the Presidents under whom I have served. Breakfast at
nine, lunch at one-thirty, dinner at seven-thirty, were almost
the only breaks in his day. It appeared as if the President
for some reason worked much harder to accomplish the
same results than other men who have occupied the office.
He dictated but little, preferring to write practically everything with his own hand. It was no uncommon thing for
him to remain in his office until two or three o'clock in the
morning, diligently laboring on some important document.
On various occasions he was known to remain there the
entire night working on a message to Congress or something
of the sort which he considered unusually urgent.

His leisure hours were few, and he only grudgingly permitted himself to be coaxed from his office for a walk or a
game of billiards. Occasionally he went for a short drive
with Mrs. Cleveland, but he took no regular or systematic
exercise of any kind. It was for this reason more than any
other that a home was maintained in the suburbs where the
family would always sojourn in early spring, prior to their
visit to their summer home, and again in the fall, before
returning to Washington. This in itself would have accomplished the desired end with most individuals, but not so
with Mr. Cleveland. The ride to and fro each day he considered quite enough leisure, and it was back to a desk
practically as soon as he arrived in his suburban home. The
family did not see much of him. He had little desire for
company and he never seemed to sleep. It was work, work,

work, all the time. He came about as near earning his
salary as any President, if work of that kind is what counts.

His only diversion was his few fishing trips during the
summer season. Of his company he was very choosey and
he seemed to prefer moneyed people. Looking over the
list, one might term it a 'millionaire crowd.' Among others
were the Benedicts, the Morgans, and the Lesters — quite a
trio in themselves.

The Clevelands had but few visitors to stay any length
of time in the house and these of the very highest quality.
An epicure and a connoisseur of wines, he thought nothing
too good for those few who partook of his hospitality. Mrs.
Cleveland was fond of company, but, appreciating the indifference of the President, she had but few resident visitors.
She enjoyed the society of others while the President worked
and never interfered with his business.

A QUEEN IN A BRILLIANT COURT

No more brilliant and affable lady than Mrs. Cleveland
has ever graced the portals of this old mansion. Her very
presence threw an air of beauty on the entire surroundings,
whatever the occasion or the company. A good and faithful
wife, an affectionate and tender mother of a number of
perfect and sweet children, a true friend to everybody that
did halfway right, it was a pleasure even to know her and
an honor to do her bidding.

The much-advertised story about the deformity of the
children was a shame and a farce without a word of truth
in it. The natural tenderness of the mother, which pre-
vented the children from being thrown into the limelight
of publicity, was the only excuse for this absurd and dis-
graceful rumor.

During this time the old house saw more brilliant entertaining than it has ever witnessed before or since: the dinners,
receptions, and other social functions, unusual from every

Keystone View Co.

GROVER CLEVELAND AND FRANCES FOLSOM CLEVELAND

point of view. Here we had a lady who took real pleasure
in seeing people and making them feel at home. At the
public receptions it was the hardest kind of work to keep the
guests from returning for a second greeting. The crowds
were abnormally large, and never has the entire season attracted so many people as during this last term of President
Cleveland. A very large part of the credit must be given to
the charming personality of Mrs. Cleveland. Not alone from
a social angle were her gifts remarkable. Daily she watched
and looked after her little ones as only a mother can, not
from a lack of help — for more domestic help was around
during their time than usually — but from maternal choice.
Also her solicitude for the President was charming to behold.
She would watch over him as if he were one of the children.
Never would she permit herself to be placed first; always
it was he. This was particularly noticeable when they would
leave the house. It was always the President who must
enter the carriage first, and no matter how much he protested — which he did — it was always he first and she after.

To the employees about the house they were considerate
and kind. The President had little to say to anybody, but
that little was always friendly. Mrs. Cleveland had a sympathetic word for everybody. She took an interest in every
employee and little tokens of esteem around Christmas or
on a birthday have been and ever will be treasured as price-
less heirlooms. Mrs. Cleveland's geniality might best be
described by mentioning one occasion when she returned
to the house unexpectedly and found several of her girl help
in the library with the fireman, a German of considerable
musical talent, banging away on the piano while the girls
danced. Did she rave and discharge those whom she knew
were taking advantage of her absence to violate the unwritten rules? Not at all. On the contrary, after relieving
their embarrassment with a look of reassurance, she insisted
on the continuation of the fun while she seated herself
comfortably and looked on.

With an intimate knowledge of how things should and should not be done in the White House and knowing how best to enjoy life there, it is a fact, nevertheless, that the Clevelands spent less time in the place than any other administration. It was off to the suburbs in the early spring, with just a drive in for a few hours each day, weather permitting. To the summer home about the middle of June, returning to the suburbs again about the first of September and remaining there often until well on to the time for the New Year's reception, which marked the official opening of the social season.

CHILDREN AND FLOWERS

The Cleveland children were very interesting and much beloved by everyone around the place. We often wished that more of them had been born in the White House; of the three there during the last term but one, Esther, was a White House product. She of course was considered just a little more interesting on that account. Of all the children discussed in these pages, none have been so loved and admired by the White House household as these three little Clevelands.

The old conservatory being still in place, it was one of Mrs. Cleveland's favorite pastimes to stroll here with her children and enjoy the fruits and flowers. The collection at the time was an elaborate one, for both she and Mrs. Harrison, who had preceded her, were great lovers of flowers. Mrs. Cleveland's favorite blossom was the pansy. Colonel Pruden, then Assistant Secretary and also an artist, would often make her happy by sketching blossoms that the head gardener told him she had particularly admired and presenting the sketch to her as a surprise gift.

Mrs. Cleveland was always warm in her appreciation of anything of this kind and never failed to make known her admiration and approval of things that pleased her and her family. Her praise stimulated us to even greater effort, and made us all very fond of her indeed.

Mrs. Taft seemed to have no particular choice; to her all flowers were alike so long as they were bright of hue.

The flowers that cost the most in any season were always Miss Alice Roosevelt's choice!

The first Mrs. Wilson preferred colonial flowers; the second Mrs. Wilson, orchids. To Mrs. Harding flowers were just flowers.

Mrs. Harrison's favorite flower was the orchid, and it was principally during her time that the very large and rare collection was accumulated. Since then it has practically gone to pieces from neglect, and the former collection of thousands of plants is but a shadow of its former self.

Mrs. McKinley liked roses of all kinds and President McKinley's love for the carnation has become a national remembrance. Mrs. Roosevelt liked the varieties that bordered on the wild flowers, and any kind of flower, no matter how insignificant, so long as it had been found in the woods, was something for her to rave over.

The Cleveland Administration, in spite of the short time spent in the White House, was a most interesting one, for everything was done with a vim and a dash that bespoke knowledge of how great things should be. When the time drew near for its close, there was a feeling of sadness among all of us. This applied as much to the family as to the hired help. Many changes had taken place during the four years, and looking back over this time it seemed as if it had been a continual case of moving about. The family now consisted of five instead of the three that arrived four years before, the additions being Esther, who was born in the White House, and Marion, who first saw the light of day at Buzzard's Bay.

It was, I believe, no secret that the news of Mr. McKinley's election was very welcome, particularly in comparison with the possibility of Mr. Bryan's success. Every nerve was strained during the period of election in hoping the former would succeed.

The preparations for leaving were gone though as on many other occasions and there was an unusually large amount of stuff to be packed. The Clevelands were liberal people and in return were just showered with all kinds of gifts. These ranged from scented toothpicks to all sorts of household effects, including an abundance of furniture, wines, cigars, mineral waters, curios, and in fact about everything one could imagine being sent to a President — and many other things that no sensible person could ever imagine being sent.

The time arriving again for the welcoming and farewell dinner but small preparations were made, word having been sent ahead that Mrs. McKinley's condition would make elaborate entertaining impossible. At the last minute we were told that she would not be able to attend at all.

At the appointed time in walked the President-to-be, alone and unaccompanied. The President and Mrs. Cleveland and the President-elect were the only ones at dinner. This last was really the simplest dinner of all those during the entire four years!

As is the custom, the preparations were made for leaving at about eleven o'clock. The committee from Congress having come to escort the President and President-elect to the Capitol, Mrs. Cleveland sent word throughout the house that she would like to say good-bye to everyone. There was no need for a second suggestion, for we all gathered at once on the second floor and there, many with tears in our eyes, we said farewell. The late comers found Mrs. Cleveland seated at one of the far windows, where, without being observed, she could watch the party leaving from the front door. This charming and beautiful mistress, who had up to this time been calm and self-controlled, now gave way to her natural feelings and wept as if her heart would break. As if endeavoring to explain the cause of her sudden change, she could but say that what moved her was not so much getting out of the Presidency, so to speak, as leaving the surroundings to which she had come practically a girl, and was now leaving a mature woman. So she departed, composing herself and leaving by the south door as soon as the party for the Capitol had left by the north. Thus we said farewell to one of the most brilliant and interesting families ever to have occupied the White House.

3

THE TRAGIC ADMINISTRATION OF McKINLEY

A CONSISTENT MARTYR

FROM the very beginning of the McKinley Administration a feeling of worry and agitation prevailed at the White House. Especially was this true of the President himself. His invalid wife occupied every moment he could take from work. The rumblings of war sounded in his ears, in spite of his attempt not to notice them. All this and much more led us in the household to believe that the President was never without the burden of worry.

His geniality in the face of it all was the charming effect of his kindly and beautiful nature. No one could help being at ease in his presence. It was his one idea in life to make those around him feel he was their friend. His features instantly impressed one with their kindly expression, and with a warm handshake or a gentle touch on the shoulder he could win the heart of anyone he met.

His days all the year around varied but little. He had practically no recreation. It was either work and worry or a continual endeavor to make the existence of Mrs. McKinley livable. To this latter cause he was a martyr. Many, many times when he could have found other diversion he would tie himself to her presence and abandon the world. Her peculiar kind of trouble kept her in a constant state of wanting. This did not deter the President, for the satisfaction of her every whim and desire was his very existence and nothing was ever suggested by her but what he made an effort to see it done. His only real diversion was his cigar.

This fact being known to his friends and acquaintances, they would vie with each other in an attempt to please him. He had an unlimited stock of all kinds and varieties, the best that money could buy, and yet it was his custom to smoke those of his own buying. Only on rare occasions would he indulge in those which had been presented to him. These, he said, were for his friends to smoke, and no doubt very often someone had passed to him the very cigar he had intended the President should enjoy.

DOMESTIC LAISSEZ-FAIRE

With the coming of the McKinleys the house practically ran itself. Owing to the President's solitary habits and Mrs. McKinley's ill-health, there was no general head of the household. Everybody in a sense was his own boss. Yet things went along well, for we were all old hands at the game. It was at this time that the office of Secretary to the President was created. Prior to the coming of Mr. John Addison Porter, the position had merely been one of private secretary to the President. With Mr. Porter it was different. He considered his position on an equality with that of a cabinet officer. Fine gentleman that he was, he did not last long. Worry, work, and sickness soon got the best of him. Mr. George B. Cortelyou then came into the limelight for the first time as an office-holder. His career was brilliant and his holdings of office numerous. However, the position of Secretary to the President has never attained the prominence Mr. Porter had intended it should, though it has naturally remained one of high dignity and influence.

So it was all through the Administration. There was nothing startling in the line of household reforms. The President remained in his office practically all day, with the exception of mealtimes, and Mrs. McKinley ate by herself in the sitting-room on the second floor, quietly whiling away the time knitting or engrossed in thoughts that were kept strictly to herself. Perhaps she would go for a short drive in the afternoon or a friend might come in to sit for a while. The President might accompany her on one of the drives if he could spare time from the office, but more often the maid would be her only companion. In the evenings friends of the President would often drop in for an hour or two to chat and smoke while Mrs. McKinley would sit quietly by, apparently enjoying herself.

'T. R.' URGES WAR WITH SPAIN

But all was not so serene. From practically the beginning, first one and then another caller would broach the subject of war with Spain — a subject that seemed repulsive to the President and which he always avoided in its earlier stages, looking more than bored when it was brought up. However, the increasing importance of the topic finally obliged him to allow it to be discussed. Good listener as he was, he now had plenty to listen to. Noteworthy among these discussions was the one just a few nights after the destruction of the *Maine*. The Secretary of the Navy being absent from the city, and some important dispatches arriving from the scene of trouble, it devolved upon the then Assistant Secretary of the Navy, Mr. Theodore Roosevelt, to acquaint the President with their contents. This, upon his arrival, he proceeded to do, the President having left Mrs. McKinley and come out into the corridor where he would not be disturbed. Roosevelt's manner of presenting the dispatches made a deep impression upon everyone. He started in by reading their contents, both men being seated on a divan. So far the meeting was placid enough. At the completion of the reading they discussed the matters mentioned. The fact is Mr. Roosevelt did most of the discussing, at first merely rising to make his words the more forcible and then striding up and down until his route took in the entire corridor, which measures perhaps fifty or sixty feet

The New York Evening Journal, August 2, 1900

WILLIE AND HIS PAPA

One of a famous series of cartoons by F. Opper

in length. Never once did he stop talking. He knew his subject, and if gestures and loud words were any criterion he knew what the ultimate result of the discussion would be.

Mr. McKinley all this while did little except encourage Mr. Roosevelt with a word or a gesture until finally the latter, apparently exhausted, picked up his papers to depart. As Mr. McKinley arose to accompany him to the door, he was heard to inquire what he (Mr. Roosevelt) would do in view of all the circumstances. With a sharp turn on his heels he fairly screamed, 'Mr. President, I would order the whole American Navy to Cuba tonight if I had my way,' and left without any pretense of saying good-night.

'GOD BLESS YOU, MY BOYS'

Quite different was the scene a few weeks later when Leonard Wood and Mr. Roosevelt came to say good-bye just before their departure for the West to organize the now famous Rough Riders. Upon leaving on this last occasion, Mr. McKinley, not content with saying good-bye in his office, walked all the way downstairs and out to the front door. As they were leaving he placed a hand on each of the men's shoulders and, so that all might hear, said in a loud voice, 'God bless you, my boys.' Turning away he saw other moist eyes besides his own, for there were at least two dozen individuals who had been silent witnesses to this parting scene. Among them were a number of newspaper correspondents. They considered the episode so personal that one and all agreed not to publish any account of it.

FIGHTING A WAR FROM AN ARMCHAIR

So began the rumblings of the coming conflict with Spain, which formed, of course, the most exciting and interesting part of this Administration. The situation was tense and at times nerve-racking. The oft-repeated visits of the various

officials, both before and after the actual declaration of
hostilities, were most interesting to observe. Come as they
would at all hours of the day and night, they always seemed
to leave with disappointed looks on their faces. Apparently
they could arouse no enthusiasm in the mind of the President, for his one determination seemed to be to avert the
war if it were possible. Not being able to do so, however, he
made his plans sadly and always appeared to be quite willing
not only to listen to, but to accept, the suggestions of others
about the course to pursue. The business of waging the
war was carried on in a most matter-of-fact way. Maps were
arranged with countless little flags to denote the position
of this vessel or that regiment. Information came direct to
this map-room from all parts of the world, and it was really
from here that the war was fought. It was the custom of
the President to retire to this room at almost any time and
sit for hours studying these maps.

FISH TO FRY

If anyone found aught but worry during all these visits,
he possessed a keener perception than I. The visits of those,
sometimes high in council, who had fish to fry, in the way
of selling the Government various things that could be used
in connection with the war, were one of the worst annoy-
ances. The scandals and suspicions which arose afterwards
were but the inevitable outcome of what occurred during
the war.

It was a habit of the President during this time to lead
visitors to the window of his office which looked out over
the Potomac. After listening to them patiently, he would
divert attention from their mission by recalling the days when
he himself fought through the Civil War and, pointing with
pride to the land toward the south which had been the scene
of action, he would tell them he knew only too well what
war was. These scenes were enacted day after day with that

kind, gentle, fatherly way of Mr. McKinley's which made all comers feel he was their friend, but left a doubt in their minds as to the substantial result that they had come to accomplish. Many were unsuccessful; but others with more backing did succeed, for which the President afterwards expressed many regrets.

With the termination of hostilities and the signing of the peace treaty, he seemed to come back to himself again. The rows and insinuations following the war he took greatly to heart. No one more than he felt the sting of the publicity given to these shortcomings, especially in the face of the glorious victories achieved. He swallowed his feelings, however, and tried to resume the domestic happiness which had existed before the war.

It was during this period, and this period alone, that anyone ever saw him in the least indifferent toward Mrs. McKinley. During part of this time, it would have been a physical impossiblity for him to have maintained his former solicitous attitude. He would be literally dragged away from her by the clamorous demands of one person or another for a confidential talk. These insistent visitors came so thick and fast at one period — just after the appropriation of fifty millions was made for finishing hostilities — that he hardly had time to eat or sleep.

'THE KING IS DEAD, LONG LIVE THE KING!'

But it all ended at last and the worry of properly safeguarding the result was all that remained. While this in itself was a vast undertaking, it did not appear at the time to be the enormous responsibility that it later became. A rest had been well earned. If consideration and anxiety go for anything, Mr. McKinley had won a crown for himself. Back again to the old routine with conditions changed, he set about doing what seemed to him best.

The summer found him at the Buffalo Exposition, where

he became the victim of an assassin's bullet. The news spread, and everyone in the White House stood aghast. Hour after hour and day after day everyone waited, hoping and praying. Not a word was printed that was not read and re-read, in addition to the messages that were sent from the sick-bed direct to the White House. But in vain; the end came, and it was with a sad heart and a tearful eye that all turned to prepare for the final farewell in the great East Room, where so many great scenes had taken place. Not only this, but preparations for the new President had to be made. Short notice; but the old principle of 'The King is Dead, Long Live the King!' must prevail.

The body was returned, laid out in the famous East Room, and a military guard placed over it day and night while it remained. One of these men actually collapsed in sheer exhaustion from the strain of events. The funeral, with its solemn line of carriages to the Capitol, was one of the saddest events I have ever witnessed. There has never been such a funeral before or since from this grand old mansion. The flowers had to be hauled away by the truckload. The house could not possibly hold them and the people too. Thousands came, but few were admitted.

So ended the Administration of William McKinley. And so ended a beautiful life in the midst of universal sorrow and mourning. The story of his last moments is so well known that it will hardly bear repetition, especially since it is something about which I have little first-hand knowledge. Judging, however, from all authentic reports his last moments were spent, like his whole life, in peace and kindliness toward all mankind. But with the ending of these beautiful days and thoughts comes another and more interesting administration.

WILLIAM McKINLEY

IDA McKINLEY IN THE GOWN SHE
WORE AT HER INAUGURAL BALL

4

KEEPING UP WITH THE ROOSEVELTS

A WALTZ AND TWO-STEP

PROBABLY no administration has ever taken such a curious hold upon the people as that of Theodore Roosevelt. It made no difference where you turned, it was the same. Every little event concerning any of the family, from the highest to the lowest (if there were any of the latter), was broadcast through the newspapers. No family have ever been written up so much; and the strange part of it was that while the newspapers exaggerated the stories about other Presidential families, in the case of the Roosevelts they had to tone down the facts for fear of being disbelieved! News was always abundant, and it was a poor reporter indeed who did not pick up a column or two any day during these strenuous times.

One might have expected that the Roosevelts, coming in under such tragic conditions, would have been hesitant and subdued. On the contrary, from the day of their arrival they displayed the characteristics which were to distinguish their entire administration.

To those around the White House who had a personal recollection of Mr. Roosevelt as Civil Service Commissioner and later as Assistant Secretary of the Navy, his bold step of taking up his residence in the place so soon after the funeral of Mr. McKinley was no surprise. They vividly pictured him coming in — as he had on many occasions as Commissioner and as Assistant Secretary — and going upstairs two steps at a time expounding his positive ideas in a manner that permitted of no contradiction. As had been expected, it was a continual two-step and spirited waltz for seven and one half years. The music varied, but the pace never ceased.

A nervous person had no business around the White House in those days. He was sure to be a wreck in a very short time. This was not due to any harsh treatment, but to the novel way the Roosevelts had of accomplishing things. The unexpected was always to be looked for. Everything was at least a little different from what it had been.

After the McKinley funeral, Mr. Roosevelt himself did not appear for several days; but in the meantime Mrs. Roosevelt and her son Teddy arrived. After looking the place over, they sent word to the others to join them and in less than a week all the family were living in their new quarters. Then began the wildest scramble in the history of the White House. The children, hearty and full of spirits, immediately proceeded to cut loose.

FAVORITE STUNTS OF THE ROOSEVELT CHILDREN

The life of the employees who took their responsibilities too seriously was made miserable. The children left no nook or corner unexplored. From the basement to the flagpole on the roof, every channel and cubbyhole was thoroughly investigated. Places that had not seen a human being for years were now made alive with the howls and laughter of these newcomers. The house became one general playground for them and their associates. Nothing was too sacred to be used for their amusement and no place too good for a playroom. The children seemed to be encouraged in these ideas by their elders, and it was a brave man indeed who would dare say no or suggest putting a stop to these escapades.

One of the favorite stunts of the children was to crawl through the space between ceilings and floors where no living being but rats and ferrets had been for years. They took delight also in roller-skating and bicycle-riding all over the house, especially on the smooth hardwood floors. Practically every member of the family, with the exception of the President and Mrs. Roosevelt, had a pair of wooden stilts, and no stairs were too well carpeted or too steep for their climbing, no tree too high to scramble to the top, nor fountain too deep to take a dip, no furniture too good or too high to use for leapfrog and horseplay, no bed was too expensive or chair too elegantly upholstered to be used as a resting-place for the various pets in the household.

Giving the pony a ride in the elevator was but one of many stunts. This little fellow, spotted and handsome, had free access to any of the children's bedrooms. By means of the elevator he would be conveyed to the bedroom floor from the basement, a distance of two complete floors. As the children grew, there grew with them the idea on the part of the staff that such a situation was really necessary to the proper conduct of things. In fact it seemed as natural to the daily life of the White House as it was for an officer to arrest a crank or for the cook to prepare the meals.

These indeed were interesting days. The two smaller children, Archie and Quentin, were mere babies. Ethel and Kermit were about the same age and were inseparable, one just as daring as the other and Ethel not willing to permit Kermit to outdo her in any respect. The escapades of these two alone would set any household agog.

Alice and Teddy completed the younger part of the household, and, while both had their share of fun, it must be said they were the more subdued upon their arrival. Alice appeared more sedate than in after years. Ted seemed quiet enough, but, as time wore on, he too got his share in the way of sport and amusement.

'NONE HAVE HAD MORE FUN'

But to leave the younger set and proceed to the daily life of these exciting times. Immediately upon the Roosevelts' arrival the usual household changes were begun; only in this case they were more numerous and more radical than ever before. Instead of moving a piece of furniture here and there, whole rooms were changed outright. Where one bed might have been before, two were now placed, and *vice versa*. The children were assigned to convenient apartments and all settled down to enjoy the White House to the utmost. As the President was heard to remark just before finally leaving, 'Perhaps others have lived longer in the place and enjoyed it quite as much; but none have ever really had more fun out of it than we have.'

That describes best the everyday life of the Roosevelts. From the hour of rising in the morning, plans were immediately prepared as to how best to enjoy the day. Meal hours, office hours, school hours, were all subject to change to fit in with these plans. Nothing was ever known to interfere — neither weather, company, business, nor anything else.

THE STRENUOUS LIFE

These pastimes took on all forms. First and foremost, of course, were the horseback rides. Every member of the family was an expert rider, and the President never seemed so happy as when either Mrs. Roosevelt or one of the children accompanied him on his ride. Next perhaps might be mentioned his lawn tennis games. It was great sport for him to figure just whom he preferred to play with in the afternoon. Of course none dared refuse the invitation, but it was well known that a poor player was never invited a second time. His favorites seemed to be Garfield, Pinchot, and Murray; but Bacon, Jusserand, and Meyer were close up, while experts like McCawley and Hurstman were only invited when he was feeling especially good. No sport seemed to be amiss in this family. Boxing, wrestling, fencing, running, and walking were among the President's favorite diversions.

Entering upon the daily routine, we found the entire family down to breakfast at eight o'clock. After breakfast the President spent an hour or so in his study, perhaps reading, while Mrs. Roosevelt arranged the details of the day's program. The President went to his office at nine-thirty or ten o'clock, and Mrs. Roosevelt for a walk or shopping, often accompanied by her secretary or one of her many friends.

All returned just about in time for lunch. Those famous lunches! Something indeed was wrong when there were not two or more guests for this meal. To prepare properly for a certain number was almost a physical impossibility, for notice was continually coming from the office that someone had been invited at the last minute, and many times the family and guests had to wait until the table was made larger before they could be seated. The place was really a transient boarding-house, and how everyone got enough to eat was the wonder of the household. Lunch being over, the rest of the afternoon was given over to sport — 'Exercise' as the President used to call it.

At one time it would be the famous Mike Donovan engaging in battles royal with the President and taking on one of the boys for a side issue. Then again it would be Joe Grant, the famous District champion wrestler, who would spend two or three hours at a time trying his prowess with the head of the nation and giving his points to the younger ones. Then again there would be broadsword battles with General Wood and others and games of medicine ball with Garfield and Pinchot.

AMERICAN WRESTLING VS. JAPANESE JUJITSU

Not content with these ordinary playtimes, the President took up jujitsu and put in two full seasons learning this famous art of self-defense. Upon one occasion, not knowing just which was preferable from a defensive standpoint, he decided to try out the two schemes of American wrestling and Japanese jujitsu. The most expert exponent of the Japanese art and the wrestler Grant were to test their respective merits before the President and a few especially invited guests. The idea aroused great enthusiasm, and when the time came for the meeting the excitement was intense.

The men came together. The President was to be the referee and to decide upon some common ground on which they might meet. Two such different methods could hardly meet on any fair basis, but the President made a rule whereby, if either man was taking an unfair advantage, he would clap his hands as a signal that hostilities should cease.

So it began. First one and then the other would attempt to get a hold, but a clap of the hands would signify that it was considered not fair to the opponent. Finally the Jap grabbed the American by the shoulders, threw his feet up into the American's stomach and away went Grant over the Japanese's head in a heap on the floor. Quick as a flash Grant was up and before the Japanese knew what had happened, Grant had a hold on him and pinned him to the floor as if he had been nailed there.

In the meantime the referee had forgotten all about the clapping of hands and was so pleased at the last maneuver of Grant that he began telling those present how it all happened. Nothing more could be done, since the Japanese could not move until told by the referee to do so. Afterwards the Japanese claimed that he could have accomplished wonders in the way of breaking bones, etc., but it had been thoroughly demonstrated to Mr. Roosevelt's satisfaction that the game of American wrestling surpassed the Japanese art. So he was happy.

On another occasion famous Chinese wrestlers gave an exhibition of their prowess in the East Room, which had been especially prepared for the occasion. These were the big fellows and, quite different from the jujitsu people, they depended upon their strength alone. It was a very interesting

A ROOSEVELT FAMILY GROUP

affair and was witnessed by fifty or sixty guests including cabinet members, Senators, and a few others. This was a wholly Chinese contest and, while Mr. Roosevelt expressed offhandedly a wish to take on one of the big fellows, he did not try it.

So it went. Nothing seemed too absurd in the way of exercise and sport. Those employed around the house vied with each other to be the first to get the information of the day's doings.

NO EXCUSES ACCEPTED

In more serious matters, great stress was laid on the fact that everything must be just right down to the smallest detail. No excuse would be accepted for the slightest error of omission or commission. Everything must be perfect. This led to a state of efficiency that was a pleasure to behold. While the demand was in a measure severe, still the thanks were so profuse that one felt amply repaid for both work and worry.

QUIET EVENINGS AT HOME

The Roosevelt family did not care a great deal about elaborate entertaining. Yet the most minute details were gone into in arranging the necessary social affairs. The formalities were so keenly observed that they were sometimes tiresome to everyone rather than pleasant or brilliant.

It was more to the liking of the family to spend a quiet evening in the library, either playing cards or reading the current magazines. The whole family were fiends when it came to reading. No newspapers. Never a moment was allowed to go to waste; from the oldest to the youngest they always had a book or a magazine before them. The President in particular would just devour a book, and it was no uncommon thing for him to go entirely through three or four volumes in the course of an evening. Likewise we fre-

quently saw one of the children stretched out on the floor
flat on his stomach eating a piece of candy and with his face
buried deep in a book. The current magazines were entirely
too slow coming out, and we were kept busy trying to get
them for the different members of the family the moment
they appeared. And yet the Roosevelts were early birds,
both in retiring and arising. Very seldom, unless something
special was on hand, did they go to bed later than ten-thirty.
In going out to dinner they made it a rule to make their departure promptly at ten o'clock. Then home and immediately to their bedrooms.

MISS ALICE'S WEDDING

The only exception was 'Miss Alice,' as she was known
throughout the household. She, of course, went in for society to the limit and was never known to be home in the
evening except for official social affairs. It can reasonably be
asserted that no one within the recollection of the oldest in-
habitant was ever entertained so much as she was. For at
least two years before her marriage there was never an evening when there was not some party being given in her honor.
Sunday was no exception to the rule. It would be a wizard
indeed who could with any degree of satisfaction state just
when she went to bed and when she got up.

This went on up to the wedding day. Preparations were
made for it months in advance. Every detail was worked out
to perfection. Weeks before the day, presents of every kind
and description began to arrive. The highest and the lowest
alike sent along their remembrances. There was simply
everything. The presents were not confined to those receiving invitations alone, but thousands of individuals and firms
sent along their wares in honor of the occasion. Some of these
were simply gorgeous and others were ridiculous. A paper of
pins from some old lady, a hogshead of popcorn from a
manufacturing firm, a box of snakes from a collector, fancy

cakes innumerable, gold, silver, cut-glass diamonds, pearls, household appliances such as brooms, feather dusters, washing machines, etc., furniture, heirlooms, books by the score and precious stones of every description. As one individual remarked, 'it is enough to make one an anarchist,' for it was entirely too much to be given to one person.

For the wedding itself, seven hundred invitations were supposed to have been issued and nearly that number attended. The ceremony was held in the large East Room, where elaborate arrangements had been made.[1] The wedding march began in the dining-room on the opposite side of the house. Everything went off as planned, and when the ceremony, which took place at high noon, was over, the rioting and sport began. The breakfast-room and dining-room were immediately thrown open, and from that time on it was one continual round of good time and good cheer. No other meals were served in the house the entire day, for the domestic help seemed to be taking just as much part in the celebrating as did the most favored guests. This was one occasion when everybody was in a measure on equal terms and was amply and fully supplied with all the inner man might desire.

BUSINESS AT MEALS

A great custom of this Administration was the conduct of business at mealtimes and in the evening after dinner. It seems to have originated with Roosevelt. The President frequently had three or four guests to dinner, and as soon as the meal was finished he turned them over to the other members of the family while he himself filled additional appointments in the various parlors before bedtime. It was at these

[1] We have always said that I could never have gotten married without (Ike) Hoover. He was a White House fixture. What he could have told about the daily existence and personal behavior of the White House occupants whom he had seen come and go would make entertaining and illuminating reading. (Alice Roosevelt Longworth, *Crowded Hours*, p. 112.)

appointments in the evening that President Roosevelt really showed to the best advantage. There was infinite variety in the topics of conversation, yet he was clearly a master of any subject he tackled.

WHY WE ADMIRED THE ROOSEVELTS

No one could possibly be around Roosevelt for any great length of time without becoming an enthusiastic admirer. Short acquaintance prompted you to believe that he was more often *assuming* than sincere; but you could not go on seeing him day after day without realizing that he was perfectly genuine. The little courtesies counted with him quite as much as the greater ones. It was a common practice for him to go all over the house saying good-bye on leaving or for a greeting upon returning from a trip.

Around Christmas-time and on birthdays nothing was considered more important than a little remembrance of some kind. These were presented with all the formality of royalty and had a most delightful effect upon the entire household. Again in the case of sickness, either of the employees or of members of their families, it was quite customary to receive a dainty dish of some kind prepared in the White House kitchen by order of either the President or Mrs. Roosevelt.

Mrs. Roosevelt was a most domestic person. While an abundance of help was always at hand, still she looked after every detail of the household herself. She did not care for the limelight, leaving that to other members of the family, but she took great pride and pleasure in all the arrangements. It was most amusing at times to hear her discussing with the President the details of domestic affairs. Though he had absolutely no inclination to hear about them, he showed a patience and a forbearance which was a tribute to his character and the secret of the absolute harmony that always prevailed between them.

THE FEMALE CABINET

It was Mrs. Roosevelt who inaugurated the idea of the female cabinet meetings. Once a week at her invitation the wives of the cabinet members would assemble in the library of the house and discuss affairs that pertained to the female branch of the Administration. Naturally reputations were made and unmade, for it is no secret that these leading ladies of the land were not conspicuously different from others when it came to gossip. Knitting was a great subject on these occasions. Mrs. Roosevelt always took the initiative and many complicated and unheard-of stitches were explained by one or the other, to the advantage of all. So as time wore on everyone took these unusual doings as a matter of course. Particularly after Mr. Roosevelt's re-election there was a more confident air about everything that was done.

WHO SHALL SUCCEED TO THE THRONE?

This confidence was no doubt partly due to the absence of political ambitions for the future. Everyone knew, however, that the President was eagerly looking around for a worthy successor. He seemed worried as the time approached when he would have to decide on whom he would bestow the support of his great personality and political strength. There is no doubt, from all remarks and indications, that he looked upon Mr. Root, then his Secretary of State, with longing eyes and that he would have done anything within his power to have made Mr. Root President.

It was a long time before he finally decided that it should be Mr. Taft. Many things were weighed pro and con. It was true that once he decided to appoint Mr. Taft to the Supreme Court. Mr. Taft himself approved, and it was only through the pleadings of Mrs. Taft that he was not appointed. I can remember the exact hour of the famous visit when Mrs.

Taft, in the face of the opposition of both the President and her husband, then Secretary of War, carried her point. From that time on the President seemed to feel that Mr. Taft should be his successor, and while in his mind he weighed others and mentioned others to his friends, still he seemed to feel that Taft must be the man.

'T. R.' ON THE FIELD OF BATTLE

Then it was that the bulldog tenacity and fierceness of his friendship showed to best advantage. He found opposition along this line even among some of his closest and best friends, but he rode over them all rough shod. It was a pleasure to see him take up the gauntlet for Mr. Taft and fight to a finish. He had never been so fierce when fighting his own battle four years previously. He would stand for no quarter. As time went on he thought of nothing else. His every move was with a view of promoting Mr. Taft's interest, and nothing seemed to please him better than getting into a war of words for the cause so dear to his heart. But the sad part of the whole affair was that this situation could not go on indefinitely. Mr. Taft being elected, almost immediately there seemed to spring from some unknown source the coolness that was so often noticed in after months. During the campaign Mr. Roosevelt had assured all the employees at the White House who saw fit to inquire that their positions would be safe in case Mr. Taft was elected. So everyone felt confidence born of a winner when finally he was elected.

THE BITTER BREAK WITH TAFT

However, seeing this coolness growing and hearing things as one will, some of the household became nervous and again inquired. Now they were told that, whereas before they had been all right, things had recently taken on a sudden change and no assurance could be given for the future. Ali were told if they desired transfer to another department it would be arranged. It was not suggested but merely mentioned and some took advantage of the offer.

As inauguration day approached, relations between Roosevelt and Taft reached the stage of a positive break. There remained some semblance of pretended admiration on both sides, but it can truthfully be said that there has seldom been such bitterness between an incoming and an outgoing administration. This applies to the entire families.

The cause was appointments. Nothing more, nothing less. Mr. Roosevelt made certain recommendations which after much consideration Mr. Taft ignored. This in a nutshell was the cause of all the trouble. From it grew the painful situation in after years. Mr. Roosevelt always felt that he had been wronged. Mr. Taft, while still believing he was in the right, always possessed a conciliatory disposition, but never made any headway in his efforts to renew the former friendship. So ended a most beautiful alliance.

Knowing both of them as I do, I do not wonder it could not last. Such a difference in two individuals would be hard to find. One the most daring, fiery, indifferent person you could imagine; the other meek, quiet, painstaking to a fault. What could you expect? And so closed this seven and one half years of wonderful events.

There seemed to be no general regret in the Roosevelt family at leaving the White House. They all accepted it as a matter of course and did not murmur. They gave remembrances to all of those who had served them so faithfully and had an affectionate adieu for everyone. As for the President himself, he was content. He had his African trip all planned and was happy in the thought of it. His one regret was that, to his mind, he had made a mistake in naming his successor.

5

FOUR YEARS OF STRIFE

SORE SPOTS IN THE NEW RÉGIME

SO THE day arrived for the change. What had been looked forward to as a pleasant event now dawned as an affair of the most formal kind. This was the beginning of what might be called the administration of four years of strife. From one source or another there seemed ever to be a mix-up. I have already mentioned the feud that had recently sprung up between President Roosevelt and President-elect Taft and that seemed so ominous to the employees whose positions were at stake. The appearance at this time of the 'Insurgency Cause' also aroused concern. Another reason for unrest, which struck even closer to those about the White House, was the more than ordinary influence that was to be exerted by the female members of the household. At the very start, precedent was thrown to the winds, and Mrs. Taft decided to share the honors of the inauguration ceremonies with the President. Her insistence that she ride in the same carriage with him on his return from the Capitol, after taking the oath of office, aroused very severe criticism. However, it was but a shadow of events that were to come.

'I'M TIRED OF BEING KICKED AROUND'

The period between the election and the inauguration seemed to have told on Taft more than the campaign itself. During the campaign he was in and out of the White House seeking advice and guidance of President Roosevelt, always jolly and in good humor, quite satisfied with himself and the way things were going. Between the election and the inauguration we did not see much of him, although we heard a great deal. So when he came on the fourth of March we noticed what a change had come over him. He had lost much of his good nature and seemed cross and uncomfortable — very different from his former self. Upon his return to the White House from the reviewing stand, he threw himself into a large comfortable chair, stretched out to his full length and prefaced his first order with the remark,

'I am President now, and tired of being kicked around.'

We often recalled this remark in the four years that followed.

MRS. TAFT: HOUSEKEEPER AND POLITICIAN

From the very beginning Mrs. Taft played a prominent part in the Administration, not alone in the domestic sphere, but in official matters as well. It was no uncommon thing to see her taking part in political and official conferences. As for the White House itself, she made plans to revolutionize the place. She seemed to have forgotten entirely that the White House is, in a measure, a public institution, and made an effort to conduct it along the lines of a private household. The force of employees was reduced to what was considered a minimum working basis. The police guard, which had been stationed at the main entrance for a century, was replaced by colored footmen, who were domestic servants pure and simple. Parts of the house previously open to the public were now closed off and maintained exclusively for private use — or at least only to be seen by a favored few. A housekeeper was to take general charge of things instead of the traditional steward. In fact every detail of management was to be radically changed. There just seemed to be a disposition to change things for the sake of changing, as if there were no possibility that anything had been conducted properly before this time.

Fortunately, circumstances stepped in to prevent many of the plans becoming actualities, others failed of their own weight. Many things that had been disarranged were restored to where they belonged. Some schemes failed of execution owing to the illness of Mrs. Taft soon after the beginning of the Administration. Yet others remained through the entire four years, but few survived the coming of other families.

A familiar sight about this time was Speaker Cannon consulting jointly with the President and Mrs. Taft. Mrs. Taft seemed always to be present and taking a leading part in the discussions. At large social gatherings a guest would often entice the President to a corner for a talk on some special subject. They would always be joined by Mrs. Taft as soon as she realized the situation. The conversation begun before her arrival would continue with her taking a full share in it.

These conditions did not continue long, however, for Mrs. Taft was taken ill. Just a little over two months after the inauguration she became sadly afflicted. She was unable after that ever to take her proper place in the affairs of the White House. Certainly she could no longer take part in political discussions, for her speech was visibly affected. As time went on there were material signs of improvement, but never was there even a partial return to the situation during the first two months.

Mrs. Taft's illness was a severe burden during the entire four years, not only to herself but those near and dear to her. Especially was this so after her physical condition had improved, leaving her, however, awkward in her speech and with other slight handicaps. Only under the most careful supervision was she permitted to take her place in the doings of the household. Even so the peculiarities rising from her condition caused many embarrassing moments, especially to the President.

TROPICAL SHRUBS YIELD TO WASHINGTON DAMPNESS

The experience of public life through which the Tafts had passed had evidently built up in their minds certain notions of how things should be done when they reached the White House. Their Philippine experience had given them ideas that were to be attempted in their new surroundings. The end terraces were to be used for all they were worth. Some of the plans seemed very odd to those who for years had seen the dignity of White House entertaining. The soft ground-glass globes of the electric lights on the terraces were changed to flaring red-covered shades. Tables were constructed, chairs provided, plants and flowering shrubs all placed in readiness for elaborate entertainments. In the end it was all a complete failure. There was no comparison between the bugs and dampness of the terraces and the quiet comfort of the grand old rooms inside. Conditions, surroundings, precedent, everything favored the old way, and to this time brought a return. A number of parties were given under the new plan, but never with success.

MAJOR BUTT AND THE QUAKER COMMITTEE

It was President Taft who first employed a personal aide. In fact it was Taft who first used aides so extensively in entertaining and even in his private life. Major Butt was the President's very shadow, always in the line of duty, and many were the complications that arose from this relationship. The Major suffered in an effort to keep pace with the President in his dinner engagements. The final result was the trip abroad for his health and the sad ending on his return aboard the ill-fated *Titanic*.

An interesting incident in connection with Major Butt's position as Military Aide occurred one Sunday morning when the President had been invited to attend service in a Quaker Church. A committee came to escort him to the service. Major Butt, in full dress uniform, had preceded the committee to the White House and stood waiting at the entrance for the President to come downstairs. When the committee arrived and saw the Major in his warlike uniform and learned he was to go with the President, there was great consternation. They said plainly that no symbol of war could enter the Quaker Church. The telephones were kept busy to learn if an exception could be made. For a time there was a flurry of arguments back and forth, but no decision. Finally it was decided to lay the facts before the President. This was done, but it did not help the situation. The President would take no stand, and was apparently indifferent to the outcome. This left things worse than ever. Major Butt insisted it was nonsense and the committee that it was their rule. Finally, without any decision having been made, the President started for the automobile, the committee and Major Butt accompanying him.

It was learned afterwards that all in the party entered the church without hindrance, but that a strained feeling existed all through the service. There was no aftermath to the affair, except that apparently President Taft received no further invitations to attend the Quaker Church. There was much gossip around the White House about the incident, but the consensus of opinion was that Major Butt had won his point.

AN UNHAPPY HOUSEHOLD

It was an administration that did not stand out, at least so far as those about the household were concerned. Mrs. Taft's illness from almost the very beginning put a damper on things generally. The President's disposition was quite contrary to what we had known when he used to be an almost daily luncheon guest of the Roosevelts. The employees with whom he came in contact had grown to know him, to like him, to consider him as a friend. He always had a

HELEN H. TAFT

WILLIAM HOWARD TAFT AND HIS
GRANDDAUGHTER

pleasant smile and a word of welcome for everyone. The Roosevelts were all so fond of him that the very air about the place had been one of welcome when he came.

But what a difference later, when he became President! There was an entire change. No more did he seem considerate. The smile was replaced by orders, not always given in a pleasant way. There was rebellion in the minds of the employees, unnoticed, of course, by the family. Only by special effort could they conceal their feelings. Thus it was during the entire four years. The Administration was rather unnatural all through. It just seemed to lack the feeling necessary to make it a success.

The President was fond of entertaining, especially at dinner parties. He was good company and ever ready to engage in social festivities. He appeared to have many friends, yet no real intimates. He lacked Roosevelt's magnetism and seemed to prefer subordinates to equals. He was the first President to play golf and that drew a number to him for a time. General Clarence Edwards seemed about the closest friend he had, aside from his own family. But even Edwards failed to hold. Before the Administration was half over, he had discontinued his visits to the White House.

The changing of private secretaries shows the general trend of the times. At least four served him during his single term. One of them, Charles D. Norton, wanted the office of Assistant to the President created, and openly called himself by that title, all with the approval and sanction of the President. He left the White House eventually to take a position with the financial interests in New York.

THE RE-ELECTION CAMPAIGN SPEECHES

The President worked hard when he did work. It seemed necessary for him to do so; his dictation was labored and his messages and speeches were written over and over, before they were finally satisfactory.

I shall long remember the preparation of President Taft's speeches for his re-election campaign. He was angry through and through and his dictation could be heard all over the house. His suspicion of those about him who had served under Mr. Roosevelt increased as the days went on. The secret service men especially came in for a goodly share of the suspicion. When neither man was elected, conditions in the White House returned to normal.

THE DINNER FOR MRS. CLEVELAND

The rest of the term passed uneventfully. The one exception was the dinner given in honor of Mrs. Grover Cleveland by the President and Mrs. Taft on January 11, 1913. Mrs. Cleveland's recent announcement of her engagement to Professor Preston of Princeton and her visit to Washington with her daughter Esther had been talked of for days. They had been entertained on a most elaborate scale by others, but, from a sentimental point of view, the dinner at the White House was looked upon as the climax of their visit. Here was the scene of her early social triumphs. Here centered the Washington that she knew. So naturally we looked forward eagerly to the dinner planned in her honor. The guest list was made up of those who would add distinction to the occasion and yet be most acceptable to Mrs. Cleveland. Yet much criticism arose when it was finally learned who had been invited.

Most of the criticism was concerned with Mrs. Harrison, the former Mrs. Dimmick, who was, it will be remembered, the niece of President Harrison's first wife. Many thought her standing of no consequence at an affair of this kind and the invitation extended to her caused much gossip and no little amusement in Washington society. But be that as it may, the lady surely did not occupy the place at the table that should have been accorded her. In all reason, if the wife of one President occupied the place of honor on the right of the President, as Mrs. Cleveland did, certainly the wife of a second President should have occupied the next position of honor, on the left of the President. Mrs. Harrison, however, was seated two places to the left of Mrs. Taft. Whether she noticed the matter or was made unhappy by it will perhaps never be known.

Naturally the employees who had known Mrs. Cleveland during her reign in the White House took a special interest in the arrangements. They gave orders to put on just a little better touch here and a little harder rub there, that she might see things at their best. So it was that extra flowers and her favorite ones appeared at the different places. In view of the almost complete change that had taken place in the house since she was last there, it was decided that her carriage should be sent round to the east entrance so that she might see the new arrangement for guests to enter and leave the house. When she had walked through the lower terrace and ascended the large staircase, she was shown to the Blue Room, where the guests were to assemble. No eye present but was turned on her as she entered this room, and it was plainly evident that her inward feelings were profound. But being almost immediately reassured by the small company already assembled, she regained her composure and took her place at the right of the entrance as the honor guest of the occasion.

From here the company passed into the newly arranged dining-room. To Mrs. Cleveland it was an entirely new apartment. And yet there were several things for her to notice. The table itself was decorated with the two kinds of flowers she always liked best — jonquils and pansies. Then again, as she was seated, she must have observed the beautiful red-bordered plate that she had selected herself just eighteen years before.

After dinner there was a musicale in the East Room. To her this was a new experience, but apparently one of little interest. The musicale being over, she stayed sufficiently long to be polite and then went quietly to the side of Mrs. Hammond and suggested that they depart. With the queenly air so characteristic of her she left the presence of the company. She had come again, had conquered once more, had gone.

A LIFELESS DEPARTURE

The Taft plans for leaving the White House were made with regret. Mrs. Taft had not improved; in fact she seemed to have a physical setback after the election, for she had honestly believed the President would be re-elected. She had made plans for the second term.

Interest seemed to be lost in everything. No consideration was given to anyone except a few to whom they felt indebted. They paid some attention to the coming of the Wilsons and offered them advice. Upon leaving, Mrs. Taft said good-bye to no one; Miss Helen, the only other one of the family here at the time, left afoot and alone.

6

TAFT OUT — WILSON IN: A TYPICAL INAUGURATION DAY

LAST-MINUTE BUSINESS

MARCH 4, 1913, dawned cloudy; but the weather cleared and by mid-morning it was warm and comfortable. The President and Mrs. Taft were a little late in coming down to breakfast — their last meal in the White House together. The New York papers were taken to the President at the table as usual and he remained there reading after Mrs. Taft had retired to the second floor, where she spent her time walking around taking a last look, as it were, and finally settled down at her desk in the west sitting-room to pen last letters to her boys, Robert at Yale and Charlie at the Taft School. In the meantime, Secretary Root had asked permission to come over to see the President at once and was received in the breakfast-room. He remained about ten minutes, and upon his departure the President came out into the Usher's Room to ask if any word had been received from Senator Crane, who was to telephone him when everything was in readiness at the Shoreham, from which Mr. Wilson was to leave for the White House. Effort was made to get Senator Crane on the telephone, but without success. The President went to his study on the second floor, where he was joined by Secretary Hilles and Assistant Secretary Forster, to finish the last remaining business of the closing administration. Meanwhile all the President's aides had gathered and were on tiptoes in anticipation of the coming ceremony.

The President had not been upstairs more than a few

minutes when the sound of music announced the coming of the President-elect. The military aides in their full dress uniforms had arranged themselves according to instructions at intervals from the front door to the door of the Blue Room, where the party was to assemble. Up to this time the only other person who had arrived was Secretary of Agriculture Wilson. He was informed of the President-elect's arrival and requested to step into the next room, as it would be rather embarrassing for him to be there alone to greet the incoming administration. The Secretary readily complied with the request. As the President-elect and those in attendance alighted from the carriage, the senior Military and Naval Aides, Colonel Cosby and Lieutenant Commander Timmons, met them at the door and escorted them to the Blue Room.

A group of Princeton students had followed the President-elect when he entered the White House grounds and as he left his carriage they started to sing one of their college songs. Mr. Wilson continued on into the house apparently not hearing them or, if he heard, he passed it off unnoticed. However, when he was just about to enter the Blue Room, he turned abruptly and retraced his steps to the front porch and with hat in hand greeted the students from there and patiently waited until they had finished their songs. It was a very touching scene and the President-elect was visibly moved.

The Vice-President-elect and the committee accompanying him were also ushered into the Blue Room. In the meantime the members of the Taft cabinet began to arrive and finally all were in waiting for the President, who was still in his study on the second floor. His personal aide, Major Rhoads, had told him that all was in readiness. Still the minutes flew and the wait became tiresome, but there was nothing to do but be patient. Finally the President finished the work in hand and came down to the Blue Room, attended by his personal aide and secretary. He entered the room rather unconcerned, walked over to the President-elect, gave him a cordial handshake and remarked on the weather. Then turning to the Vice-President-elect and other members of the party, he greeted them with rather a cold formal tone until he reached Senator Crane, when his usual friendly manner returned.

MR. WILSON AND THE LADY PHOTOGRAPHER

This ended, the President again turned to the President-elect and said that the next thing in order, as he understood it, was to have their pictures taken together. The President took Mr. Wilson by the arm and they both moved through the Red Room to the South Porch, where a score of photographers had arranged their cameras. As Mr. Taft walked through the Red Room he was stopped to don his overcoat and hat, as Mr. Wilson still had his on, and some little conversation took place between them. President Taft remarked that it was just four years ago that he and Roosevelt had had their pictures taken in the same identical place. Mr. Wilson merely replied, 'Is that so?'

A large number of pictures were made and the antics of the operators in their haste was really amusing. The two men were asked to toe a line that had been made on the porch by face powder from the vanity-box of a lady photographer. They were asked to shake hands, to face each other, to look this way and that, and finally to look away from the cameras and operators entirely, that a side view might be taken. The two men had so far moved mechanically; but at this last request, coming as it did from the lady member of the party, Mr. Wilson turned in her direction and remarked that they would much prefer to look toward the lady. This brought a broad smile from everyone and the picture-taking episode ended with good feeling all around.

They were now ready to start for the Capitol. Mr. Wilson had come in a two-horse open victoria, but while he was inside the White House the landau, drawn by four horses, had been substituted. Colonel Cosby and Lieutenant Commander Timmons led the way to the carriage. President Taft entered first and sat on the right, after he had graciously suggested that the President-elect precede him. With a blare of trumpets the party was off.

MRS. TAFT LINGERS ON

Mrs. Taft and Miss Helen had watched the departure from the latter's bedroom on the second floor. They were entirely alone, so what their feelings were can only be surmised. Mrs. Taft had arranged beforehand to leave at eleven o'clock to go to the home of her sister, Mrs. Thomas Laughlin, and there to be joined later by Mr. Taft and proceed to the station. Miss Taft had arranged for a friend, Mr. Chauncey Hackett, to call for her at ten-thirty, when she planned to take her dog Cairo and walk to Mrs. Laughlin's to join her parents later. However, after the party had left for the Capitol, all these plans were delayed. It was really distressing for a while. Nothing ever more resembled a household from which a funeral had just departed with the corpse. Mrs. Taft wandered around the second floor hardly knowing what to do with herself and finally settled at her desk to finish the two letters to her sons. In the meantime one of the ushers turned over the house register to her for final keeping, calling her attention to the fact that a similar book had been presented to Mrs. Cleveland when she left here after the first administration and that, when she brought it back at the beginning of the second term, it formed a connecting link between the two. This suggestion of a possible return of the Taft family brought a real smile to her sad and forlorn face. Then with a parting good-bye the usher left to be about his duties in arranging for the incoming administration. In the meantime Mrs. Taft had changed the hour of her departure from eleven to eleven-thirty. There is no doubt that her regrets at leaving were many, for with all her worries and trials, she had reveled in the life she had lived for the past four years.

Miss Helen having left, everyone just waited for Mrs. Taft to depart. No one cared to go ahead with any visible preparation for the incoming people while she still remained around. An automobile had been in readiness for a half-hour; in fact everyone had merely been standing around waiting for the end so as to prepare again for the beginning. Finally at eleven-thirty Mrs. Taft arose from her desk, put on her hat and furs, and came down on the elevator for the final parting. She had the two letters to her boys and several numbers of recent magazines in her hands and also a large bunch of orchids that had been presented to her earlier in the morning by Colonel Cosby. She was visibly affected when she came into the Usher's Room. In the effort to hand me the two letters, she dropped all the magazines. Everyone who witnessed this last effort was moved to sympathy. Her feelings were so evident that practically no one even attempted to say good-bye to her.

A NERVE-RACKING INTERLUDE

Back in the house everything was as dead as the traditional doornail. For a time there was no mistress, no one to give or approve necessary orders. Those in recognized authority must proceed of their own volition. The cooks and butlers were busy preparing the luncheon that was to be served upon the arrival of the party from the Capitol. The cleaners and maids were giving the last touch to a bare household. The place was so bereft of any bric-à-brac or ornamental furnishing that it was hard to know just what to do to make the best appearance. The ushers and officers were making their plans to receive the new family and their guests. At twelve noon the flag that had floated from the pole was hauled down and a new one put in its place. This

old flag was taken by Colonel Cosby, who had sent a new
one to replace it.

Then all being in readiness it was just a case of sitting
down and waiting for the arrival of the new people. This
is in a way a most interesting moment and some of the conversations are truly amusing. Of course they have to do
with the policy of the incoming administration — not the
great policies that concern the country at large, but the
question of who will hold his job under the new régime.
Everyone sees some particular reason why he should be
retained and yet each without exception is just a little worried.
On this occasion the word had been passed around that
there were to be no immediate changes in the household,
yet we all felt a bit shaky just the same.

NEW FACES

It was just two-fifteen when the guests began to arrive.
The first comers were strangers to the doorkeepers; a face
here and there would be known, but they were as a rule an
entirely new lot of people. Finally Mrs. Wilson and her
daughters arrived and were shown to the second floor of
the house where they were to spend many of their future
days and nights. They seemed bewildered, but in a happy
frame of mind. They had some meager knowledge of the
surroundings from a plan of the house that had been taken
to them at Princeton. From this the girls had evidently decided what rooms they were to occupy. They immediately
proceeded to locate these rooms, but found them very different from what they had pictured. They marveled at the
size of the apartments and only acknowledged that they
felt lost.

In the meantime most of the guests had assembled in the
East Room and were chatting and enjoying themselves to an
extreme. They numbered well on to two hundred and included the men who were to form the new cabinet. The

names of these gentlemen had not as yet been made public, yet they had to be known in order that we might admit them to the house. In applying for cards of admission to the Capitol ceremonies and inaugural stand, the request had been made from Princeton that the proper number be furnished in blank. It was done in this case, but admission to the White House was another proposition. So after many requests a list of the names of the new cabinet was supplied. It was looked upon with curiosity by those who had access to it.

Mrs. Wilson and her daughters had been upstairs but a short time when they were asked to proceed to the lower floor and join the guests in the East Room. It had been planned beforehand that those assembled should proceed to the dining-room and begin the lunch in advance of the arrival of the party from the Capitol. This after many difficulties was done. It was a hard matter to get the presiding lady and her daughters to go to the dining-room, for they rather hesitated to take the initiative in this, their first social function in their new home. Finally the sound of music told of the approach of the parade and returning party and, in sheer desperation, I exerted strong persuasion on the ladies. They were escorted to the State Dining-Room by the various aides who had returned from the Capitol.

A FAUX PAS

This was just about accomplished when the carriage containing the new President and the ex-President drove under the porte-cochère. Both men alighted from the carriage very quickly, walked rapidly through the entrance door to the center of the vestibule, and stopped just over the Seal of the President of the United States of America, which occupies a panel in the floor. They were both plainly embarrassed, now that they were free from the clamor and shouts of the multitude. President Wilson seemed much more composed than the ex-President, but neither seeming to know just what should be the next move. Presently one of the ushers approached and informed Mr. Wilson that the luncheon party had already assembled in the dining-room. The new President, taking the hint, gallantly turned to Mr. Taft and invited him to join him at lunch. At this point the rest of the official party entered, including Mr. Taft's Secretary, Mr. Hilles, who suggested that there was not time for the ex-President to lunch at the White House, as his train left at three-ten and he had to call for Mrs. Taft. As a matter of fact there was ample time, but this was a plan prearranged by very close friends of the Tafts, who had been appalled when they learned that he intended to remain and attend this luncheon in honor of the new Administration.

I have no doubt that Mr. Wilson expected Mr. Taft to decline his invitation, for he looked ready to say good-bye. On the contrary, however, Mr. Taft was determined to have that lunch, and regardless of Mr. Hilles's suggestion, which would have been adopted by nine hundred and ninety-nine men out of a thousand, he replied that surely there was time enough for him to eat a sandwich anyhow. And the way he said it! No one who heard it but whose sympathy was excited. He said it in such a sad way, as if to convey the idea either that he was actually hungry or else just wanted to eat once more within those portals that had been so dear to him for the four years past. Nothing more was said, but those who were aware of the previous efforts to prevent this very thing choked down a feeling of regret, as the two men proceeded to the dining-room together.

As the two men reached the door of the dining-room, the new President excused himself momentarily, but not before he had received the plaudits of the assembly. He returned in a few minutes and was the center of all eyes. The ladies of the household were scattered throughout the room engaged in conversation with those whom they knew, but when the new President entered all tried to reach him for a handshake. It was really sad to observe Mr. Taft. No one seemed to pay

any attention to him. It was now necessary for him to do a
little hustling for himself, but he managed somehow to get
hold of a bit of salad and a sandwich. Word finally came that
Mrs. Taft would not wait for him any longer, but would continue on to the station. This was not told to Mr. Taft, but instead he was again reminded that the time was so short he
would not have time to go by for Mrs. Taft and to the station
unless he left at once. This had the desired effect and he was
practically dragged away from the scene of his former
achievements.

The episode was an embarrassing and painful one. I don't
believe it had ever occurred before, and may it never happen
again! After his successor is actually inaugurated, the retiring
President should make himself scarce just as soon as possible.

TUMULT AND SHOUTING

In the meantime President Wilson was partaking sparingly
of the lunch, appearing anxious to get out to the parade that
he knew was being kept in waiting. Several times he made
inquiries as to whether it was the proper time for him to go to
the reviewing stand. It was not until he finally sent word
rather brusquely to General Wood that he was ready to review the parade that the latter cut his lunch short and made
preparations for this part of the ceremony. Finally at three-
ten word was given the President that all was in readiness,
and without a moment's hesitation he laid aside his plate
and, escorted by the chairman of the Inaugural Committee,
proceeded to the reviewing stand erected in front of the
house.

At the conclusion of the parade he immediately made his
departure amid the tumult and the cheering of the crowd. It
was now practically night. As he left the stand he was surrounded by metropolitan police officers and secret service
men. Once in the house he breathed a sigh of relief, and after
saying good-bye and cordially thanking those of the Inaugural

Committee who had accompanied him, he retired immediately to the second floor where he joined his wife and daughters. In a short time the entire family, with the guests who
had been invited to stop in the house, appeared for dinner.
It was a happy occasion, everybody just bubbling over with
joy at the new surroundings and all trying to talk at once.
The President alone in the midst of all the festivities remained silent, as if in deep study. His manner was impressive,
especially in comparison with Mr. Taft's happy-go-lucky
style on such occasions.

After dinner the family found a little time to inspect their
new quarters. There was a continual running through the
house from one room to another, a shrill voice screaming to
someone else as a new place was discovered. Relatives from
the hotels going in and out, visitors and acquaintances seeking admission but added to the turmoil. What a difference
there was in the type of visitors, especially in their language!
The spick-and-span Northerners, with their peculiar twang,
had given way to the free-and-easy Southerners, with their
drawl and their soft speech. Over the telephone especially
one had to learn a different language.

CARY GRAYSON GETS HIS CHANCE

In the midst of all this turmoil came a call for a doctor.
The President's sister had somehow cut a big gash in her fore-
head. What doctor should it be? There were three of them
waiting within call for just such an emergency. It is on occasions like this that subordinates many times decide the fate of
their superiors. Then it is, that old scores are repaid. So now
the lucky doctor got his call, and to his credit be it said he turned
out to be just the right one, not only for this particular case,
but for a very long time after. His name was Cary Grayson.

So it went during the course of the entire evening. First one
thing, then another kept the place in an uproar. The President
with his youngest daughter, Miss Eleanor, left the house to at-

tend a smoker at the Shoreham Hotel given by the Princeton
Alumni. This took him away for possibly an hour and a half.
Upon his return, finding the same condition prevailing as
when he left, he in his quiet way attempted to enter into the
spirit of the occasion. We all remarked on the contrast between this evening and other inauguration nights that had, as
far back as could be remembered, been celebrated by an Inaugural Ball.

So along toward midnight the day was considered closed.
One by one the family and guests wended their way to their
rooms. It was not long after the President had gone upstairs
that he rang several bells in the house, not knowing at the
time which was which. One of the doorkeepers answered the
call and when the President appeared he was clothed in his
underwear only. He asked for his trunk, which had gone
astray and unfortunately contained his night clothes. Immediate search was made and it was located at the station where
an automobile was sent for it; but it did not get to the White
House until one o'clock in the morning after the President
had already retired.

Thus concludes the story of an inauguration day at the
White House. In many ways it is typical of them all.

7

THE COURTSHIP AND MARRIAGE OF A PRESIDENT

THE DEATH OF THE FIRST MRS. WILSON

FROM the very beginning President Wilson appeared retiring, uncommunicative, and rather ill at ease in company; but with his own family — who were all of the gentle sex — he was at his best. They pampered and petted him and looked up to him as their lord and master. He could do no wrong in their eyes.

It was not long, however, before Mrs. Wilson was stricken with disease. After a lingering illness she died on August 6, 1914. A lovely person had passed away. The unusually simple ceremonies at her funeral were impressive. After her death, the place took on a new atmosphere. It was strangely lonesome and different. Mrs. Wilson had lived just seventeen months after the inauguration. In that space of time she had endeared herself to all. But now new conditions must be met, and no one could be better fitted than the President to undergo such an ordeal.

He set about it with characteristic patience and resignation. That he was lonely was quite evident. He surrounded himself with his family and added to the household by insisting that several of the guests who had come for the funeral remain for an indefinite visit. He delved more deeply into affairs of state and seemed more absorbed than ever in his new policies. He went to the Executive Offices more regularly and spent hours alone in his study. He never seemed to be outwardly disturbed, but accepted the inevitable with a grace and a charm that was inspiring to all about him. Never an extensive reader — never at least since he had taken up his residence in the White House — he did not resort to this means of diversion. He found more comfort apparently in conversation with members of his family, and spent many evenings with them in the library, sometimes talking, sometimes reading aloud. The mealtimes were little social gatherings, the ladies vying with each other in an effort to please the President. He accepted their solicitude and their sympathy in a manner that delighted them, and each in her turn was happy when she could say or do something to command his approval.

The President came to be an ardent golf player during this time, not so much for the game itself as for the objective it gave him to get out in the open. His opponents were few, and he never attempted proficiency at the game. In fact he seldom kept his score and paid little attention to it when he did. He would play at all hours, sometimes as early as five in the morning and sometimes late in the afternoon. Good or bad weather was just the same to him. When there was snow on the ground, he would have the balls painted red and find amusement in driving them around on the ice and snow. For amusement it was, never sport.

During the summer months, immediately following the death of his wife, he took to motoring. Methodically he arranged his various rides and numbered and named them to suit his fancy: 'Number one ride,' 'Southern Maryland ride,' 'Norbeck ride,' 'Potomac ride.' No change from a previously arranged route would be permitted. He loved the rides into Virginia and would often comment on them upon his return. He was heard to say that Alexandria pleased him because it was the only 'finished' city in the United States. On these rides he would always be accompanied by one or more of the ladies of the household.

There was no special period of mourning observed. The ladies would go out to call and have their friends in. The one married daughter had come home for a visit and during that time a son had been born, which added greatly to the interest of the household. Thus the time passed from midsummer to late in the next winter season. There was no official entertaining until January, when there was a moving-picture entertainment. All the cabinet members and their families were invited and served with refreshments afterwards. This might be considered the end of the period of mourning.

A PHYSICIAN COURTS AN OFFICER'S DAUGHTER

In the meantime other things were happening. Doctor Cary Grayson, who had now become an intimate of the household, spent much of his time with the President. But he had an affair of his own which kept him busy. Being interested in a young lady, the daughter of a former officer in the Confederate Army, it behooved him to make the best showing possible in the face of his numerous rivals. Through her he met an impressive widow, Mrs. Edith Bolling Galt, who lived in the northwest section of the city. At her home the doctor evidently found sympathy and encouragement in his suit. In return he sang the praises of Mrs. Galt in the White House, with the result that she was asked there for tea, apparently without object other than the one of friendliness for Doctor Grayson.

This slight beginning led to more numerous visits, but it was some time before the President first met her. He had heard her spoken of, however, for all liked her. She was an attractive lady — good to look at and with a taste for clothes. After her first meeting with the President, he found more opportunities to join the ladies at teatime. Thus it came to pass that one afternoon early in the spring Mrs. Galt was invited to take a motor ride along with the President and his cousin, who was now her close friend. It was just a routine sort of ride, but the ice was broken. From this time on it was evident the President found pleasure in having the lady present whenever he was able to lay aside affairs of state. She helped to make up the party on many rides, and the visits back and forth became more frequent. It was now quite evident which way the wind was blowing. All did not look on his interest in the lady with favor, but they dared not make known their objections.

The middle of spring was here, nowhere more beautiful than in the nation's capital. The casual meetings now became appointments and Mrs. Galt came for the first time to dine. The President was all expectancy and had arrayed himself in his best manner. Mrs. Galt looked young and handsome and was dressed to perfection down to the last detail. A single purple orchid, pinned high on her left shoulder, set off the picture. She was just the type a man of the President's keen discernment would admire. When she spoke her voice was soft and musical, with a Southern accent. Her every characteristic was pleasing beyond measure.

There were three at dinner, only one member of the President's family being present. Before taking Mrs. Galt home they went for a long drive, accompanied, of course, by a secret service car. Presidents are handicapped, especially in affairs of this kind, for they must ever be attended by secret service men wherever they go. 'A necessary evil' this President described it. 'A nuisance' and 'a pest' other Presidents have called it, when they wished to do something or go somewhere known only to themselves.

The President but seldom dines out at a private household. He cannot with propriety show favor to one and slight another. Those who dine with him must come to the White House. So it was in this particular case. Invitations to Mrs. Galt now went thick and fast. But the President never went to her home or appeared with her in public without a third party present.

However, he was not deprived of the pleasure of being alone with her. In the evening they would often retire to the President's study and the rest of the company would find amusement in other parts of the house.

THE SITUATION GETS OUT OF CONTROL

It was now about nine or ten months since the President's wife had been buried. Everyone about the place still had sweet memories of her and yet their sympathies were with the President in his new enterprise — possibly with the exception of the immediate members of his family. They could hardly believe their own eyes. Doctor Grayson and the President's cousin were, I think, afraid lest they had brought about a situation, now beyond their control, that would not be approved either by the people in general or by those close to the President. Their anxiety was justified, but they were now helpless and could but watch the drift of affairs, make the best of it, and obey orders from the commander-in-chief.

Every activity now revolved around the lady; every plan included her. At every place where the President was to be, provision must be made for her to be there also. Dinner at the White House at least three times a week; motor rides sometimes twice in a day; a trip to New York for the naval review; a trip to Baltimore — and so it went.

Spring passed and summer came on. When plans were made for a summer vacation, the lady must be included. Thus it was that along in June she with several members of the household motored to the hills of New Hampshire to the same spot where, two years before, the President had spent the summer months with his first wife and his family. That family had been broken now by death and marriage, but someone had come to fill an ever-widening gap. Whereas he had occupied these summer quarters but a few days at a time on other occasions, the President would now stay a month when he went to visit. When he was not there he was lonesome and unsettled. He wrote to Mrs. Galt constantly and the Library of Congress was put to a test to find quotations to express his feelings.

WOODROW WILSON, ELLEN AXSON WILSON, AND THEIR
DAUGHTERS, JESSIE, ELEANOR, AND MARGARET

WOODROW WILSON AND EDITH BOLLING GALT
Philadelphia, October 8, 1915

MEETING THE FUTURE IN-LAWS

September first found all back in Washington. The President had returned a few days ahead of the ladies, looking forward to the time of their coming with as much interest as could be manifested by the most enthusiastic lover. No sooner were things settled than the President began to 'step out.' He went to the theater for the first time since the death of his wife. He stayed up later in the evenings, took more interest in details of household affairs, endeavored to improve his own personal appearance, was more tolerant of those about him, more considerate and understanding. In short, he was a changed man.

Mrs. Galt was now almost a daily visitor. Along in this same month she brought her family — that is, her mother and her sister — to the White House to meet the President. She had a large family and they could not all conveniently come for this first visit. The mother and sister came in the afternoon. The President received them in the Red Room and never was knight more gallant than he. He left not a stone unturned to make them at home and comfortable under most trying circumstances. He was very happy and no doubt felt the battle was going in his favor. The approval of these two relatives meant as much to this great man as it would have to the plainest of everyday citizens. He was no more the President but a prospective son-in-law and brother-in-law to them. As for them, they must have been delighted at the prospects. Their departure was like the triumphant march of a powerful army which had just been through battle and come out victorious. It showed in their every act. They came in hesitant, but left confident and understanding and full of approval. From this time on, all seemed set.

BUSINESS CAN WAIT

For the next month the President missed no opportunity to be with his lady. He had a private wire installed between his room in the White House and her home and spent hours and hours composing letters to her. Flowers were sent to her daily and when she was to come to dinner or go to the theater orchids were delivered to her. The orchids carried a certain significance, and when she appeared it would always be with just one of them worn high on the left shoulder. Many are the worries that attended the getting of these orchids, for they are scarce always and during this time seemed scarcer than ever. But they must be had and the flower shops were put to a test to furnish them.

The President was simply obsessed. He put aside practically everything, dealing only with the most important matters of state. Requests for appointments were put off with the explanation that he had important business to attend to. Cabinet officers, Senators, officials generally were all treated the same. It had always been difficult to get appointments with him; it was now harder than ever, and important state matters were held in abeyance while he wrote to the lady of his choice. When one realizes that at this time there was a war raging in Europe, not to mention a Presidential campaign approaching, one can imagine how preoccupied he must have been. There was much anxiety among his political friends, who just had to accept the inevitable, but who began to look about for a way to postpone it until after the election, for fear lest the people would not approve. They lay awake nights in an effort to find a way out — all unknown to the President, of course. How could a postponement be brought about? Who would mention the subject to him? First one and then another was suggested, but when it came to the actual performance of the feat, no one was willing to undertake it. They understood the depth of the President's feeling and they knew his determination when once he had made up his mind to do a thing. They feared lest they encounter his displeasure, and none wished to do that, even with the stakes so high. So all the talk went for naught.

A SOLEMN ANNOUNCEMENT

At length the President decided to relieve the strain and end the suspense. He approached the business with the same confidence he had manifested from the beginning. He sent for his secretary and ordered that his engagement be announced from the Executive Offices that very afternoon.

The President had been in his study all of the morning. His lunch had taken but a few minutes. During that time he was quiet and uncommunicative. After lunch he returned to the study. He was in deep thought, for he was about to make what he considered a very solemn announcement. What thoughts were in his mind it would be hard to guess. He strolled about over the floor of the house. Returning to his study, he rang the bell for one of the attendants who had been just a little closer to him than the others. As the latter entered, he was leaning in deep meditation with one arm on the bookcase. Calling the attendant by name he said, 'I want you to be one of the first to know that I am going to marry Mrs. Galt.' Then he waited. 'I am both glad and sorry,' was the answer. The President seemed to comprehend the meaning of the words with all their honesty of intent. He knew that the person whom he was addressing was a great admirer of the first Mrs. Wilson and yet he knew also that there was nothing this man would not do to add to his happiness and comfort. After a moment's silence he said, 'I believe if Mrs. Wilson could know, she would approve.'

This was a serious day at the White House. When it became known that the die had been cast, there was quiet rejoicing and anxious solicitude. Everybody seemed to like Mrs. Galt, but there was deep sympathy for the members ot the family who would now have to take a back seat. Then, too, things had been going on so well, and everyone had grown quite accustomed to the situation brought about by the death of the first Mrs. Wilson.

The remainder of this day in early October the President spent in seclusion. He made no attempt to do anything else. He had made up his mind and awaited results. Through his secretary at the Executive Offices he arranged that word should be given to the public that evening at eight o'clock. In the meantime it was planned for the lady to come to dinner, and while she was seated at the table the announcement went out to the world.

A new order of things now began. The lady brought more of her relatives to dine at the White House. The President's family evidently felt he was traveling a little too fast, that they were being subordinated with too much of a rush.

OUR RESOURCE IS PUT TO THE TEST

In good time the President announced his plans. The date, time, and place were proclaimed: The ceremony was to take place on December 18, 1915, at eight-thirty in the evening, at Mrs. Galt's residence.

When it became known that the wedding was to be held in Mrs. Galt's rather small home, there was consternation. It made the arrangements doubly hard. At the White House, where facilities are ample, it would have been a different matter. But the President wanted simplicity.

According to instructions I called on Mrs. Galt and found her perfectly open-minded concerning the arrangements and quite willing to leave them all to me. Under any circumstances, preparing for an affair of this kind is no easy proposition. Receptions, dinners, social affairs of various kinds were everyday affairs, but a President getting married was a new experience. I realized that the house was small and inadequate for such a use as the wedding, but I set about the arrangements vigorously. The whole world was looking on and the interest was immense.

The first question naturally was: How many would be invited? When the President mentioned forty people, there was immediate conjecture about who they were to be. Even that number would tax the capacity of the two small rooms where the ceremony was to be held. Fifteen or twenty would be a crowd. But the task of arranging was begun. There was the license to be obtained, floral decorations to be arranged for, the caterer to be engaged, invitations and announcement cards to be printed, details of the ceremony to be planned, especially as to the getting away afterwards and the spending of the time of the honeymoon. These are but a few of the things that had to be thought out.

In the meantime Doctor Grayson was making headway in his own cause. The President gave a little dinner party at the White House a couple of days before his wedding at which the doctor and the young lady were guests of honor. The President had the young lady sit on his right and Mrs. Galt had the doctor on her right. The young lady could not help but be impressed with the importance of the doctor's status on this particular occasion. Both of the principals, of course, felt they owed him something and took this way of showing their appreciation.

PLANS AND PRESENTS

Presents of all kinds soon began to pour in. Every manufacturer, producer, and merchant seemed to feel he was privileged to send a sample of his wares. Soap of every description, toilet preparations, perfumes, brooms, brushes and dusters, pieces of furniture, mineral waters of all kinds, candy by the crate and cakes in large box lots, much handiwork of good housewives, a barrel of sugared popcorn and enough fruit and vegetables to open up a large market — these were but a few of the gifts. Others, much more valuable, were received at the same time. There was hardly a friend or acquaintance of short or long standing but contributed to this general collection. It was a big job simply to take care of this avalanche of favors. A list was started, but the presents were received in such numbers and from so many sources that the problem got away from the most experienced. Only the more important gifts were listed and acknowledged. Silver and glassware came in quantities, pictures and prints, carpets and rugs from the most select of collections, novelties by the score, jewelry and ornaments of all kinds, table linen, tapestries, and works of art. A quick list, made up by one of the principals for the purpose of answering inquiries, included: Tiffany glass and brass desk set, cut-glass punchbowl and twelve cups to match, silver ladle, superb silver loving-cup from a state delegation in Congress, magnificent white bearskin rug, vicuña rug from South America, filet table spread from Porto Rico, tablecloth of Russian lace, numbers of vases of silver, glass, and pottery, ancient Chinese Ming bowl of sixteenth century, Swiss traveling clock, magnificent diamond and sapphire brooch, sapphire and gold flexible bracelet, alabaster Florentine lamp, four wonderful fans, mahogany dining-table, ancient Chinese box.

In making plans for the wedding and surveying the possibilities of the modest little house, it was clearly evident that many radical things would have to be done. There were just two rooms that could be used. In these the service would have to be held and the supper served. All furniture would have to be removed to start with. A portable table could be arranged in the extreme rear from which a buffet supper could be served. All the caterers of any prominence in the city were anxious to serve this supper regardless of compensation. One of the best was finally selected and his charge was nominal. He was to furnish all service, linen, china, silver, glass and candelabras, supply all waiters, bake the bride's cake and furnish the small boxes of wedding cake so generally used in these days as souvenirs. The menu consisted of:

Oyster Patties
Boned Capon — Virginia Ham — Rolls
Chicken Salad — Cheese Straws
Biscuits with Minced Ham
Pineapple Ice — Caramel Ice Cream — Cake
Fruit Punch — Coffee
Bon-Bons — Salted Almonds — Chocolates

Let me add, there was plenty of everything and the punch was real punch. Music was to be furnished by a small orchestra from the United States Marine Band, and it was some job to find room for it! Eventually it had to be placed on the bedroom floor, and from there the strains of the wedding march poured forth. The principals themselves, of course, arranged for the minister. The license had to be procured in the regular way, for there was no exception to be made even though the person being married was the President of the United States. He had to pay his fee of a dollar out of his own pocket, and answer all questions just like the humblest citizen. Police arrangements had to be made, since there was sure to be a tremendous crowd of curiosity-seekers. When these various details had been worked out, we turned to the florist for the final touches. For this purpose we had not only the resources of the leading floral decorator in Washington, but also the privilege of the Government greenhouses. The two combined eventually transformed these two small rooms into a paradise of flowers that delighted all who were privileged to see it.

Fortunately the front room had a window recess at the extreme end. Here the ceremony was to be held. The three windows were to be entirely closed off from the rest of the room. A wire framework was so arranged that it formed tier above tier of shelves where the most delicate of maidenhair ferns were placed, forming a semi-circular bower in which the bridal couple were to stand. This was the basis of the entire decoration. Overhead there was a canopy of green in the form of a shell, the inner side being Scotch heather, symbolic of the origin of the President's forbears. There was a mirror placed in the back of this green bank which enabled the President and his bride to see all the guests as the service was being performed. It was afterwards learned that the President took advantage of this privilege but the lady did not. She remarked afterwards that she was so impressed with the occasion that she saw little of what was going on.

Here and there in the green was placed a spray of the beautiful purple orchid, the bride's favorite flower. On either side were massed great pyramids of American Beauty roses. The prie-dieu was of white satin covered with a small cluster of orchids on either side. This same prie-dieu has been used by a number of couples who have been married within the circle of the Presidential household.

The remainder of the space in the two rooms was as handsomely decorated. The mantels were banked high with the rarest of flowers; ferns and palms were placed in every niche and corner where they would not interfere with the space for the guests. Meanwhile the guest list, which had originally been limited to forty, was undergoing a terrible ordeal. When the members of the two families were counted, it was seen they would constitute almost that number by themselves. A few personal friends were added, very few, and there were many keen disappointments. Adding to these the President's 'official family,' consisting of the members of his cabinet and their ladies, the number went beyond the original estimate. There were a few over fifty present.

As the day for the wedding approached, there was great chatter among the women-folk about what was going to be worn. Everybody was having a new dress made. These included a black silk velvet, a sapphire blue velvet, a blue silk brocade, a rose charmeuse, a yellow silk, a turquoise-blue and gold, a robin's-egg blue chiffon, a richly jetted net, a white crêpe and silver net, etc. Altogether it became a real fashion show.

THE GREAT DAY

At last the day set for the wedding arrived. It dawned clear and pleasant both inside and out. Though the ceremony was not to take place until eight-thirty in the evening, the President was up bright and early. He left the White House a little after nine for the home of his fiancée, returning just before eleven. He did some work with the stenographer and had the work written out at once, so he could sign his mail and have business out of his way. At lunch there was but little conversation. All the members of his family and the guests of the household were present. Under almost any other roof and with any other person there would have been some jest at the near approach of such an event, but not here. It was much too serious an affair and the President took it so solemnly that no one dared even to mention it, much less speak of it in a light vein.

In the afternoon the President took his lady for a drive, returning to the White House at about six o'clock. He immediately proceeded to confer with me about the arrangements and checked up on every detail. At seven-thirty he left for the scene of the ceremony.

As the guests arrived at Mrs. Galt's home, they were amazed at the transformation. It was a bower of fragrant blossoms. After leaving their wraps they moved about as far as space would permit and remained standing all through the service. On the appointed hour the minister came down the staircase and took his position back of the prie-dieu. At a signal that all was in readiness, the Marine Band began to play the Lohengrin wedding march and the President and his fiancée descended the stairs. During the reading of the service every sound ceased, every neck was craned. The guests could not but realize that they were witnessing a most unusual scene.

Only when the final words had been uttered and the strains of the music again pealed forth did a normal state of mind return to the assembly. The family of the bride rushed forward to congratulate her and the President. Then the other guests greeted the newly-weds on the spot where they had been united.

The band continued to play and the party became general. The bride and groom made their way to the table where, piled high in layers, stood the wedding cake. All looked on as the bride went through the time-honored ceremony of cutting it. She did it well, for not only did she place the knife in the cake, but herself served several pieces to those near-by, including the President. All partook freely of the buffet supper and remained standing all the while. Moving from one person to another the bride and groom mixed with the company quite as much as any of the others. It became quite a homey sort of an affair with everybody talking at once.

In the midst of all this the bride and groom slipped quietly upstairs and made ready for their departure. They were at least half an hour ahead of schedule and some hustling had to be done to prepare for the getaway.

When word was passed around that they were preparing to leave, there was considerable excitement, for everybody tried to get near the small space at the entrance. A great cheer went up as the newly married couple made their way to the waiting automobile. The secret service car was very close behind and both with engines running were ready to make a fast start. The President waved his hand at the cheering throngs, both as he appeared from under the canopy and when the machine started off. Newspaper people from far and near had come to write up the story. None were admitted to the wedding ceremony, so they were all on the outside waiting. Many had swift cars, intending to follow wherever the wedding party should lead them.

It was a wild ride. I was privileged to be in the secret service car which followed, or at least attempted to follow, the car in which the President and his bride were riding. There

was also supposed to be a police escort, and at least ten newspaper cars started out in our wake. They did not know where
they were going, but just followed. Even the police did not
know. The driver of the President's car was about the only
one aside from the principals who knew what was going to be
attempted. For a while the pursuing cars managed to keep
up in the face of the tremendous speed at which the President's
machine was traveling, but they dropped off one by one and
gave up the chase. We got so far behind on several occasions
that it was a question whether we were following the right
car or not. After twelve or fifteen miles all the rest had been
shaken off. So a much more deliberate pace was taken. The
shades were drawn in the limousine in which the President
and his bride were riding to prevent identification by the
new-gatherers who he knew would be watching from every
vantage-point. The crests on the doors of the car had been
covered temporarily with black carbon paper. How well all
this succeeded can be seen by the fact that two of the newspaper cars had actually guessed the place where the party
was to take the train, but, not finding the President's car,
were on their way back.

The party arrived at the station ahead of schedule and,
knowing this, the President ordered the cars parked back in
the shadows until the approach of the train from Washington,
when the couple would make a quick exit. A short step
through the baggage part of the station into the private car
and they were lost to the world for a while at least. Except
for a couple of secret service men, they had no one with them.
Their baggage had all been arranged for in advance and
there was no delay. One or two recognized the President as
he stepped aboard the car and they were so surprised they
seemed spellbound. Thus off into the night and on into the
Southland went the happy President of the United States and
his bride. His last words were in thanks and appreciation of
all the efforts put forth to make the ceremony the success it
had turned out to be. With smiles and a last farewell they
departed.

8

TO PARIS WITH WILSON

[THESE extracts have been chosen, as being of general interest, from the many personal letters which Ike Hoover wrote to members of his family during his two trips abroad with President Wilson. Since he would often continue one letter from day to day, it has been impossible to give the exact date of each selection.]

THE CONQUERING HERO

Left Washington Tuesday evening, December 3, 1918, at 10.00 P.M.
Sailed from Hoboken, New Jersey, Wednesday, 10.15 A.M.

Friday, December 13. Is this not the President's lucky day? We are just entering the harbor of Brest and I write these hurried lines before leaving the ship. We have been joined by other ships all through the night. There are now about sixty ships about us and the gun salutes are deafening. First came to meet us nine big battleships, then twenty destroyers, all American. Then as we get closer the French ships join us until the ocean becomes one moving mass of ships as far as the eye can see.

Wednesday, December 18. All the big officials of France were at the Paris station. There was a long walk over a platform all draped in flags, to waiting open carriages which took us to the Prince Murat Palace where we are stopping. Nothing of the kind has ever equaled the reception given the President on this ride from the station to the palace. It was beyond description. The people were wild. Soldiers from many

countries lined the streets. Back of them as far as the eye
could see was one writhing, milling mass of humanity. They
did not applaud; they screamed, yelled, laughed, and even
cried. They threw flowers by the tons. Hats, flags, coats,
everything was thrown in the air and at the carriage until it
seemed that all the noise in the world had broken loose and
turned adrift in Paris. No conquering hero was ever greeted
so. The people of France are certainly wild about the President of the United States of America.

I TAKE CHARGE OF A PALACE

The Prince Murat Palace is a palace indeed. On the first
floor there are three large parlors, much larger than those in
the White House, a large state dining-room and many large
halls and corridors. One of these parlors I use as my office.
On the next story is the greatest conglomeration of all kinds
of bedrooms and sitting-rooms that you can possibly imagine.
There are so many servants in the place they cannot be
counted. Certainly thirty or forty and running around all
the time. At the table where I eat my meals there is a butler
for each person, all dressed up in the funniest kind of uniform
according to the hour of the day. Now picture me walking
into this place and taking charge of it. That is absolutely
and literally what I did. Neither the President nor Mrs.
Wilson has uttered one word as to how things should be done.
They have just brought me along and taken the rest for
granted. I have had to work from eight or nine in the morning until ten or eleven at night.

We had hardly got settled in the palace before the President of France came to pay his official call. He is a prepos-
sessing looking fellow, but all French. Something like 'Leon'
the hairdresser, though a little more dapper-looking. Short
and inclined to be stout. His actions are impressive. His
wife is very nice-looking and makes an excellent impression.
She looks more like an American woman.

Last Sunday afternoon was passed in seeing people, among whom was Mr. Hoover, the American Food Administrator. On Monday the President was made a Citizen of Paris. The French are wild about him. Every time he goes out there are thousands to cheer him. He is beginning to look tired and worn. He is working hard.

'MY GOD, MR. PRESIDENT!'

On Thursday the King of Italy came to town and was received late in the afternoon. He was disappointing. I had thought of him as a tall, stately man, but on the contrary he is a short little fellow. He was very pleasant. Speaks very good English and seems a good sport. His understanding of English idiom, however, seemed somewhat weak, for after meeting the President he looked around the room and said, 'My God, Mr. President, I cannot give you a place like this when you come to Italy!' The President laughed out loud without making answer.

SIGNS OF STRAIN

Everyone has worked hard, the President included. I looked at him critically last night, and he had the appearance of a tired old man. He is feeling the strain and seems to realize the enormousness of the proposition he is up against. I should like to tell you all about it, but it seems too serious a matter to try to explain in a few words. Just on the surface it looks like the statesmen of the more important countries of Europe, especially, have stacked the cards against the President.

BUCKINGHAM PALACE

In the evening was held a state dinner in Buckingham Palace. It was some dinner. I saw about everything going on. They got out all the gold plate. Everything used on the table was gold. Candelabras, knives, forks, spoons, dishes, plates, everything, and to top it off on three different sides of the large room the walls were hung with gold dishes that were not used during the dinner. These latter were very large, about the size of tea-trays. Honestly it was so gorgeous it was vulgar. There were one hundred and twenty-five covers, more than we ever seat in the State Dining-Room at the White House.

A SAVIOR COME TO EARTH

It is really remarkable how wild the Italians are about the President. It is amazing. They seem to consider him as another Savior come to earth: the most wonderful signs about him everywhere and they simply seem to worship him. He could be elected to anything he might choose in Italy. I really believe they would make him King if he wanted them to. The French, too, are wild about him, but not so much as the Italians.

THE 'Y'

I find myself from time to time inquiring about the status of the various organizations who collected so much money at home for the soldiers. The general consensus of opinion expressed among both officers and privates seems to be that the Y.M.C.A. was a fake all the way through, that the Red Cross did very good work and the Knights of Columbus also. But they say the Salvation Army was the best and they all swear by it.

A FEEBLE SEND-OFF

The departure [on the return trip to Paris] was not so demonstrative as on the first occasion, the crowds were not so large nor the noise so boisterous. In fact, to be honest, there was only a feeble send-off compared with the one that had gone before. The President, who stood on the bridge at the time of leaving, seemed by his expression to feel the lack of enthusiasm. There were the salutes and the convoys of cruisers and destroyers and a squadron of airships that hovered over all the way down the harbor, but still there was something lacking.

KING ALBERT

The Belgian King is a very imposing-looking person. He is the best-looking King I have seen among the lot that has passed in review. His appearance justifies all the nice things that have been written about him. He is tall and rather handsome, while the others were neither. He is well built, with light flaxen hair standing straight up, carries himself well and seems quite unaffected. He had but one aide with him, which, from our standpoint, was very much to his credit.

The President received him in the best parlor and stayed with him for a full half-hour. Afterwards he was taken downstairs to be presented to Mrs. Wilson. She received him in her salon. The King made an excellent impression on everyone — and most everyone in the house was peeping at him from somewhere.

A KILLING PACE

I often marvel that the President is able to keep his poise and bear up as well as he does. It is so different from the way he works at home, and if he does not break down when it is all over, he will be a wonder indeed. I sometimes think it is the excitement and extreme interest alone that is keeping him up, but he goes on and on from day to day, working hard from ten to twelve hours and sometimes even longer. I get so I cannot understand why he does not crumble up. Yet the truth is he really seems better than ever, right now. He is so busy he never dresses for dinner any more. He goes right to that meal in the clothes he had worn all the day. This is so different from his usual custom that I mention it to illustrate what is happening to him.

CONFUSION IN CONFERENCE

The conferences these days are very mixed-up affairs. There is no one particular order in the discussions, no system whatever. They have the unfinished portion of the Austrian Treaty and the reply to the German proposals before them at one and the same time. First one and then another problem is taken up for consideration as it is made ready by the experts to whom it has been referred. Thus, one minute they may be considering the German colonies in South Africa and the next minute deciding what mountains or rivers shall form the boundary between Italy and Jugo-Slavia. How they manage to get any reason at all out of the numerous and varied discussions is hard to understand.

Then, too, these European nations are all the time looking for just a little advantage. The schemes resorted to for this purpose are sometimes laughable. One favorite trick is to have the expert of a particular nation heard all alone when a certain subject is being considered. It is customary to have the experts of all the four nations present at the same time when a certain subject is to be discussed. But at times the English, French, or Italians, knowing certain matters are to be considered, with no experts present, will bring their own along in what they think a diplomatic way, and plead to have them heard, thinking to gain some advantage thereby.

These schemes are not often successful, but I have seen some of them go through. The President is very watchful and also tactful. He has a horror of experts at best and is firm in holding them in check. He likes more to have their conclusions in writing that he may look them over and study them at his leisure.

POPULARITY FADES

Friday, May 16. It is curious how things have changed. No one seems to be satisfied any more. Even the people who were so wild about us when we first came seem to have lost interest in us now. It is a selfish bunch over here and they are all alike. I shall be glad to get back to the old U.S.A.

Another day and it has been a very full one. That you may see the number and variety of appointments I am attaching the list of engagements. In addition to these there were two more that are not listed.

A BUSY DAY
PRESIDENT'S ENGAGEMENTS
Friday, May 16, 1919

DELEGATIONS

11:00 A.M. Prince Charoon, and the other members of the Siamese Delegation.

11:15 A.M. Hon. Charles Mayer, Acting Chairman and the other members of the Commission on Industrial Enquiry of the National Civic Federation. (New York City.) (To pay their respects.)

11:30 A.M. Dr. D. A. Markoff, Mr. Paul Dzonchyk and Mr. P. P. Hatalak, delegation of Carpatho-Russians. (With reference to the Carpatho-Russian cause.)

11:45 A.M. Mr. Olivier, President of the National Union of Railwaymen of France. (Wishes to inform the President of the work, and the humanitarian and sanitary program of the National Union of French and Belgium Railwaymen.)

12:00 P.M. Mr. J. Jacob, President of the Celtic Circle of Paris. (To present 'The Anthology of the National Bards and Poets'.)

12:15 P.M. Dr. Juan Antonio Buero, Delegate from Uruguay, and brother-in-law of the President of Uruguay.

12:30 P.M. Turkham Pasha, President of the Provisional Government of Albania. (To present the 'just claims of Albania.')

12:45 P.M. Signor Villegas, ex-Secretary of State, Chile, Minister of Chile, Rome.

2:15 P.M. Dr. Edward Beneš and Mr. Kramar. (On the question of Silesia and Teschen.)

2:30 P.M. M. Damour, French Deputy, Chairman of Committee. (For the purpose of explaining the plans for the erection of a statue at the mouth of the Gironde River, to commemorate the arrival of the American troops in France.)

2:45 P.M. The Delegation of the Parliament of Kouban. (Northern Caucasian.)

3:00 P.M. Chrysanthos. (Archbishop of Trebizond.)

3:15 P.M. Governor Manning.

3:30 P.M. Mr. Joseph Reinsch.

The part I have to play can be more or less guessed at.

More than two thirds of these people do not understand a word of English. They bring no interpreters with them and we keep no one here for that purpose. As a rule we have a hint as to the object of their visit and the President manages somehow to listen with attention and generally sends them away happy.

PADEREWSKI

This morning we have Paderewski with us. He is before the Conference pleading the cause of Poland. The small nations, the new ones just created, are giving considerable trouble these days. It seems to me they have lost all trace of what should be their life gratitude and are biting the hand that has fed and even created them. It is interesting to note Paderewski's movements when he comes. He is always late and comes in just as he does at his concerts on the stage. He rumples his hair, does all the bowing and scraping as if he were appearing before a regular set audience, and even sits, as if he were at the piano, out on the edge of a chair.

THE GERMANS DIE HARD

Monday, June 23. Everyone connected with the conference is on tiptoe with expectancy. This is the day when the time limit granted to Germany expires. By seven o'clock this evening they must make answer. All through the day messages have been flying back and forth. The Germans are dying hard. They have jumped from one position to another, but the end is near. They seem to be worrying now about the 'war guilt' clause and the trial of the former Kaiser. They have abandoned all other claims and now dwell on these two items alone. This morning they asked for an extension of time, forty-eight hours, but it was denied them. So it is just a case of waiting and the hours are slipping by.

In the meantime there has been a conference during the morning in which the final clauses of the Austrian Treaty were considered. This was held at the usual time, eleven o'clock, but previous to that the President had been over to Mr. Lloyd George's apartment, at nine, meeting Mr. Clemenceau there, when they considered the request for delay which had come overnight. The morning conference here adjourned at one-fifteen to work on Austrian matters. It was to meet again at four, to consider any word received from the Germans in the meantime.

They had been in session only a half-hour when a message came from the Germans, reiterating their request to be exonerated from responsibility for causing the war and making another appeal for the Kaiser and others, saying they would sign if these two features could be eliminated. The original text in German had been brought over and a French translation along with it. But this latter was not satisfactory, not even to Mr. Clemenceau, for when I handed it to him he told his confrères the substance of it, but asked that an English translation be made immediately. This was evidently believed to be Germany's final answer, for there was a nervous excitement among them to know the true contents of the dispatch. The experts who were present immediately retired to translate. It was read from the German to the French and was just about to be dictated into the English when another messenger came rushing in from the French Foreign Office. This fellow was one of the higher officials and was passed right on to the conference room. He told Mr. Clemenceau they had a telephone message from Versailles, through the German mission there, of the intention of the German Government to sign unconditionally and that the official memorandum was on its way from Versailles. There was deep silence and all seemed to heave a sigh of relief. There was no comment of any consequence except that they hoped for the early arrival of the original text. This was not long in coming and then the meeting practically disbanded. All present engaged in animated conversation and commented on the fact of how hard the Germans had died.

Many suggestions were made about the plans for the actual signing, but nothing could be settled without definite information. Everybody was in a happy mood, especially Mr. Clemenceau, and when the conversation became rather animated he attempted to soften it somewhat, by remarking that there need be no anxiety. 'We have done it many times,' he said, meaning that France was an old hand at treaty-making and treaty-signing. It was but a few minutes longer before it was decided to adjourn and with good feelings and elation at accomplishment they parted.

PANDEMONIUM

Immediately after the conference, the President and Mrs. Wilson went for a short drive. The news by this time had begun to spread and all the sirens were sounded which had been used to announce air raids during the war. Cannons too began to fire salutes. The chauffeur was ordered to take back streets to avoid the crowds. There was good feeling everywhere which continued on through the entire evening and night. They returned in time for dinner and immediately after the President left for a meeting at the hotel. This time it was impossible to avoid the boulevards and it soon became known that he was at the hotel. A great crowd gathered and upon his exit they cheered and raved and his car just had to fight its way through the people to get back home.

The celebration in the evening was the occasion for all kinds of noise-making. People were on the streets by the thousands, principally on the downtown boulevards. The Boulevard des Italiens was one writhing mass of humanity. The crowd paraded up and down in groups and in bands, girls, boys, women, children, soldiers and civilians. Those in uniform especially seemed to go the limit. Flags, all kinds of costumes, wagon loads of soldiers and girls, soldiers carrying girls on their shoulders and hundreds in lock step — everything. The cafés were thronged, everybody seemed wild, and none more so than the American soldiers. Someone in authority told me there were twenty-five thousand of them loose in Paris that night and they made as much noise as a million. They were the lions of the hour and all the others followed in their wake. The scene is beyond description. At eleven-thirty, the closing time of the cafés, most of the lights were extinguished, but the celebration went on more furiously than before. One of their particular sources of amusement was to drag the big cannons from their places in the parks, load them up with girls astride, and drag them through the street. They would pick up the light taxicabs almost bodily and turn them in the direction from which the driver would be trying to go. And yet there was good humor everywhere, there was no real disorder, and they all just took it good-naturedly and had the time of their lives during that one evening.

9

COLONEL HOUSE

THE story of the remarkable friendship between Colonel Edward M. House and President Wilson, and of the tragic break between these two men, is perhaps without parallel in American history. Having been on close terms with both during the critical years, I can, without attempting to pass judgment, record the facts I knew at first hand.

For purposes of comparison let us recall for a moment other men who, in times past, have held positions of trust and responsibility similar to that of Colonel House under the Wilson régime. During more than forty years in the White House, I have known many of them. Benjamin Harrison had his Dudley of Indiana; Grover Cleveland his Benedict, the famous New York banker; William McKinley, his Mark Hanna; Theodore Roosevelt, his Henry Cabot Lodge; William Howard Taft, his brother; Warren G. Harding, his Harry Daugherty; Calvin Coolidge, his Frank Stearns or his Dwight Morrow; Herbert Hoover, his good Administrator friend. Yet none of these men was nearly so close to his President as House was to Wilson. In their case, the crown, so to speak, was shared by others; in the matter of Wilson and House, there were no others. No one else seemed to count. There was nothing too big, too important, too secret, or too sacred to discuss with Colonel House. He was simply the President's one confidant, the one outlet he gave to his innermost thoughts, plans, and purposes. He was a constant visitor at the White House, and it was very evident that the President looked forward to his coming with great pleasure and always regretted to have him leave. These visits

were seldom sought out by the Colonel; in fact, he seemed to
have a strong disinclination for them. He was constantly
asked to come and always urged to stay on, and when he
was at the White House the President would so arrange his
time that he could be with him constantly. On at least one
occasion when he could not come to Washington, the President went all the way to the North Shore of Massachusetts
to confer with him. Hours and hours they would sit and talk
and the President always seemed much benefited by his
visits. His deference and consideration for the Colonel were
pronounced. On one of these visits when House was taken
suddenly ill, and wished to leave either for his home or a
hospital, it was the President alone who insisted that he stay
at the White House during this illness. And contrary to the
President's every principle, he arranged that doctors, medicine, and nurses from the Government service should be supplied without expense to anyone.

THE MOST SOUGHT-AFTER MAN IN THE WHITE HOUSE

During these visits Colonel House was the most sought-
after man who has ever come to the White House. His sphere
of influence was recognized by everyone; foreign representatives, cabinet officers, officials of the departments, Senators,
and members of the House all sought his council. His suggestions were apparent in all the appointments to office. The
changes in the Cabinet and in the State Department could
easily be traced to his conferences with the President. Even
the Supreme Court was not outside his influence, for he was
frequently sought by members of this august body who had
ideas they wished to put across.

It became a custom in the White House, if anything unusual was desired, to seek the aid of the Colonel. There
were many household matters arising from time to time that
required the President's approval, yet about which he could
not be personally approached. An increase of salary or a

change in the daily routine could generally be relied on to get the President's sanction if it were sponsored by Colonel House. Even the family would often take him into their confidence when they had something to be done that they feared would not meet with the President's whole-hearted approval.

PERFECT INTIMACY

As time went on, House's position became stronger and stronger. During the War he seemed indispensable to the President. He was sent for and consulted about everything. His visits became more frequent and the two men corresponded almost daily. I was the intermediary through whom many of these letters passed. They were always received in an outside envelope addressed to me and contained a sealed inside envelope addressed to the President. I delivered them to him in person and neither secretary nor stenographer knew of their existence. The President generally wrote his letters to Colonel House on his own typewriter, and no carbon copies were made.

The most intimate and personal affairs of the President were shared by Colonel House. His second marriage was one of these; every detail of this event, especially in its political implications, was determined by what House thought of it. On his various trips to Europe he was the President's mouthpiece.

The original draft of the League of Nations became Colonel House's pocket-piece. Long before the ending of the War, even before America entered the contest, the Covenant of the League of Nations was talked about. House had taken it back and forth to Europe with him several times. The President had it on his mind always and it seemed such a great relief for him to discuss and analyze it with the Colonel, who certainly had more to do with the making of it than Wilson himself, especially in its original form. The President, of course, had whipped it into shape on his little typewriter, but it is reasonable to guess that not a soul other than Colonel House had seen it in its entirety up to the time the President landed on the shores of France. House was then in Europe, having preceded the President's party. He had gone to prepare the way and never was a representative better equipped than he. The President had seen that every detail was arranged even down to personal expenses and credentials of all kinds.

THE SEEDS OF STRIFE ARE SOWN

These satisfying conditions prevailed when the War ended and the President made ready to sail for Europe. I happened to be one of the immediate party, which consisted of only nine people. Attempts had been made to add others, but they met with no success.

A new situation had arisen during the months immediately preceding. The War had brought into the limelight many persons, distinguished and otherwise. Many of these had come into personal contact with the President. They plainly felt the importance of their positions, regardless of the patriotic side, and wished to bask in the sunshine of Presidential favor. This was no easy matter. The President was generally aloof and unapproachable from this angle. They all knew of the close, almost brotherly, relationship existing between him and Colonel House. This aroused a feeling of resentment, of envy, of jealousy, although the Colonel was always considerate of those people and those things in which the President was interested. It just seemed to be his nature.

The friction which later arose between the President and Colonel House can be attributed to these causes and to nothing else. Every little opportunity was seized upon to discredit him. It began as soon as the President went aboard the *George Washington*. The arrangements for the passage and the personnel had been left to the State Department.

The President had made clear that it was to be a business proposition, not a junketing trip. He had kept his personal party down to a minimum. He had given permission for a couple of ambassadors to go along, but aside from that he did not know in detail who were to be aboard. Somewhat surprised when the passenger list was shown him, he felt there had been some looseness in its arrangement. Much encouraged in this view by several of those near him, he began to look for a cause. Through guarded suggestions it was made to appear that Colonel House had presumed much in drawing up the list and had taken advantage of the confidence of the President to make it a junketing trip for those in whom he was interested.

This was the first open blow struck at Colonel House. His detractors pointed to several of his relatives and friends among the names on the passenger list and hinted that he was getting all he could out of the making of the Peace Treaty. And now, for the first time, doubt entered the President's mind; he began to question whether, after all, the Colonel was the unselfish, loyal friend that he had always appeared to be.

The President was particularly nervous and keyed up when he went aboard the *George Washington*. His condition can be judged by the fact that he went straight to his suite of rooms and did not emerge for two full days and nights. When he did, he seemed much refreshed and quite his normal self again. All the suspicion about the passenger list seemed to have disappeared. But the incident had laid the foundation for the undoing of Colonel House and it was with a feeling of satisfaction that certain rivals looked on.

PARIS, 1919

When the party arrived in Paris the relations between the two men seemed perfect. They visited back and forth between the Palais Murat and the Hôtel Crillon and there was apparently not a ripple of misunderstanding. The Covenant of the League of Nations was the one objective of both men and they seemed to be working along in perfect harmony. I was surprised at this, for I could clearly see the other influences that were at work in an effort to discredit the Colonel.

The matter of the League of Nations was practically completed and the time came for the President to return to the United States for the closing of Congress. All other members of the Peace Commission were to remain in Paris and make preparations for the general conferences at which the treaty itself would be framed, for up to this time practically all of the effort had been put forth to perfect the Covenant of the League of Nations. Colonel House was left behind to keep the coals alive while the President was gone. During this period of about three weeks, he was naturally sought out by different elements, held many conferences, and saw many people. Upon the President's return to Paris, the critics of the Colonel got busy. Directly and by inference they pictured him as having taken unto himself the influence, prestige, and responsibility of the President. They pictured him as undermining his chief. The President was very serious, very conscious of his influence, very intent on his purpose, and very egotistical about his new position in world affairs. He was jealous of his power and responsibility. In addition, he was not well. He showed signs of nervousness in many ways and had clearly been working too hard. So it was that these innuendoes about Colonel House took root, grew as time went on, and finally terminated in the complete alienation of the two men.

'I WISH HE WOULD LEAVE ME ALONE!'

The effects were numerous and interesting to us on the inside. Colonel House would from time to time be placed in the most embarrassing positions. In the conferences that were held daily at the Palais Murat, Clemenceau, Lloyd George, and Orlando often found themselves in opposition to Wilson's views. For days an important question would go unsettled. In the meantime these statesmen would endeavor to bring influence to bear to make the President see things in their light. Knowing of his influence, their first thoughts would turn to Colonel House, and conferences would be arranged with him. These were invariably brought to the President's attention with the idea of illustrating how his own influence was being subordinated and belittled.

Frequently after these very conferences, Colonel House would seek out the President and discuss the subject matter with him, as had always been his custom and his privilege. But now, for reasons stated above, the President seemed to have lost patience. Once when the Colonel called him on the telephone and asked for an appointment, I heard him say, 'I wish he would leave me alone!' at the same time granting the request. Lost confidence was followed by a suspicion of treachery, the President feeling that House was trying to make himself too conspicuous and important. How foreign this was to the truth! Colonel House saw the situation coming on, but he was helpless. There was nothing that he had done for which amends could be made. I am sure if there were he would have gone to the very limit of his endurance in his loyalty and his faithfulness to the President. No one was more loyal than he.

TOO MUCH FOR ONE MAN

One fact greatly aggravated the situation. In these conferences the other members were always surrounded with a staff of assistants, secretaries, interpreters, etc., while President Wilson had no one with him. All alone he battled and argued, and it was felt that he was at a great disadvantage. It was a subject much discussed at the time, not only by Colonel House, but the other members of the Commission.

It was suggested to the President that he have an assistant and he was partly favorable to the idea until the name of Mr. Gordon Auchincloss was mentioned. That put a different light on the whole proposition. He thought that the other members of the Commission, and Colonel House in particular, were trying to keep an eye on him. Of course such was far from the case, but the President by this time was suspicious of everybody and everything. I believe that he was a sick man and his later collapse had its inception in those trying days.

The President fought the battle all alone; fought it valiantly, wonderfully, masterfully. There was no limit to his endeavor. But that he did fight it alone, through choice, is undeniable. Whatever was good was his; for whatever was bad, he was responsible. He could not see the selfish influences that were at work all about him to discredit Colonel House. What was to be attained I do not know. But an important object there must have been, for it was pursued with determination.

THE FRUITS OF INTRIGUE

So as the time went on, the Colonel became less and less an object of the President's confidence. Yet there was no actual break. Not a word of discord had passed between them. Though he realized there was something wrong, House just went the even tenor of his way doing the best he could. True, he could not know all that was going on, and those of us who sympathized with him were not in a position to tell him. He was not privileged to inquire about it from the President. It would have been a liberty he dared not take. He knew he was being silently ignored, but, rather than complain, he took his medicine, evidently hoping that the sky would clear and things would right themselves.

Until the end of the Paris trip and the final signing of the treaty of peace this situation continued. Still there was no break, just suggestions, hinted suspicions, inferences that, owing to the President's nervous condition, fell on fertile ground.

Wilson returned to the United States; Colonel House remained behind in Paris. The Colonel's detractors returned with the President. They were happy, for they had maneuvered themselves into a favorable position. The President himself seemed so different under these influences! He was now associating with individuals of whom he had once strenuously disapproved. He really seemed a changed man. Much of his poise and consideration for others had left him entirely.

SUSPICIONS TURN TO HATRED

His return, his presentation and championing of the treaty, are well known. Then came his illness. Colonel House did everything within his power to help. He put aside any feeling of disappointment that might have lingered from the days in Paris and sought in every way to live up to his ideal of a faithful friend. He sent messages of cheer, admiration, devotion, loyalty.

I feel that, had not illness overtaken the President, all would have been well. With his keen discernment, he would have seen things in their true light. He needed Colonel House and, in a way, fully realized the fact. But this illness changed the entire aspect of things. The President was sicker than the world ever knew, and never afterwards was he more than a shadow of his former self. Even when conscious, he was unreasonable, unnatural, simply impossible. His suspicions were intensified, his perspective distorted. Unfortunately those about him had to encourage him in these notions, for it was the only way to get along with him. His feeling about Colonel House become an obsession. He could see no good in him at all. Encouraged by those around him, his obsession apparently turned to hatred. Yet he talked of him incessantly. Letters were coming from Colonel House pertaining to the closing up of the affairs of the Peace Conference, but they were never opened. They accumulated for months. None, I believe, was ever acknowledged. The matter of the misunderstanding with Secretary Lansing was but an echo of the obsession about Colonel House. All the talk about cabinet meetings being held unknown to the President and without his permission was but a pretext advanced by a third party. He knew all the time about these cabinet meetings and, in his feeble way, approved of them.

'MAN'S INHUMANITY TO MAN'

Colonel House tried by every honorable means to place himself in the right position toward the President, but all to no avail. The former great man was no longer himself. He went on to the end with the same animosity, falsely aroused within him, and there was no one to repeat to him the lines he had so often quoted:

'Man's inhumanity to man
Makes countless thousands mourn.'

After the President had left the White House, and become a comparative recluse in his own home in Washington, Colonel House came to visit several times with the intention of paying his respects to his old friend 'the Governor,' as he always referred to the President. He was advised by those who had his best interests at heart not to do so. By taking this advice I am sure that he saved himself deep embarrassment, for there was no time, even to the end, when he could have overcome those false suggestions and hinted accusations that had poisoned the President's mind. It is a sad state of affairs when misunderstandings come between two such men as these. Both suffered in more ways than one, for until the break came they were the personification of team work that brought results.

10

THE TRUTH ABOUT WILSON'S ILLNESS

THERE has been so much guessing on the subject of President Wilson's illness that I am prompted to record the facts as I knew them at the time. The guessers have many times hit close to the mark, but none seem to have sufficiently correct information to make a truly historical record. Those in a position to know — and there are but few — seem disinclined to tell the truth, or, if they do, it is so meager or purposely distorted as to lose its value.

It has been said that President Wilson was always, more or less, a sick man. I saw nothing of the kind during the six and a half years I served under him, prior to this last illness. On the contrary, he was exceptionally robust, much more so even than his appearance would lead one to believe. He was heavy-set, muscular, and courageous. He had an unusually strong chest and stout limbs and had a good appetite. He did have a little twitching in one eye, but it was hardly noticeable. He was a man who took excellent care of himself. He knew how to work and when to work and how to rest. He could lie down any time of the day, banish all thoughts from his mind and go off to sleep in a few minutes. Likewise he could wake up just about when he wished without being called. He prided himself on these two faculties and I have often heard him discuss them.

It was in this satisfactory condition that he left for Europe. I was one of the few who personally accompanied him. When he started out, I believe he was tired, but surely not sick.

THE STRAIN OF THE PEACE CONFERENCE

In Europe there were trying times for him. It was so different from what he had been passing through the previous five or six years. Now he was certainly the whole show — at the beginning at least. The responsibility seemed tremendous. I was by his side for twelve or fourteen hours every day. My hours were his hours. There was not a let-up, all days were alike. He was so intent that it was a positive burden to try to keep up with him. The others of us in the party wanted to see Europe and especially Paris, but our opportunities were limited on account of the intensity and concentration of the President. But the day came when he wavered. The load was too much. Some saw it from one angle, some from another. He went to bed ostensibly with a cold. When he got on his feet again he was a different man.

Even while lying in bed he manifested peculiarities, one of which was to limit the use of all the automobiles to strictly official purposes, when previously he had been so liberal in his suggestions that his immediate party should have the benefit of this possible diversion, in view of the long hours we were working. When he got back on the job, his peculiar ideas were even more pronounced. He now became obsessed with the idea that every French employee about the place was a spy for the French Government. Nothing we could say could disabuse his mind of this thought. He insisted they all understood English, when, as a matter of fact, there was just one of them among the two dozen or more who understood a single word of English. About this time he also acquired the peculiar notion that he was personally responsible for all the property in the furnished palace he was occupying. He raised quite a fuss on two occasions when he noticed articles of furniture had been removed. Upon investigation — for no one else noticed the change — it was learned that the custodian of the property for the French owner had seen fit to do a little rearranging. Coming from the President, whom we all knew so well, these were very funny things, and we could but surmise that something queer was happening in his mind.

One thing was certain: he was never the same after this little spell of sickness.

BACK HOME

Returning to America after the close of the Conference, he arrived in Washington at midnight on July 8, 1919. The rest and diversion on the boat had apparently done him a lot of good. He was quite his normal self again. He seemed to feel that he had left many of his troubles behind. He was looking to the future with satisfaction and confidence. I am sure he did not realize what he was going up against or, if he did, he felt complete master of the situation. In speaking of the future he pictured himself back at Geneva as the Head of the League of Nations in all the power and prominence which that position would give him. On one occasion he asked me if I would like to go back to Geneva.

During the two months between his return from Europe and his so-called Western trip, he went about the even tenor of his ways. He motored a great deal, played golf several times, attended the theater, and saw a number of visitors. Still it was evident that those about him, and even the President himself, were making an effort to conserve his health. He had several notable appointments during this time, especially the one with the Foreign Relations Committee of the Senate. To those of us who just looked on and listened, the President was not at his best at that meeting. In fact all through this period he manifested an over-anxiety toward his guests. He had one short spell of sickness which kept him confined to his room for a couple of days.

But what struck us most was that he refrained from going to the Executive Offices during this time. Most of his appointments were made for the White House proper and it was noticed that he was doing a lot of resting, retiring to his room from time to time during the day, shutting himself off from all the world.

In the meantime, by his orders, arrangements had been made for his Western trip and on the evening of September 3, 1919, he left the White House for the station to join the others who were to accompany him. He returned to Washington on the morning of September 28, after his collapse, or whatever it was, that overtook him in Wichita, Kansas.

Upon his return he appeared no worse than when he left, except that he looked a little peaked and seemed to have lost some of his spirit. His face was a little more florid than usual, but there was apparently nothing alarming in his condition. Those of us who knew, however, remembered the days in Paris, the suspicions of the French servants and of the moving of the furnishings in the palace. He took up his daily routine, went motoring, and, though he stayed close to his private quarters, he gave the impression that after a little rest he would come around all right, as he had done after his illness in Paris.

THE CRASH

Thus the days went on, four in number, until Thursday, October 2, 1919, when the crash came.

The story of this, his last and lasting illness, is tragic. The whole truth, of course, can be told by only one person in all the world, Mrs. Woodrow Wilson the second. Especially must all that is known of the climax come from her. I doubt whether she will ever tell the world just what happened. Those of us who attempt it must be given credit for honesty of purpose in narrating the facts as they came to us, and due allowance must be made for most unusual and startling circumstances at the time.

At exactly ten minutes before nine o'clock on this memorable day (I noted the time in writing the same day), my telephone on the desk in the Usher's Room at the White

House rang and Mrs. Wilson's voice said, 'Please get Doctor Grayson, the President is very sick.' The telephone used was a private one that did not go through the general telephone switchboard. Mrs. Wilson had come all the way out to the end of the upper hall to use this particular telephone instead of the regular one in their bedroom. I reasoned at the time that it was done to avoid publicity, for there had been talk about the operators of the switchboard listening in and disseminating information they picked up. I immediately called Doctor Grayson at his home, repeated the message as Mrs. Wilson had given it to me, and ordered one of the White House automobiles to go for him with all haste. I then went upstairs to see if there was anything I could do. Upon reaching the upper floor I saw that all doors were closed; I was helpless so far as being of any assistance was concerned. The servants were about, but none of them had heard Mrs. Wilson telephone and they knew nothing of the President being sick. I waited up there until Doctor Grayson came, which was but a few minutes at most. A little after nine, I should say. Doctor Grayson attempted to walk right in, but the door was locked. He knocked quietly and, upon the door being opened, he entered. I continued to wait in the outer hall. In about ten minutes Doctor Grayson came out and with raised arms said, 'My God, the President is paralyzed! Send for Doctor Stitt and the nurse,' mentioning the name of the latter, the same one who had been in attendance upon the first Mrs. Wilson and who was with her when she died.

The remark of Doctor Grayson made an indelible impression on my mind. Paralyzed! What a fate for such a great man! I am free to say I never heard the word mentioned thereafter in connection with the President's condition, by those who were in a position to know the facts. When Doctor Grayson returned to the President's room, there was not much excitement. The second doctor and nurse arrived and were shown to the room. The employees about the place began to get wise to the fact that the President was very ill, but they could find out nothing more. Other doctors were sent for during the day, and the best that could be learned was that the President was resting quietly. Doctor Davis of Philadelphia and Doctor Ruffin, Mrs. Wilson's personal physician, were among those summoned. There were doctors everywhere.

A consultation of them all together was held about four o'clock. An air of secrecy had come over things during the day. Those on the outside, including family and employees, could learn nothing. It was my privilege to go into the sick-room in the late afternoon. Some rearrangement of the furnishing had to be made and the domestic attendants on the floor were not allowed in. So Doctor Grayson, the nurse, and I did the job.

The President lay stretched out on the large Lincoln bed. He looked as if he were dead. There was not a sign of life. His face had a long cut about the temple from which the signs of blood were still evident. His nose also bore a long cut lengthwise. This too looked red and raw. There was no bandage.

Soon after, I made confidential inquiry as to how and when it all happened. I was told — and know it to be right — that he had gone to the bathroom upon arising in the morning and was sitting on the stool when the affliction overcame him; that he tumbled to the floor, striking his head on the sharp plumbing of the bathtub in his fall; that Mrs. Wilson, hearing groans from the bathroom, went in and found him in an unconscious condition. She dragged him to the bed in the room adjoining and came out into the hall to call over the telephone for the doctor, as I have related.

For the next three or four days the White House was like a hospital. There were all kinds of medical apparatus and more doctors and more nurses. Day and night this went on. All the while the only answer one could get from an inquiry as to his condition was that it 'showed signs of improvement.' No

details, no explanations. This situation seemed to go on indefinitely. It was perhaps three weeks or more before any
change came over things. I had been in and out of the room
many times during this period and I saw very little progress
in the President's condition. He just lay helpless. True,
he had been taking nourishment, but the work the doctors had
been doing on him had just about sapped his remaining
vitality. All his natural functions had to be artificially
assisted and he appeared just as helpless as one could possibly
be and live.

He lived on; but oh, what a wreck of his former self! He
did grow better, but that is not saying much. I was with him
at some time every day and saw him, even up to the end, at
his private residence. There was never a moment during all
that time when he was more than a shadow of his former self.
He had changed from a giant to a pygmy in every wise. He
was physically almost incapacitated; he could articulate but
indistinctly and think but feebly. It was so sad that those of
us about him, who almost without exception admired him,
would turn our heads away when he came along or we went
near him.

A NATION WITHOUT A LEADER

It is interesting to note what happens when the President of
the United States is incapacitated. During his' early illness
everything in the way of business came to a standstill. But
there came a time when something had to be done. For at
least a month or more not one word, I believe, was mentioned
to him about the business of the office and he was so sick he
did not take the initiative to inquire. No secretary, no official,
no stenographer, no one with business had even seen him.
He was lifted out of bed and placed in a comfortable chair for
a short while each day. He gradually seemed to get used to
his helpless condition. At times Mrs. Wilson would read to
him. Finally, when it could no longer be delayed, some mat-

ters of importance requiring his signature were read to him and with a pencil, his hand steadied and pointed, he would sign where the hands had been placed. I saw many of these signatures and they were but mere scribbles compared to his normal signature. Even this mechanical process seemed to exhaust him.

This original stroke, or whatever it was, simply put the President out of business, for at least a month. At the end of that time he could be lifted from the bed, placed in a chair beside the bed, and chair and man moved to another part of the room. After a few days of this an invalid rolling chair was tried, but it soon proved a failure. He could not sit upright. It was evident that more rigid braces for his body were necessary. I suggested one of the single-person rolling chairs like the ones used on the boardwalk at Atlantic City. This was agreed to and arrangements were made to hire one from a dealer at Atlantic City. The original arrangement was to hire it for five dollars a week, but as time went on, and it was seen that the chair was to be a permanent affair, it was bought outright. When it arrived, we changed the footrest part of it, making it to stand out straight on a line with the seat, thereby avoiding the necessity of bending his legs when he was placed in it. This chair was used every time the President got out of bed for the remaining days at the White House. I pushed it about day after day during the entire time. Even in the few journeys out of the house, he would be rolled to the elevator and practically carried the rest of the way to the automobile in waiting. His several trips to the theater were pitiful. I would accompany him and with much assistance get him awkwardly into his box. We were always driven to the rear entrance of the theater.

HOW THE GOVERNMENT WAS CARRIED ON

If there was ever a man in bad shape he was. He could not talk plainly, mumbled more than he articulated, was helpless and looked like a man fatally ill. Everybody tried to help him, realizing he was so dependent for everything. At all of the cabinet meetings he would be rolled into the cabinet room in his old chair and fixed up prior to the coming of the members. He took little part in the proceedings, the others doing all the talking.

When the Senate Committee came, the President, who had been sitting up in his rolling chair, was put to bed, propped up with pillows, and covered over entirely, except his head and right arm. Mrs. Wilson stood at the foot of the bed, the nurse at the side of the bed, Doctor Grayson in the doorway, which was left open, and I behind Grayson. Their visit was very short, apparently limited to brief consultations. They made no effort to cross-examine or inquire about his condition, and he went through with it well. Everyone was happy afterwards that nothing more serious had happened.

GRAYSON, TUMULTY, AND MRS. WILSON

So it went through the fall and into the winter. On sunshiny days he would be wheeled out into the south grounds for an hour or so. If there were some papers requiring his attention, they would be read to him at this time — but only those that Mrs. Wilson thought should be read to him. These would reach her through Doctor Grayson. To him they had come from Tumulty or from some other official. He would tell Mrs. Wilson what had been said about the matter and she would tell the President. Likewise, the word of any decision the President had made would be passed back through the same channels.

There was but very little even of this sort of business. Tumulty tried hard to get to the President during all these months, but he was kept away. He was loyal to the core; there was no position he would not have taken under the circumstances for the President's best interests. He never gave up in spite of the awkward position he was occupying. It was

Tumulty and Swem with the help of the cabinet members who prepared the President's message to Congress. This Swem was a fine young fellow, smart and understanding. Even when the President was well, he played such a part in handling his correspondence and in the preparation of all his papers that it became easy, when the necessity arose, for him to prepare additional papers, for the Wilson style was second nature to him.

THE DEMOCRATIC CONVENTION

The winter passed and the spring came. Some motor rides were suggested. One might have noticed that the President never rode in the rear seat of the car, but always in front with the driver. He could not sit up in the back. He would slide down or topple over as the car rolled along. The front seat was braced for just one person to sit in and here he would be placed. He always wore his cape coat; he could not get on an overcoat, could not get his poor limp arm in the sleeve. With spring came the prospect of the Democratic Convention and at the so-called cabinet meetings the nomination was discussed from time to time. Through this source it became evident that the President was in a receptive mood for the nomination. The truth is he was not only receptive, but anxious and expectant. There was not a member of the cabinet present who did not know that it would be an impossibility, physically, mentally, and morally, even to harbor such a thought, and yet there were some who did encourage it. Whether they did it for sentiment, charity, or really expected to put such a thing over on the Convention, only they can answer. It was really sad how they deceived him. The disappointment they caused him could have been avoided if they had just kept silent.

When the Convention was over and Cox had been nominated, there was no interest left in the campaign, so far as the White House occupants were concerned.

On their return to Washington, the cabinet members met with a cold reception from the President. It was days before any of them got even the slightest notice and yet they were anxious to explain their positions at once. He had not much patience with them and it was rumored that one would be asked to resign. Daniels was the first to make headway, for he had Doctor Grayson's help. Colby gradually got back in some degree through the influence of Mrs. Wilson; but one of them never did get back. He had no friend at Court or perhaps he did most of the talking and promising before the Convention met. He became a sort of outcast around the White House; the only one who even in a small measure helped to keep him afloat to the end was Tumulty.

'I AM TIRED OF SWIMMING UPSTREAM'

The President never had any more actual initiative after that early October day of 1919. Every effort was made to save him from coming in contact with people or considering anything except what seemed to Mrs. Wilson important. Persons who could not be put off were received by her. Information she received would be passed on to the President, many times to be heard of no more. Some few persons gained access to him, but in such cases he was watched and prompted during the audience. Interviews like those said to be held with Mr. Baruch or David Lawrence were all arranged by Doctor Grayson at the suggestion of Mrs. Wilson. From the first day of his illness no one ever got close to the President again.

The usual routine for weeks and weeks, in fact practically to the end, was for him to be taken from his bed about ten o'clock, placed in the chair, and rolled to the south grounds; or, in bad weather, to the porch or to some other room. The last year of his stay saw him in the East Room every day at twelve o'clock to look at a motion picture. We scoured the country that he might have a different picture each day. He would return to his bedroom at one o'clock, have his lunch, and be placed back in bed, where he would remain until the next morning. Until his last hour in the White House he had a corps of nurses in attendance and everything under the sun was resorted to in an effort to help him. My own opinion is that he never really got much better from the very first day of his trouble.

I visited him after he left the White House at his S Street residence. He was not much changed. A little of the mystery surrounding him had disappeared, but in so far as he himself was concerned I saw no difference. When I remarked that he seemed to be getting on well, he replied, 'I am tired of swimming upstream.'

It was indeed a sad ending for a great man. In his prime he was a giant among men. I saw him at his best and there were but few to equal and none to surpass him. I bow to his memory and believe that the generations to come will do the same when the works of the days of his genius will prevail and the horrors of his illness will be swallowed up in the glory that will be his.

11

NOTES ON THE EARLY YEARS

EMBARRASSING MOMENTS

THE old steward in Harrison's time went to the East Room to announce a state dinner with one leg of his trousers up, showing his underwear. The next day Mrs. Harrison asked him if he had adopted the English style of his breeches and, if so, why only one leg.

I remember once in the old days a policeman was discovered fast asleep on duty, dressed in a nightgown with a pillow and blankets.

OLD JERRY AND THE WATERMELON MINISTER

Old Jerry, the Negro janitor in the Executive Offices, saw ghosts, and as he swept the floor with a feather duster, he would sing to himself to keep his spirits up. He also served as carriage caller and once shouted, 'The Watermelon Minister,' for the Guatemalan Minister.

It was Jerry who one morning raised the White House flag upside down. It blew that way for about ten minutes before it was discovered and righted. Sometime afterwards, one of the newspaper men at the Executive Offices called on the telephone and inquired about it. He was told that it was true, but was asked not to publish the story, since it was not a matter of public interest and would only get the colored man who made the mistake in trouble. He promised he would say nothing. The matter was then forgotten, but, lo and behold, when his paper came out that afternoon, there was on the front page a headline story and a picture of the White House with the flag upside down. He had gone to the trouble of faking this picture and writing the story, in spite of his promise. Fortunately, no harm came to the man who made the mistake. When spoken to about the matter afterwards, his only excuse was that he feared some other paper would get hold of the story and publish it. I tell this to illustrate again one of the difficulties of being at the White House where the news-gatherers consider every grunt, groan, or smile a piece of news that the world must have.

The newspaper men detailed at the White House know about many private affairs of the Presidential families which they don't dare to write, or which their publishers will not print. There are dozens of human-interest stories every day which are never known outside the White House.

THE SPANISH WAR

There was more excitement at the White House during the time of the Spanish War than during the World War. More officials came running around to see McKinley than to see Wilson. McKinley seemed to do more of the actual planning, while Wilson left the preliminary work to others and only passed on finished plans. The fifty-million-dollar bond issue during the Spanish War seemed quite as large as the billions during the World War.

RAT HUNT

In the old days, it was no uncommon thing for a rat or a mouse to present himself in the dining-room at mealtimes. During the Roosevelt Administration, I remember at least two occasions when the family dinner party was broken up to chase a rat around the room. It was great sport for the male members of the family, the President included.

STATIONERY

Roosevelt changed 'The Executive Mansion' to 'The White House' on his stationery. He pointed out that every state had an Executive Mansion and that the President's house should be distinctive.

TAFT

When Taft came to the White House, a large tub had to be placed in his bathroom, since the one already there was not big enough. The President would stick in it when bathing and had to be helped out each time.

The Taft cow was one of the real novelties of Presidential life. Automobiles having come into vogue with the Tafts, the stable was free of horses. Here is where the cow made its home. A man was assigned to the cow. He had nothing else to do. He was hired for the purpose and would bring the milk to the White House kitchen twice a day.

When President Taft told Cardinal Gibbons that he was expected to deliver an extemporaneous address, the Cardinal replied, 'Mr. President, do you realize generally speaking there is no such thing as an extemporaneous talk, for everything you will say, you have heard before, or at least it has been said sometime by someone.'

WILSON

When I went to Princeton to arrange for the removal of President Wilson's effects to Washington, I noticed that his books were autographed in various forms:

Thomas W. Wilson
Thomas Woodrow Wilson
T. W. Wilson
T. Woodrow Wilson
Woodrow Wilson

It is interesting to note how he changed his signature from time to time.

There was a campaign to let Joseph Tumulty, Secretary to the President, out in the Wilson second term because of Tumulty's religion. Wilson seemed to agree for a while, but later, realizing Tumulty's loyalty and devotion, kept him on.

President Wilson had an album made containing pictures of all the members of the Senate and House, so that he could recognize them when they came to see him. He spent many hours studying the pictures, which were taken by a prominent photographer.

Mr. Sayre, Wilson's son-in-law, would wear his shoes until the rubber heels were worn down on the outside and would then have the heels shifted. This idiosyncrasy was much a topic of discussion among the domestics.

President Wilson had an old cape he always carried when motoring from the White House. He had worn it on a bicycle trip through Europe. It got many rides without use.

When Wilson left the White House, we cut at least ten large oil paintings from their frames and sent the frames to auction, the employees keeping the canvases. We also demolished thirty-two busts of the Presidents, both plaster and metal. We smashed them with a sledgehammer.

'I NEVER DO THE SAME THING THE SAME WAY'

One day when President Wilson's daughter Margaret was going for an automobile ride with her father, she waited for him on the stone path outside the White House door, where she could see him coming over the terrace from his office and be ready when he arrived. On this occasion, the President did not come over the terrace, but instead came underneath. He arrived at the car and had to wait for Margaret. As she ran up, she remarked, 'Why, Father, I thought you always came over the terrace.' 'No, my dear,' he replied, 'I never do the same thing the same way.' Knowing President Wilson

and his way of doing his own thinking, I felt that the remark
had great significance.

FORD'S PATRIOTISM

While at 'Shadowlawn' in the summer of 1916, President
Wilson asked Ford to finance his campaign, since Ford was
always talking peace. Ford refused outright, but suggested
he would send a letter to every purchaser of a Ford car in
America, advocating Wilson's election. The President agreed,
and Ford did so, setting up an office in New York City for the
purpose. Wilson remarked afterwards that Ford's patriotism
was measured along with the sale of his cars.

FIREWOOD

An autumn storm during Wilson's time blew down a large
elm tree in front of the White House. The President, looking
out of the window of the Usher's Room, saw men chopping it
up and hauling it away. He inquired what they were going to
do with it, and being told it was to be thrown on the dump,
he remarked, 'What a waste!' He gave orders that it should
be sawed into proper lengths and split, to be used in the open
fireplaces at the White House during the coming winter. He
went on to mention the tremendous waste of that kind which
was permitted by the American public, explaining how the
people in other parts of the world used every particle of a
fallen tree, even to the twigs and leaves. From then on, all
the fallen timber around Washington, especially in Rock
Creek National Park, has been used for firewood at the White
House. I believe the practice continues to this day.

HARDING

Harding would often say, 'Let the rankest come first.'
Harding died in San Francisco on August 2, 1923. Coolidge took the oath of office at his home in Vermont at midnight. When he arrived in Washington, he made his head-

quarters at the Willard Hotel. The funeral services in Washington were on the seventh, followed by burial at Marion. On the eleventh, Mrs. Harding returned to the White House, and Coolidge dined with her in the evening. She left on the seventeenth, and for the next three days the White House had no occupant. The Coolidges moved in on the twenty-first at three o'clock in the afternoon.

When the body of President Harding arrived at the White House, the undertaker — who offered his services free — laid it out in the East Room as McKinley's had been, with the head to the south. From the mass of flowers, Mrs. Harding selected those which she said Warren would like and placed them near the casket. She was wonderfully calm under the ordeal.

Owing to the delay of the funeral train, the services originally planned for the evening of its arrival were postponed until the next morning. There was a short prayer at the White House. The Diplomatic Corps and the members of Congress waited in the Blue Room until the procession was ready to start. A question of precedence caused a mixup on entering the automobiles; which should come first, the Supreme Court or the Ambassadors? The matter was settled by appointing the Justices of the Court honorary pallbearers, so that they might go ahead with the cabinet. Wreaths were placed on the casket by representatives of the three branches of the Government; Coolidge for the Executive; Taft for the Judicial; and Gillett and Cummings for the House and Senate.

WHITE HOUSE CHILDREN WHO HAVE GROWN UP

It has been most interesting during the latter part of these forty years to see those who have once been babies at the White House grow up and come back with families. The McKee children were about three and five years old when I went to the White House. During the Coolidge Administration, the former 'Baby McKee' returned, a grown-up married

WARREN GAMALIEL HARDING AND
FLORENCE KLING HARDING

GRACE COOLIDGE

man, and Mary, his sister, came in the Hoover time with husband and three children. The Cleveland children whom I have carried around the house on my shoulders have been back several times since they are grown up and married.

The Roosevelt family when they came to the White House in 1901 were practically all babies, with the exception of Ted and Alice, who were in their middle teens. They came back later, all with wives and children. Ethel had grown into a woman just like her mother when she was in the White House. Archie comes with a large family and when he asks for Mr. Hoover and is directed to the Executive Offices, by an attendant who thinks he wants to see the President, he blurts out, 'I want to see *my* Hoover.' The men at the door take the cue handily and I am called to the front. The other Roosevelt children come also and ask for 'Hooie,' as they all, including the President and Mrs. Roosevelt, used to call me when they were there. Poor little Quentin, who was killed in the War, was the pride of the place. Everybody took an interest in him and loved him and all looked forward to the time when he would grow up to look just like his great father. In the younger days he was the one who was most like him. It is he who scratched 'Ike Hoover' in one of the glass window-panes with a diamond ring, and it still remains after these twenty-five years have passed.

PART II
A SPOTLIGHT ON YESTERDAY'S HEROES

12

THE WHITE HOUSE FROM THE GROUND UP

BEFORE I begin my story of the Coolidge and Hoover Administrations, and of the many celebrities whom we entertained at one time or another, I should like to give the reader a systematic description of the White House as it is today. The major alterations in the old building took place under the Roosevelts, as a result of the construction of the present state dining-room. [See Chapter 32.] Here, then, is what one would see if he were allowed to explore the White House from top to bottom.

BETWEEN THE POLICE AND THE SECRET SERVICE

On the ground, or basement, floor as one enters by the east is the guard-room, which is the headquarters of the White House police, and a long cloak-room that takes up the entire area beneath the east terrace. Entering the basement floor of the house proper, to the left are three rooms used for general purposes and open to the public — two of them living-rooms, the third used to house the china exhibit. Next comes the billiard-room, which is also used as a doctors' office, then two servants' rooms, one of them a dining-room for the help.

Back again, going to the east entrance on the same floor and entering as before, on the right is a large room used for employees' lockers. Then in the middle on this side is the very commodious engine-room, divided into several compartments. This large space was the original kitchen of the house, and here can still be seen the old open fireplaces where the cooking used to be done. Adjoining this room on the west is the present kitchen, made up of one large and two smaller rooms.

The space under the west terrace is partitioned off into numerous rooms for various purposes. There is the white servants' dining-room, a large room for the florist, a small room for the President's military and naval aides, and two rooms for the so-called Social Bureau. Adjoining is a room used by the State Department representative who is supposed to have something to do with the social side of the establishment. At the extreme end are three rooms, two of them used as secretarial offices and the third as an office by the secret service detail. Thus you note at the extreme east end is the police room and at the extreme west end is the secret service room!

THE SCENE OF OFFICIAL LIFE

As one enters the White House from the front or north door, on the main floor, one comes first to the entrance hall and the long corridor running between the famous East Room at the one end and the State Dining-Room at the other. In between these two on the south are the three parlors, the Green, Blue, and Red, looking from east to west.

The East Room is used for many purposes. It forms the principal assembly room for all social affairs. Here the President receives committees and delegations. Here are held all musicales and dances. The mantels are made of American marble from different States of the Union. The gold piano was donated to the Government in 1903. The large blue vases, as well as the bisque figures of Washington, Jefferson, Lincoln, and Franklin on the mantels were presented by the French Government. The electrical fixtures form a special feature of the room.

The Green Room is one of the three private parlors. It

was used by Mrs. Hoover to receive her guests at afternoon tea-parties and also by many Presidents for private conferences. The furniture is truly colonial of the period of the original White House — 1792. The walls are covered with specially made tapestry and the rug is of unusual design. On the walls hang the portraits of Jefferson by Andrews, John Quincy Adams and Van Buren by Healy, and James K. Polk. The mantel is one of two original mantels of the house which have survived. The other is in the Red Room.

The Blue Room is the formal room, the State Parlor of the house. Here all foreign representatives are received when presenting their credentials. Here also the President and his wife stand when receiving on state occasions. The walls are covered with silk brocatelle, made for the room. The furniture is of special design. The clock and ornaments on the mantel are Napoleon heirlooms, presented to the United States Government by Lafayette on the occasion of his second visit to America in 1825.

The Red Room is another of the private parlors, used principally for informal affairs. Here assemble all guests for meals when they are being privately entertained. It is also used extensively for afternoon teas. The furnishings were selected by the Roosevelts. The walls are hung with silk tapestries. On one wall is the famous painting of Washington by Gilbert Stuart, saved from the fire of 1814 by Dolly Madison, and the portrait of Martha Washington by Andrews. Here also is John Adams,[1] the first President to occupy the White House. This painting is a copy from a Stuart. Grant by Ulke, considered one of the best of the General, is also in this room.

The State Dining-Room is used not only for official entertaining, but for daily lunch and dinner, even when the President and his wife are alone. Separate tables are arranged for all large parties according to the number of guests. The largest one is semi-circular and seats ninety-two persons.

[1] See Coolidge's comment, page 128.

The walls are of English oak. The furnishings were made specially for the room. Particularly fine are the eagles, carved out of solid mahogany, which form supports for the side tables. The famous Cogswell painting of Lincoln hangs in this room.

Adjoining the State Dining-Room are the breakfast-room and the pantry. The one other room on this floor is the so-called Usher's Room. This is used for every purpose under the sun and in fact is a sort of clearing-house for the establishment.

WHERE THE FAMILY LIVES

Mounting the grand staircase to the second or bedroom floor, we find another long corridor stretching out from one end of the house to the other, from east to west. In the southeast corner is a suite which was once Lincoln's office and cabinet room. Later used as a bedroom, it was restored to its original purpose by Hoover, who greatly valued the Lincoln tradition.[1] Next on the south side, going west, is what is now the Rose Drawing-Room, arranged as such by Mrs. Hoover when the President gave it up as a study. Adjoining this is the Oval Room or Library, as it is sometimes called. Then comes a bedroom and another suite at the extreme southwest corner consisting of a large bedroom, a dressing-room, and a bath. These have been the sleeping quarters of almost all the Presidents in recent times.

Crossing the corridor to the corner on the north side, we find another three-room suite. This is known at present as the Lincoln Suite, for here has been assembled all the furniture known to have been used by the War President. Cleveland and McKinley were the only Presidents I knew who slept here. Moving eastward there is a small hall room that is cut into by the elevator shaft, the blue bedroom, and the yellow bedroom. This brings us back to the grand staircase

[1] See page 181.

again. In between the staircase and the extreme east end is one more suite, the Rose Suite.

THE EVOLUTION OF AN ATTIC

The grand staircase ends at this floor and we must, to get to the story above, either take the elevator or return to the other end to mount the domestic stairway. Originally this story was an attic accessible only by a ladder. Roosevelt had a stairway built up to it and a couple of rooms arranged up there. The Tafts added a few more rooms and the Wilsons still more. It was the one place in the house that gave room for expansion. But it remained for Coolidge to put on a new roof, remodel the entire floor, and make it a habitable place free from cobwebs and rats. Going up either by the stairway or the elevator, we find ourselves in a long central corridor running east and west with rooms on both sides and a suite at either end, the one on the east being used by the colored female help, such as the cooks and housemaids. On the south side of the corridor are six rooms. Four of them were furnished and intended to be used as guest-rooms, but were used as offices by Mrs. Hoover's three secretaries. The other rooms are a sewing-room and a valet's bedroom. On the north side of the corridor are all kinds of rooms — two are used by the housekeeper, two are linen-rooms, three general storerooms, one cedar-room for winter storing, and finally a very large space over the north portico is used to store the chairs used at musicales and dinner parties.

There is not an idle inch of space in the house. Every nook and corner is made to serve one purpose or another, and I believe that we could easily use twice as much space as we have. To try to define just which rooms are private for the President's family is difficult. Of course the entire second and third floors are strictly private. The two dining-rooms and the three parlors are only semi-private. The lower floor and the East Room are open every day to visitors, but can easily be closed off if they are desired for private use, as is often the case. Connected with these various rooms are fourteen private baths, about ten lavatories, and several small retiring-rooms. These baths are all modern, the first one having been installed about the time of the Arthur Administration. It is hard for us today to realize how the early occupants of the mansion got along without them.

13

LIVING WITH THE COOLIDGES

IT IS fair to say that the Coolidge régime was the most expensive to the Government of any up to its time. There were many reasons for this. The Coolidges were the first for whom the new law by which the Government pays for official entertaining was put into effect. The Hardings had the law passed, but never got a chance to benefit by it. There were more officers from the Army, Navy, and Marine Corps detailed to the White House as aides than ever before. A colonel of the Army was given a job which always heretofore had been filled by the officer in charge of the Public Buildings and Parks. A representative of the State Department was detailed to do what had been done for a century by a clerk, and he in turn had a stenographer and a messenger. For a long time there were two Social Secretaries, one being superseded by the aforementioned State Department expert. There were more domestics than ever before in the house: three regular cooks and one or two extra help in the kitchen and the same in the pantry. There were more maids and more men cleaners than in times past. The secret service detail was increased on account of the early rising of the President, who would often walk for ten or fifteen minutes before seven o'clock in the morning.

The summer trips were extended and required the services of a large staff. The summer Executive Office force, which was always established in perfect form and size, was no small expense in itself. An Army and Marine guard of unusual proportions, numbering a hundred or more, was always maintained.

Since many of those expenses would not appear on the books as 'White House upkeep,' it would be hard to say how much they amounted to. But the Government certainly paid out more for these various activities than it had previously done. Probably these increased expenditures were the more noticeable because they were in contrast with the President's private ones. In connection with the latter there was the most rigid economy, as exemplified by the purchasing of supplies for the household from such sources as the Piggly Wiggly and Sanitary Grocery chain stores, much to the dismay of those of us who thought 'The President should have the best.'

Economy note. Swannanoa called from Virginia for a copy of *Colliers*, in which President Coolidge was reading a serial, two days before it was out. Cost of telephone: $1.00. Left word to be notified if it could be got. Message sent back it would take some little time. Another $1.00. President out when message sent. Upon return had man call and say to get it and send it in first mail. Another $1.00 for telephone call — Total $3.00 for messages to get one five-cent magazine.

THE FAMOUS WHITE HOUSE BREAKFASTS

Other administrations would have considered such breakfasts as those given by President Coolidge as rather important events. Not so Coolidge. They were simply one of his diversions. He would have one whenever the notion presented itself and many times on very short notice. Often we had to seek guests at midnight for breakfast the next morning. Generally he would ask members of both parties, and the meal was charged to 'official entertaining.' Many of the Democrats, and even some of the Republicans, would hesitate about accepting. They did not like the early hour, eight o'clock. Many would plead sickness, sometimes of their wives or even their friends, as an excuse. Some would inquire, 'You are sure the President means me?' A Socialist member suggested that he was a Socialist and surely *he* was not wanted. Two or three Senators in particular were all the time sidestepping, and did not hesitate, even when talking themselves over the telephone, to say they could not be reached that evening.

Those who did come would arrive rubbing their eyes, especially the older statesmen who were not accustomed to getting out so early. As a rule the guests were prompt, but occasionally there would be a delinquent. The excuses telephoned in by those who could not get there in time were often very amusing.

Once Senator Pittman's excuse was telephoned by Mrs. Pittman, who said that a wheel had come off their car down the road and the Senator couldn't make it. Senator Hale pleaded that his man forgot to call him. Senator Johnson's alibi was that his barn had burned down. One Congressman had been out all night and couldn't be found.[1]

However, the President never waited for them. He would join his guests promptly at eight and start off with the meal. The late comer would have to run the gantlet of the jeers of those who had assembled as he was shown to the dining-room and proceeded to make his excuses to the President. With few exceptions the breakfasts seemed to have little object. In fact, we frequently heard a guest inquire upon leaving, 'What did he have us here for?' The question would go unanswered.

Coolidge would join his guests in the Red Room and after a formal handshake would lead the way to the dining-room. The two or three highest would be placed near the President on his right and left; the others just scrambled into any seats

[1] The following note, referring to one of President Coolidge's breakfasts, was found among Hoover's papers:
Senator Heflin: Regrets, sick.
Senator Norris: Unable to locate.
Senator Pittman: Regrets, sick.
Senator Reed, of Missouri: Regrets, sick friend.

that were convenient. He never made any effort at arrangement and never seemed to care how or where they were
seated. It was always embarrassing at the beginning, for
everyone looked to the President to start off the conversation
and he never did. The fruit course would be eaten before a
word was said; everyone seemed to be looking around for the
other fellow to say something. No general conversation was
ever indulged in, and it became a matter of each guest
amusing himself by a few words back and forth with his
neighbor on the right and left. The entire meal would continue on in this wise, every man for himself. The breakfasts
seldom lasted much over a half-hour, and when the President
had finished he would rise and proceed to the door, the
guests filing by singly with another handshake and a good-
bye, some of them thanking the President for the 'nice
breakfast,' as they would describe it. As they left the dining-
room, I would get many a significant wink from guests I knew
personally. They seemed always to enjoy the food — bacon and
eggs, sausage and cakes, fruit, toast and coffee — but they
never seemed to understand the idea of having them there
either for social purposes, of which they saw no evidence, or
for official matters, of which they heard nothing. It was
just a breakfast!

In inviting three Congresswomen to one breakfast, Congresswoman Langley, of Kentucky, was somehow overlooked.
She came two mornings later with fifteen men.

JOHN ADAMS'S BALD PATE

The oil painting of John Adams hung in the Red Room,
where it could be seen from the table in the State Dining-
Room. The head was bald and the varnish made it shine.

President Coolidge sent for me one luncheon-time and,
pointing to the picture in the next room, said, 'I am tired of
looking at that old bald head. Will you have some hair put
on it?'

I got an artist and some turpentine was smeared on the head, taking off the shine and giving the appearance of a little hair.

At the next meal the President thanked me and said he 'saw that Mr. Adams had grown some hair on the top of his head.'

COOLIDGE CHICKENS AND ROOSEVELT MINT

An admirer in Cleveland, Ohio, sent two dozen live chickens. President Coolidge had a wire fence put up to keep them in until they were wanted for the table. He pointed out a place just beside the office building. It turned out to be the old Roosevelt mint patch. It was late in the fall and the mint was in flower. The chickens throve and, when eaten later, the flavor of mint was clearly discernible all through the meat. We never knew whether he selected the mint bed on purpose or not. If he did, it was in keeping with many other odd things the President was up to.

LUNCH WITH THE ROCKEFELLERS

February 26, 1927. John D. Rockefeller, Jr., and Mrs. Rockefeller came to lunch. Mr. Rockefeller had come down from New York for the Gridiron Dinner and had written several days before asking that he might be permitted to 'pay his respects' to the President. He was invited to lunch and accepted. When he arrived in Washington, it was learned that Mrs. Rockefeller was with him and she was invited to accompany him.

As soon as it was known he was coming, there was a feeling of excitement all about the place. Why? Wealth. Strange but true how much it counts. When the menu was made up, it was given a special touch by Mrs. Coolidge and the housekeeper. The butler put his best linen on the table, and the china, glass, and plate were given just a little extra touch and polish.

Mr. Rockefeller was received upon entering no differently from hundreds of other guests. And yet there was the feeling that it was an important occasion. It was evident that the President felt the importance of his guest. He went out of his way to be considerate. He offered his arm to Mrs. Rockefeller and escorted her to the place at the table on his right. This was unusual, for it was his custom to lead the way alone, unheralded, and generally in a hurry.

Mr. Rockefeller makes an excellent impression. Good-looking, composed, considerate. Perfectly at ease with no sign of conceit or egotism. He was just about as easy to handle and to converse with as anyone who ever visited the White House.

DINING UNDER DIFFICULTIES

Saturday, April 23, 1927 — 8:00 P.M. Dinner to the President of Cuba. Two dates before had been set. We rather wished that he would not come, but he was determined. The reception during the day was very cordial. The dinner was small, twenty-six covers.

Happenings: One Cuban lost his necktie, one American broke off his front tooth, another Cuban pushed through the bottom of the cane seat of his chair and would not permit it to be changed while the dinner lasted. At the conclusion it hung from him as he arose. There was a fire in the chimney all during the dinner. The oil-burning apparatus was extinguished and men placed on the roof to watch and control the fire.

At a Cabinet Dinner on November 8, 1928, two days after Hoover's election, the President's mind was so upset that he left the table before the meal was finished. As soon as he had eaten his ice cream, he abruptly rose from the table, though others had not yet been served. Mrs. Coolidge with signs and nods tried to correct him, but in vain. The fruit and candy and bonbons had not yet been passed. Everyone was taken by surprise and embarrassed, for the aides were not lined up, those in attendance in the dining-room were not in their places, and the butlers were running around getting ready to change plates when they should have been at attention to remove chairs. The band was in the midst of a heavy score with no march ready to play, as is customary when the President leaves the dining-room. Mrs. Coolidge tried to remedy the break by having candy served in the parlor, but this simply emphasized it. The incident but goes to illustrate the state of mind of the President about the election and his coming retirement from the limelight.

FISH STORIES

In South Dakota President Coolidge went fishing in white kid gloves. He always wore gloves when fishing, but this time Mrs. Coolidge made such fun of him that he went back to the darker shade afterwards.

In fishing he just held the rod. Bait was put on for him and any fish he caught were likewise taken off the hook for him. The secret service men complained bitterly when it fell to their lot to perform this most unusual function, which they did not consider a part of their duty of protecting the President.

A man once caught some fish from the stream in front of the house in South Dakota. The President said, 'They are my fish,' and sent a secret service man out to get them, which he did.

A MAN OF FEW WORDS

For over four years I never had a conversation with President Coolidge. Other Presidents were apparently eager to hear about what had been done by former administrations. Coolidge answered all questions with just 'Yes' or 'No,' or made inquiries which could be answered in a similar manner. The whole atmosphere among the employees was one of fear and trembling, lest they lose their jobs just on a notion of the President. He never appeared to appreciate any efforts they put forth to serve him and kept them in a state of constant anxiety. This interfered with their best efforts and it could easily be seen that he was not getting the most out of them. Half of them were pouting all the time.

COOLIDGE ECCENTRICITIES

Coolidge permitted no one to ride in the automobile with him except Mrs. Coolidge and John. Other Presidents took their aides along, but Coolidge made them ride in a separate car behind. Even guests in the house going to church had to obey this rule. It was amusing to see the President alone in one car and Mr. Stearns alone in one following. Sometimes it was embarrassing for those who did not understand the President's eccentricity.

Coolidge used to have his head rubbed with vaseline, regularly, while eating breakfast in his bedroom. A couple of times he actually had his hair cut while eating breakfast.

One summer day at his Adirondack Camp Coolidge felt a mosquito bite his head. He turned to the secret service man and asked whether he had seen it. 'Yes,' the man replied. 'Then why didn't you kill it?' snapped the President.

Neither Mrs. Coolidge nor anyone ever presumed to ask for or make a social appointment for the President, other than official entertainments, at the White House proper. He saw everybody at the office or not at all.

Coolidge set a record at one Army and Navy reception. The line started at 9:05 and ended at 10:10 with 2096 persons received, an average of thirty-two plus per minute. At 10:45 the reception was over, dancing and all. (Harrison, Cleveland, McKinley, Taft, and Wilson were slow in their receiving. Roosevelt was gracious. Harding was overly slow and gushy.)

Coolidge bestowed what he thought were funny nicknames on some of the employees. He called John Mays, a doorman, 'the mink.' Thomas Roach, a butler, was 'bug.' James M. Haley, secret service man, he called 'that long-legged Haley man.'

Mrs. Coolidge could whistle well, the President couldn't, so he usually blew a whistle for the dogs, and blew it like a locomotive. Once, when the President was trying to whistle in the dogs at night without the aid of the whistle, Mrs. Coolidge asked: 'What's the matter, poppa; don't your teeth fit tonight?'

To a guest who refused a cigar after lunch, saying that he could not hold one in his false teeth, Coolidge suggested that he ought to have a little wire platform made to attach to his chin to rest the cigar on.

14

THE PRINCE OF WALES COMES TO LUNCH

AUGUST 31, 1924. Months in advance the Prince's visit had been heralded. As the time approached and the arrangements were taken up by the State Department, it grew more and more important. Everyone wished to take some part in his reception. When an aide was assigned to accompany the royal visitor during his stay, jealousies promptly arose. For instance, the aide selected being an Army man, the Navy thought they should be represented, especially since, as they pointed out, His Royal Highness was an officer in the British Navy. But suggestions were of no avail. The one aide was considered quite enough.

The President and Mrs. Coolidge being more or less indifferent about the whole affair, it was easy to put over almost any arrangement. Thus the visit of His Royal Highness was advertised as being very informal in so far as the White House was concerned.

As the actual time of arrival drew near, there was more or less anxiety. The crowds which had begun to gather in the grounds had to be driven out, for it was evident that there would be an awful jam. The two senior aides, representing the two branches of the service, had arrived long in advance and it was interesting and refreshing to hear them discuss their duties in connection with the Prince's arrival. They seemed to feel one might get closer than the other and get more prestige out of the contact with His Royal Highness. Duties that would be ordinarily assigned to domestics, or that the civilian force would regularly perform, they took upon their own shoulders.

So the preliminaries were all set, even as to the dress, for the Prince had telephoned in the morning asking that he might come to lunch in informal dress. So word was passed around to that effect and the President and the Secretary of State decided to appear in business suits.

THE PRINCE IS NERVOUS

The train pulled in at one o'clock sharp and the car containing the Prince reached the White House gate at exactly one-twenty.

His appearance was informal all right. He looked positively shabby. He had on a dark, everyday suit, possibly once navy blue, a much-worn gray fedora hat, a blue shirt and a collar of the same color, perhaps attached to the shirt, no cuffs that were visible, low shoes so well worn that it was hard to tell whether they were black or very dark tan, a small dark four-in-hand scarf, and socks that were either faded blue or gray in color. His clothes generally gave no distinct impression of any particular fashion. On entering he seemed quite at ease, affable, and at home. As he walked to the parlor there was quite a slouch in his bearing and he seemed to have a slight limp.

Here he was made as comfortable as possible and the President was officially notified of his arrival. The President's greeting was very cordial. The Prince during this time seemed quite nervous. He would stand first on one foot and then on the other, his hands were continuously in and out of his coat pockets and he buttoned and unbuttoned his coat several times during this short interview. But in a few minutes the two secretaries bade adieu for the time being and took their departure, leaving the two men alone. The President invited the Prince to a seat and they stepped to the side of the room and so remained for about ten minutes, the aides waiting outside.

At a signal, which was the President's arising from his chair, the aides stepped into the room — one to escort the President to the private apartments, the other to show the Prince to his rooms. This was what is known as the Rose Suite, consisting of a very large bedroom, a dressing-room, and a bath. The Prince seemed much relieved as he mounted the stairs and immediately reached in his pocket for a cigarette. This he lighted even before entering the room and puffed with a relish, as if to relieve the nervous strain under which he was laboring. It had been previously arranged that he should be brought down to the Red Room at one-twenty-five, five minutes before lunch-time; but it was already one-thirty when he went upstairs, so it was just a case of finishing the cigarette and coming down to meet Mrs. Coolidge and John Coolidge before lunch.

The meeting was simple, the President presenting the Prince in very informal style to Mrs. Coolidge, she in turn presenting her son John. It sounded strange to hear Mrs. Coolidge and John address the Prince as 'Your Royal Highness,' but they had drilled themselves in advance to do so and carried the matter through with all the ease of a royal household.

COOLIDGE TALKS FOR ONCE

All during lunch the Prince seemed ill at ease. The conversation took many angles, the President and Mrs. Coolidge doing most of the talking, John saying nothing, and the Prince only chiming in occasionally, generally when he was asked a question. I am sure he was glad when the meal was over, even though the President had outdone himself in the talking line. It was remarked afterwards, even by the family, that he was never known to be so communicative before. He seemed to realize the Prince's embarrassment and did all in his power to make him comfortable.

Luncheon over, the President took his guest to his study

for a smoke They had twenty minutes of uninterrupted conversation. Again the President was observed to be doing most of the talking; apparently he was digging into his storehouse of historical memories in an effort to be entertaining. Coolidge smoked a cigar and the Prince several cigarettes of his own. The conversation continued beyond the allotted time, for at two-forty-five it had been arranged for the members of the cabinet and their wives to come to the White House and meet His Royal Highness. The young ladies of the cabinet circle were not invited.

'A HORRIBLE PICTURE'

The aides and I had to break up the tête-à-tête, which, as I said, had already lasted overtime. It was just a little embarrassing, but with the stamping of feet and the rattling of sabers it was finally accomplished.

The Prince was then escorted to his rooms for a little rest before joining the company. There was great clamor among the employees and officials for the Prince's autograph. They thought this would be a good opportunity to ask him for the favor. Accordingly one photograph that had been previously purchased and six small cards with the White House crest upon them were placed upon the desk in the room. After he had entered and lighted another cigarette, they were called to his attention and he was asked if he would sign them.

The request apparently did not appeal to him. He walked over to the desk and remarked it was 'a horrible picture,' and clearly did not want to autograph it. He asked rather impatiently who they were for and was told, 'some of the officials.' About this time he was left alone, after he had autographed two of the cards. Upon returning in about ten minutes, we noticed the picture was also autographed, but not another word was said about it.

A COOL FAREWELL

The Prince was now taken to join the President and Mrs. Coolidge in the Blue Room, where the guests had been arranged in a semi-circle. After the formal presentations, they all stood around and talked, everybody with an eye on the Prince. He still appeared ill at ease and the President had now got back in his old stride of talking but little. This left rather an inhospitable gathering and all concerned were wishing for it to come to an end. In a few minutes the President and Mrs. Coolidge, with their son John, bade good-bye to the Prince and left the room. After the President left, the Prince stayed on, seeming now much more at ease. But when it was suggested to him that he make his adieus, he acquiesced with considerable grace, and along with his suite immediately left for the station.

The impression he left behind was a very pleasant one. Generally speaking, there was no fuss made over him at the White House, though we tried to make him comfortable. The newspaper reports of the affair were greatly exaggerated.

15

AN INAUGURATION THAT FELL FLAT

'COOLIDGE WEATHER'

THE White House. March 4, 1925. The day dawned clear and comfortable. 'Coolidge weather,' as Mr. Stearns remarked, radiantly happy.

The White House was very calm. Those of us who had weathered the storm of other inauguration days could not reconcile the calm of this day with what we had known. It seemed unnatural that such an important event should arouse so little outward feeling. It seemed as if, could it have been so arranged, the President would have liked to keep on with the regular routine, just merging one day into the next, one administration into the other. He would have preferred to take his little walk of ten or fifteen minutes in the morning, spend the day at the office, take another short walk in the late afternoon, retire early, and let it go at that!

BUSINESS AS USUAL

The family arose as usual at about seven o'clock. The President went for his walk at seven-thirty and was back before eight o'clock, at which time he breakfasted in his bedroom with Mrs. Coolidge according to custom. The other guests in the house likewise had their breakfast in their bedrooms. No special arrangements of any kind were planned. After breakfast the President went to his office as always to look over the mail, returning to the White House at ten o'clock and going immediately to his private apartment. He here busied himself with what preparations he planned to make for the exercises of the day. These were very few and did not take long. Soon he was in conversation with Mr. Stearns, waiting to be notified of the start for the Capitol.

In the meantime the guests, principally the cabinet members and their wives, who were to accompany the President, began to arrive and assemble in the Blue Room on the main floor. As the hour approached for leaving the house, the guests and the cabinet ladies were sent on in advance. The Vice-President-elect and Mrs. Dawes arrived a little before eleven o'clock, the hour set for leaving.

Upon being notified of the arrival of the guests and the coming of the Vice-President-elect, the President and Mrs. Coolidge immediately descended to the main floor and joined those assembled in the Blue Room. The most informal of greetings were exchanged and the President and Mrs. Coolidge led the way to the waiting automobiles for the journey to the Capitol.

WILL THE GUESTS GO HUNGRY?

After the party had left the White House, there was nothing for us to do but wait. There were none of the customary preparations to make, since the lunch that had heretofore been served on inauguration day was to be omitted, in the interests of simplicity. We who had known many previous inaugurations felt it was a mistake. We had previously made an effort to have this feature of the ceremony included, but the best we could do was to persuade the President to permit the Vice-President and his wife, on their return from the Capitol, to go to the second floor with them and partake of coffee and sandwiches. We foresaw an embarrassing situation. Remember, the cabinet members and their wives and other officials were to wait downstairs while this little coffee and sandwich act was going on upstairs! Of course they had the privilege of going out to the reviewing stand; but it would have been bad form to have done so, and the wait without a lunch of any kind would not have been pleasant.

THE REVIEWING STAND AT THE WHITE HOUSE FOR THE FIRST
INAUGURATION OF WOODROW WILSON

THE SPECIAL BATHTUB BUILT BY THE J. L. MOTT IRON WORKS
FOR PRESIDENT TAFT

THE ARMY SAVES THE DAY

Fortunately, it appeared that Colonel Sherrill, the Military Aide, had, without the President's knowledge, prepared in the State War and Navy Building a lunch for the aides on duty. Since there was an abundance of good things provided, all the guests who came to the White House from the Capitol were invited to the other building. When the time arrived for the President and party to go to the stand, there was no one to go — not even an aide to accompany the President. All were over at Colonel Sherrill's lunch. They came straggling into the reviewing stand for the next hour after the President had arrived, looking satisfied with themselves and smiling like the cat who had eaten the canary.

We thought there would be a reckoning when the facts became known, but, on the contrary, aside from some caustic comment about the Military Aide presuming and being fresh in the matter, nothing came of it.

The progress of the inaugural parade is kept track of through telephone messages from different merchants along Pennsylvania Avenue who call up the White House when the head of the column reaches their place of business, so that the President may be notified when to go out to the stand. They are very glad to do this and feel a peculiar pride in calling the White House. Unfortunately, on this occasion the report from the last point came too soon, as the parade halted just afterward, and when the President arrived at the stand the parade was nowhere in sight. There was a scurrying of ushers, secret service men, and regular police from the city force, all without avail. A wait of nearly half an hour was experienced, which tested the patience of the occupants of the reviewing stand. However, the President did not seem to mind, except for an inquiry two or three times as to the cause of the delay. Aside from this he sat perfectly quiet, saying nothing. A review in silence, as several were heard to remark. The parade ended, the usual return to the White

House was made amid the applause of the people. Still it seemed less spontaneous than usual. Why? The only cause I can assign is the apparent lack of appreciation of the President for such demonstrations. The people certainly like to be noticed and the President could not or would not warm up to them.

CELEBRATION CONSPICUOUSLY ABSENT

Upon the return to the White House there was to be a reception to all the visiting governors and their parties. Previous to this, the regular lunch was served, but there was a little time for rest between the ending of the parade at three-forty and this reception at four-thirty. Advantage of this respite was taken by the President, who immediately after eating retired to his bedroom and threw himself across the bed. Evidently he was tired out.

Following the reception to the governors, several delegations came to be received.

As the guests were received in the East Room, they made their way to the State Dining-Room where an elaborate buffet luncheon had been prepared. They all partook of this freely, the President and Mrs. Coolidge joining them for a few minutes before they retired to their own private apartment. Later dinner was served in the usual way. No outside guests were invited; there were only the house guests: the President's father, Mrs. Coolidge's mother, and a friend, Mrs. Hills of Northampton, Mr. and Mrs. Frank W. Stearns, and a Miss Skinner, a close friend of Mrs. Coolidge.

John Coolidge, the President's son, came for the day only, arriving at eight in the morning and leaving at seven in the evening. John wanted to stay on, but it was felt he could not spare the time from college.

In the evening the President attended a dinner that was being given by a special delegation down from Massachusetts. It was made up principally of men with whom he had been associated during his official life in that State. He returned to the White House at nine-thirty and by nine-forty-five was in bed. So ended the inauguration day of Calvin Coolidge 'in his own right.' It was a most unusual inauguration day, quite different from anything that had gone before. The occasion had always been looked upon as one for celebration. Certainly there was nothing of the kind this time. I am sure the President would have had even less had it been physically possible. It was remarked by those who knew that he would have liked to walk to the Capitol, take the oath of office, and return to the White House for his nap!

16

WE ENTERTAIN QUEEN MARIE

'PLEASED TO MEET YOU'

OCTOBER 21, 1926. 'Her Majesty, the Queen of Rumania!'

'I am so pleased to meet you, Mr. President.'

'Pleased to meet you.'

The advance arrangements and plans for the visit of the Queen of Rumania and her party had been in the making for several weeks previous to their arrival. When it was first mentioned there was a rolling of eyes and much incredulity. No one seemed to have considered whether or not such a visit would be agreeable to the Administration. But we made the best of it and went ahead with our plans, though with only half-hearted enthusiasm. It had been decided to give a dinner for the Queen and to ask no one but those on the official list, making it about the size of a small state affair — forty-six covers.

A BREACH OF ETIQUETTE

The Queen arrived in the city at six o'clock on October 18. She was immediately escorted to the Rumanian Legation. Her appointment to be received by the President was made for the next day at four o'clock. It was most unusual for a visitor of her rank to be here for such a length of time before being received. Mrs. Coolidge, however, had personally arranged that a goodly quantity of flowers were sent to the Legation for the Queen. These were accompanied by her personal card. The next morning came an acknowledgment of the compliment when the automobile from the Legation drove up to the front door of the White House and the messenger handed in a letter, saying it was from the Queen. This, as is customary, was taken direct to Mrs. Coolidge. True, it was an acknowledgment of the flowers, but not from the Queen. One of the ladies-in-waiting had penned the note at her direction. This was considered a bad breach of etiquette and thought to show a lack of consideration and appreciation. At the very least the Queen could have acknowledged the courtesy that Mrs. Coolidge had personally shown her by acknowledging it in her own handwriting. The incident made a bad impression and built up an antagonism that was hard to dispel.

THE LADIES DO THE TALKING

The Queen and her party were to be received at the White House at four o'clock and the President and Mrs. Coolidge were to return the call at four-thirty.

At the appointed time two White House cars, each fully manned with a footman and an aide, went to the Legation to convey the royal party. In the first car rode the Queen, the Chargé d'Affaires of Rumania, the Assistant Secretary of State, and an aide. The second car carried the Prince and Princess and an aide.

The royal family arrived at the White House exactly at four o'clock. Quickly alighting, they crossed the corridor to the long hall where the Queen and others were presented to the President's military aides. Stretched out in single formation down the hall stood six other aides, forming a lane to the Green Room where the visitors were to wait until President and Mrs. Coolidge appeared.

Having been informed of the arrival of the royal party, the President and Mrs. Coolidge descended to the main floor and were escorted to the Blue Room. The Secretary of State had previously arrived and he joined them for the presentation.

The Queen, the Assistant Secretary who was to make the presentation, and the Chargé d'Affaires were then escorted along the hall into the Blue Room, attended by the six aides. With dignified acclaim the Assistant Secretary announced, 'Her Majesty, the Queen of Rumania!' But here dignity seemed to disappear. With rapid step the Queen left behind those who accompanied her and proceeded to take matters into her own hands. A quick word of inquiry from the President, a volley of words from the Queen, with Mrs. Coolidge breaking in at a chance opening, occupied the first few minutes of the audience, after which the party retired to the Red Room. It had been planned that the President and the Queen should be seated on the sofa and the Secretary of State and Mrs. Coolidge in two separate chairs, facing them. But the Queen immediately selected for herself a large comfortable over-stuffed chair at the end of the group of chairs arranged in a semi-circle about the fireplace. There was nothing for the President to do but to take the next chair, which was a little cane-seat affair. He sat sidewise in it most of the time. Mrs. Coolidge took the next chair to the President and the Secretary of State the last one of the group. Conversation proceeded with the Queen and Mrs. Coolidge doing most of the talking. The sound of the President's voice was seldom heard. However, as previously arranged, he asked that the Prince and Princess might be brought in that he might meet them. They all this while had been waiting in the Green Room with one of the junior aides. When the President made this request, a signal was given to the Military Aide standing outside the door, and the two children were escorted to the Red Room, where the Queen personally presented them to the President and Mrs. Coolidge and the Secretary of State.

All had risen at the entrance of the royal children and it had been planned that there would be no more sitting down, but that, after a little talk, the signal would be given for ending the audience and the Queen and her children would take their departure. This was all fully gone into in advance and the Queen was supposed to be familiar with all of the details and arrangements. But instead of taking her leave as expected, the Queen immediately, without a suggestion from anyone, proceeded to take her seat again. There was nothing for the President to do but accept the situation and himself be seated. All others followed likewise. It now became a problem how to end the audience. We who were standing around outside knew a mistake had been made, but we were helpless. There was nothing to do but wait developments. The President was equal to the emergency, for after a few minutes of conversation he arose and, after some form of parting words, left the room with Mrs. Coolidge. Immediately the royal party made their way behind the escort to their cars and back to the Legation. The cars that took the party there immediately returned to the White House, the President and Mrs. Coolidge entering the first car and two aides the second, and went to return the call at the Legation. Thus Her Majesty and their Royal Highnesses, the Prince and Princess, were formally received. In truth, it turned out to be more informal than otherwise.

THE PHOTOGRAPHERS GET A BUM DEAL

All during the day photographers had been clamoring for the privilege of making pictures of the Queen, especially of the Queen and Mrs. Coolidge posing together. Every request had been refused, for it was felt that it would interfere with the dignity of the occasion. But when the President and Mrs. Coolidge returned from the Legation, we learned that, upon arrival there, they found that complete arrangements had been made for photographing them with the royal party. There was nothing for the President and Mrs. Coolidge to do but to submit to the inevitable with as much grace as possible. So it was that most of the visit was occupied in the unpleasant ordeal of being photographed. Poses of all kinds were made and published in the daily papers, with captions explaining that they had been taken at the White House.

THE QUEEN IN ALL HER GLORY

Then for a few hours there was a lull. Nothing more was planned until the dinner at eight o'clock.

At eight the Queen's party drove up to the entrance. All inside was a-flutter. The Marine Band, in their scarlet uniforms, had been instructed to rise at her entrance. The aides were drawn up in formation, looking their finest in all the gold braid at their command. Just inside the glass doors, the footmen took the visitors' wraps and there stood the Queen arrayed in all her glory. The setting was perfect.

Personally I had been privileged to take part in her reception on two previous occasions when in Paris at the Peace Conference. She seemed to be much thinner now than when I had seen her before and, while she retained all the grace that has made her famous, I felt disappointed. She looked well but not unusually attractive. She seemed overdressed. Her headdress reminded me of the helmet of a football player. Of course it represented great value, but one could not get away from the foreign impression it made. Her other adornments were abundant and prominently displayed: bands of pearls about the neck and massive arrangements that hung about the ears. The gown was white and quite short, gauged by White House standards.

The Queen, the Prince, and the Princess were ushered into the Red Room. The rest of her party — ladies-in-waiting, aides, and officials attached to her suite — were shown to the Blue Room, where all the other guests of the evening had previously assembled. Here the company was arranged in semi-circle according to rank. The royal party were now escorted in from the Red Room and 'made the circle' of all the guests, being presented personally to each one by the

Naval Aide. The President and Mrs. Coolidge then went through the same procedure.

THE PRINCESS MAKES A HIT

The Queen appeared somewhat ill at ease while the President and Mrs. Coolidge were going the rounds. Finally, she stepped out of line and walked down to where Mrs. Longworth was standing and engaged in conversation with her. She was there when the President and Mrs. Coolidge completed the presentation ceremony and from here she was escorted over to the President in preparation for the march to the dining-room. The Prince, who was to escort Mrs. Coolidge to the dining-room, was perceptibly nervous — actually to the point of trembling. But fortunately, Mrs. Coolidge took his arm in a friendly manner and spoke a few words that seemed to work wonders with him. So all through dinner she seemed bent on making him feel comfortable and succeeded admirably. The Princess seemed the most composed of the three. She calmly stood and waited for the Secretary of the Treasury, Mr. Mellon, and with grace and confidence permitted herself to be escorted in the line of march. To the strains of music the party wended its way to the dining-room. The President had the Queen on his right and the Princess on his left. On the right of the Queen was the Secretary of State, Mr. Kellogg, and on the left of the Princess sat the Secretary of the Treasury, Mr. Mellon. The Prince was on the right of Mrs. Coolidge and on the other side of him was Mrs. Dawes, the wife of the Vice-President. Mr. Dawes was on Mrs. Coolidge's left.

The dinner proper was not different from hundreds of others. Of course all eyes were on the Queen, especially during her efforts to engage the President in conversation. In this she was not any more successful than others who had tried it before. Before the dinner was over, the Queen realized that most of the published reports of the President's uncommunicative disposition were true. She also seemed to appreciate that the President was paying more attention to the Princess than he was to her, for she was heard to remark to the Princess, upon leaving the White House, that the latter had made more impression during the evening than she had herself.

The dinner lasted exactly one hour and forty-five minutes. It was just nine-forty-five when they left and they had arrived at eight o'clock. There was no time lost in any ceremony. When the President went to his study for cigars, they remained but fifteen minutes.

Yet withal it was a pretty party, a successful party, a party that any American could feel a pride in. There were features to give one a thrill. Mrs. Coolidge was everything that the wife of the President should be and filled the rôle 'to the Queen's taste.' In her beautiful simple gown, practically without ornamentation, she was superb.

17

WILL ROGERS OUT OF HIS ELEMENT

JANUARY 17, 1927. Reading in the *Saturday Evening Post* Will Rogers's story of his visit to the White House prompts me to record what really happened on this occasion.

Mr. Rogers had written the Secretary to the President of his intended visit to Washington and had asked permission to pay his respects to the President. When this request was placed before the President in the usual routine of such matters, he suggested that Mr. Rogers be invited to be his guest at the White House. This was done and the invitation was accepted.

On the day of his arrival, word had come from him that he would be here at six-twenty in the evening. He did, as suggested in his story, telegraph from Philadelphia to Secretary Sanders that he was on his way and that if there was a catch or a joke of any kind in the invitation, please to let him know and he would discontinue the journey. Word was sent back to him that the invitation was a genuine one and that a White House car would meet him upon his arrival at the station.

His train was late, on account of a railroad accident of some kind. At best he would have been just in time for dinner, which was always served at seven o'clock during the Coolidge Administration. When we learned that he would be late, we wondered whether he would have time to change and put on his dinner clothes. This was mentioned to the President, who remarked that if Mr. Rogers did not get there in time to change, he would not himself dress for dinner. However, as time went on, the President

retired to his room and came forth arrayed in his dinner
coat, having apparently changed his mind about not
dressing.

The train arrived at six-fifty and at exactly seven o'clock
the White House automobile drove up to the door. The
President and Mrs. Coolidge had just come down in the
elevator on their way to the dining-room and were told that
Mr. Rogers was at the door. They made no effort to wait,
but proceeded on to their places at the table.

'TRUE DEMOCRACY'

We tried to hurry Mr. Rogers, but it took some little time
to relieve him of his overcoat and hat and to take care of
his suitcase. I also had to explain that the President and
Mrs. Coolidge had just gone in to dinner and that it would
be necessary for him to go direct to the dining-room, with
no chance to change his clothes. He looked rather embarrassed when the matter of clothes was mentioned, but there
was no time for discussion. So he was shown immediately
into the dining-room, where the President and Mrs. Coolidge
were already seated alone at the table. Mr. Rogers had on a
blue double-breasted business suit and a soft collar.

Having been announced, he walked toward the President,
remarking on the way, 'This is what I call true democracy,
the President and his wife waiting dinner on me, such as I
am.' Of course they had not waited at all, but the remark
went over well, drew a smile from the President and something a little more than a smile from Mrs. Coolidge. The
President half-arose, shook hands, and presented him to
Mrs. Coolidge, who had not met him before. She invited
him to be seated on her right.

The President took the lead in conversation by mentioning
the train delay, the trip to Washington, and eventually the
matter of Mr. Rogers's recent trip abroad. From then on
Mr. Rogers held the stage, the President and Mrs. Coolidge

just adding enough from time to time to keep the flame of
his narrative alive. The remainder of the evening was spent
in the west sitting-room. Some jigsaw picture puzzles were
brought out and worked on for a while. Mrs. Coolidge did
some knitting, the President smoked, and all retired at
twenty-five minutes past ten. Mr. Rogers had been assigned
to what is known as the pink guest suite, in the extreme
northeast corner of the bedroom floor. It consists of a large
room with a four-poster bed, a small dressing-room, which
also has a single brass bed in it, and a private bath. He was
escorted halfway down the hall by the President and his
room pointed out to him. A doorman was summoned to
have one last word with Mr. Rogers and learn if there was
anything that could be done for him before he retired.

Upon entering the room, Mr. Rogers seemed rather hesitant about occupying the large four-poster bed that had been
prepared for him. Turning to the doorman, he inquired if
he had to sleep there. He was told of the small bed in the
dressing-room and chose that in preference to the large one.
The man turned down these covers and left Mr. Rogers with
his own thoughts, to spend the night in the White House
with all the thrills he afterwards described.

MR. ROGERS TRIES TO BE SERIOUS

As was the custom during these times, Mr. Rogers had his
breakfast in his room. After breakfast time rather dragged
on his hands. He seemed to have no plans, except that he
appeared anxious to get away as soon as possible. He really
seemed uncomfortable. He did mention that he would like
to go by aeroplane back to New York and inquiry for his
benefit was made. He then sat around for quite a while
in the Usher's Room adjacent to the main entrance. Here
he met a number of people, principally those attached to the
place. He engaged them in conversation, telling about some
of his European experiences and mentioning also that he did

not wish to be considered always as a humorist, but liked, at times, to be taken seriously. In fact he really tried to be serious during his White House visit. Referring to his late arrival the night before, and to the fact that he had been expected to dress for dinner, he said he had never owned a dinner coat in all his life.

He sat around for quite a while, and then at the suggestion of an official he decided to go over to the flying-field to arrange for his trip back in the afternoon. He went in a White House automobile and as he started out he said he was going to see Jimmy Davis, meaning the Secretary of Labor. This was about ten in the morning, and when he returned at twelve o'clock he apologized and explained that not only had he been to see Mr. Davis, but had also called on 'Alice Longworth and Mrs. McLean.'

A COMMONPLACE AFFAIR

He had lunch with the President and Mrs. Coolidge alone. He was then bidden good-bye and expected to be on his way. He was shown to his room, where he found his bag already packed, and immediately left in a White House automobile for the flying-field.

Thus ended Mr. Will Rogers's famous visit to the President and Mrs. Coolidge in the White House. It was just a plain everyday visit like hundreds of others. That he afterwards made so much of it, in amusing his audiences, is to his credit, for in reality his field was very limited. He seemed to interest Mrs. Coolidge just a little, and the President a great deal less. In fact, when someone remarked later to the President that it was hoped he got a good 'kick' out of Mr. Rogers's visit, he replied casually, and without a smile, 'Oh, Will! he is all right.'

OFFENSIVE SATIRE

Will Rogers later offended Coolidge when he imitated him over the radio. He sent a letter apologizing, but never got back into the President's good graces. Coolidge especially disliked the nasal tone adopted in imitating him. He remarked that Rogers had been a guest in the house once, but, if he was to be again, some other President would have to do the inviting.

(Rogers also offended Harding with a sketch of a cabinet meeting, the President telephoning and talking golf all the while. Harding refused to go to see the show, after having promised to do so.)

18

LINDBERGH — THE PERFECT GUEST

JUNE, 1927. Charles A. Lindbergh was returning to America as a conquering hero. He had accomplished the unbelievable feat of crossing the Atlantic in an airplane from New York to Paris. The whole world was sounding his praises; foreign nations had outdone themselves in an effort to recognize the greatness and the importance of his feat. It now remained for his own country to do him equal honor.

The officials at Washington were in a quandary, for they had no precedent to fall back on. To be sure, there had been plenty of celebrations for returning heroes, but nothing quite like this. They wondered how best to do justice to the occasion, and felt uncertain as to proper procedure. The subject was taken up in public and in private. The cabinet laid aside affairs of state to discuss what would be the most appropriate way to honor this youth who had, overnight, become the world's most popular figure. A committee of high officials, including cabinet members, were appointed to weigh the matter; out of this grew the large local reception committee. They got to work immediately, arranged for the arrival of the hero, the financing of the celebration, the order of ceremonies. The part the President should play remained in doubt.

The committee faced many perplexing questions. In what ship should Lindbergh come? Where should he stay in Washington? What part should his mother take in the program? Many papers were busy offering suggestions and

announcing plans before they had been made. Still they accomplished something, for it was through their influence that
a warship was sent to bring him back from France and that
he was invited to be a guest of the President at the White
House. But when it was announced in the press that Mrs.
Lindbergh would also be a guest in the same household,
there came a hitch. The young man had been invited, but,
unfortunately, the mother had not. Still the papers continued to publish the fact that she would be, with the result
that she finally was.

THE SEARCH FOR MRS. LINDBERGH

So at last all was settled. The U.S. Cruiser *Memphis*, on
which the hero had sailed, was already at sea. No word came
from Mrs. Lindbergh, however, as to her plans. A telegram
had been sent asking her to let us know the time of her arrival, that she might be met by a White House car and conveyed to the temporary residence of the President on DuPont
Circle. This message, however, did not reach her. As the
time drew near for the arrival of the *Memphis*, the papers
published the story that Mrs. Lindbergh had left Detroit on a
certain train for Washington. No preparations had been
made to meet her, for we had had no word from her. The
next morning, again through newspapers, we learned at the
White House that Mrs. Lindbergh had left the train on the
outskirts of Baltimore, planning to go to the city by trolley
car; that she had been recognized by some official and had
accepted a motor ride to Baltimore. We telephoned several
hotels and finally found her. We told her that the President
and Mrs. Coolidge desired her to be their guest and that one
of the White House automobiles was ready to go for her.
She accepted the invitation. Accordingly the car, with
driver, footman, and one of the President's junior aides,
proceeded to Baltimore for the lady and returned with her
to the temporary home of the President. This was late in the

afternoon of Friday, June 10, the day previous to the scheduled arrival of her famous son.

Mrs. Lindbergh appeared to me a very agreeable person. She was self-possessed and seemingly unspoiled by the excitement her son was causing. She had a very pleasing personality and showed every evidence of a proper sense of proportion. She certainly made an excellent impression with everyone with whom she came in contact and conducted herself perfectly under most trying circumstances.

When Mrs. Lindbergh arrived there was a crowd assembled outside the house, the word somehow having leaked out that she was coming. A group of photographers had also collected and they promptly got busy as she alighted from the car. With grace and smiles she submitted to all their attentions. Upon entering the house she was shown to her room on the main bedroom floor, overlooking DuPont Circle, where the crowds had assembled. She was made to feel as comfortable as possible and permitted to rest before seeing the President and Mrs. Coolidge. Miss Randolph, the social secretary, joined her and explained what would be expected of her during the visit.

In due time Mrs. Lindbergh was taken to the President's study and formally presented to Mrs. Coolidge. The two engaged in conversation for fifteen or twenty minutes, until the arrival of the President from the Executive Offices. He joined them and remained for possibly another quarter of an hour, after which Mrs. Lindbergh was shown to her room again, where she remained until dinner-time. At this meal, in addition to the President, Mrs. Coolidge, and Mrs. Lindbergh was Mr. Dwight Morrow of New York. He had only by chance remained on until this time and it was fortunate for the Lindberghs that he did so, since he took a special interest in them and was of material help, both in Washington and later in New York. After dinner the party broke up, for the President and Mrs. Coolidge had to attend a government budget meeting. Mrs. Lindbergh was entertained a while by Mr. Morrow and later retired to her own room to await the coming of her son in the morning.

There seemed to be some confusion as to the procedure on Colonel Lindbergh's arrival. Where and by whom should he be met? It was planned for the President and Mrs. Coolidge to go direct to the reviewing stand, but it was uncertain where he should first meet his mother. After considerable discussion it was decided that she should go to the Navy Yard and meet him at the boat. This she was willing to do, but she did not wish to have this first meeting between a mother and her son take the form of a public demonstration. At length it was arranged that, when the boat docked, Mrs. Lindbergh should be the first to go aboard and that she should be taken to a private room furnished by the Captain, where she could meet her son undisturbed by the public.

THE PRESIDENT PLAYS SECOND FIDDLE

The ceremonies attending the arrival of Lindbergh in Washington — the parade up Pennsylvania Avenue to the reviewing stand, the exercises there, and the return to the temporary White House — formed one continuous ovation. In the first car came the President and Mrs. Coolidge and immediately behind, also in a White House car, rode Lindbergh and his mother. The cheers were for Lindbergh. For once the President and his wife were playing second fiddle.

Before going into the house the four people posed for pictures on the front steps. Once in the house, preparations were made to go to lunch; but the crowd outside was clamoring for Lindbergh, so lunch was delayed while the President and Mrs. Coolidge, Lindbergh and his mother went out on the veranda over the front entrance that the people might have another look at their hero. At his appearance they went into a frenzy of excitement. All through lunch they could be plainly heard calling for him. In fact there never seemed an hour while he was the guest of the President but what there were cries for him from the people assembled.

'CHECK!'

The lunch was very informal. When it was over, the young man was shown to his room, where, after greeting him and assuring him that I desired to be of service to him, I told him what was expected of him during his stay with the President and Mrs. Coolidge. All of this he calmly and graciously agreed to. He seemed especially pleased that someone should take the initiative in advising him. He was anxious to do 'what's right,' as he put it. So his entire stay was mapped out.

It was interesting to note his agreement with everything I suggested. He would reply 'Check!' meaning 'Yes!' I wondered how he came by this expression, but it was very characteristic of him. There were a lot of things to talk over with him; plans to be made for his visit and for the disposition of the mail and the gifts that were pouring in. His mail was arriving by the sackful. It would have been a physical impossibility for him to handle it personally and yet something had to be done with it. Among the gifts was about everything that could be imagined, some of it of real value, and much of it worthless. Every baker seemed to feel he must send him a cake; there was so much candy a store might have been started; there were fruits of all kinds, jewelry, art works, a number of flying-machine models, two suits of clothes, and so many cards and letters they almost filled a small room.

Alone with him in the quiet of his room it was easy to form an opinion of him. He was just a plain sweet character. He seemed rather bewildered, unable to realize what it was all about. When we had finished with these arrangements, he asked that his St. Louis friends be permitted to see him. He named Messrs. Knight, Bixby, Robertson, Blythe, and Mahoney. He did not have to wait long, for these very gentlemen were standing outside the door, hoping to be in at the first roll-call. So an appointment was made for them with the approval of the President and Mrs. Coolidge, as is customary in such cases. I suggested to him that some of these friends should be named to look out for his immediate affairs, especially to care for his mail, etc. This appealed to him, for he was anxious to see them, in his own words, 'form some sort of an organization.' They called him 'Slim' and were glad of the privilege to serve him. When they left they took with them two taxicabs loaded with mail and presents.

Lindbergh seemed greatly relieved after this arrangement had been made. He could now turn his thoughts to the program that had been prepared for him. There was nothing scheduled for this first afternoon. He had opportunity to rest and he took advantage of it, pulling off his coat and stretching out full length on the bed. He spent some time alone with his mother and received a delegation of mail pilots who had come to Washington from all over the West to be here when he arrived. They all seemed to know him personally or so well by reputation that they addressed him as 'Slim.' No 'Colonel' with these boys; he was just one of them.

AN OLD-TIMER GETS A THRILL

When Lindbergh's baggage was delivered, it consisted of one lone suitcase. Fortunately he had a dress suit with him, since there was to be a formal dinner that evening. It was a very select affair, the guests few and strictly of the official set. There were many efforts to have others asked, but the President was firm in his decision that the list should be limited. Even Commander Byrd, who was in the city at the time, was not invited, though his name was suggested by a high official. The dinner list, in order of precedence, was as follows:

> The President and Mrs. Coolidge
> Colonel Charles A. Lindbergh
> Mrs. Charles A. Lindbergh
> The Secretary of State and Mrs. Kellogg
> The Secretary of the Treasury
> The Secretary of War
> The Attorney General

The Postmaster General and Mrs. New
The Secretary of the Navy and Mrs. Wilbur
The Secretary of the Interior
The Secretary of Agriculture and Mrs. Jardine
The Secretary of Labor and Mrs. Davis
The Secretary to the President and Mrs. Sanders
Mr. and Mrs. John Hays Hammond
Colonel Blanton Winship
Captain Wilson Brown

The dinner hour was set for seven o'clock, so that the evening program might be carried out. The guests were all prompt in arriving and shown to the main parlor on the second floor. There were the usual aides in attendance, in addition to the two chief aides who were dinner guests. The Marine Band Orchestra was stationed in the balcony. When everything was ready, Colonel Lindbergh and his mother were ushered in and, in true royal fashion, 'made the circle' of the guests, being presented to each by one of the aides. Then, taking their places at the head of the line, they awaited the coming of the President and Mrs. Coolidge. After they had gone through the presentation ceremony, the President escorted Mrs. Lindbergh to the dining-room. Mrs. Coolidge was escorted by Colonel Lindbergh, who was seated on her right. The picture of this youth, but a short time ago an unknown mail pilot, taking precedence over all these officials actually sent a thrill through the old-timers like myself.

The Lindberghs, though they were the object of all eyes, seemed as composed as any of the others. Everyone seemed to feel that he was being especially honored at being permitted to be present.

'WE WANT LINDY!'

At the conclusion of the meal the ladies retired to the library, the men to the large parlor where coffee and cigars were served. Lindbergh did not smoke, but he was, of course, the center of conversation and each one had an opportunity to say something to him. The immense throng that had assembled outside the house at his coming in the early afternoon had continued on, being reinforced from time to time. By evening it had become a multitude. As far as the eye could see from the windows there was a milling mass of people. They would yell and applaud at every possible provocation. 'Lindy!' 'Lindbergh!' 'Colonel!' 'Lone Eagle!' could be heard continuously above the din. 'We want Lindy!' was begun in chorus and practiced until it became a perfect unison. When the men returned to the library from the parlor, they found the ladies of the party amusing themselves looking out of the windows at the people assembled on the street. Lindbergh walked over to one group, which included Mrs. Coolidge, and being immediately recognized there was a wild scramble outside by the people to get to that side of the house. It almost caused a panic and many accidents were narrowly averted by the prompt action of the police, who had been detailed in large numbers to hold the masses in check. The President and Mrs. Coolidge bade good-bye to their guests and retired to the private part of the house. But the guests made no attempt to leave until after Lindbergh had gone. Even the sage Secretary of State stayed on when he should have been the first to leave, not only because he was the ranking guest, but because he was to take part in the reception for Lindbergh by the Minnesota Society, to be held at the Willard Hotel. It was an interesting coincidence that the Secretary of State, Mr. Kellogg, had at some previous time directly opposed Lindbergh's father when both were candidates for the Senate. It seems that Mr. Kellogg won out, but that considerable feeling had remained even until now, to the possible embarrassment of both parties, in the light of the prominent part the Secretary of State had to play in welcoming his rival's son.

A White House automobile was placed at the disposal of

the local committee and in this they took the Lindberghs to the reception of the Minnesota Society and also of the National Press Club in the Washington Auditorium. At both of these he received a wonderful ovation, so much so that upon his return to the home of the President at midnight he remarked that 'they nearly mobbed me.'

COOLIDGE ON SUNDAY SUITS

After a good night's rest, Lindbergh was clearly refreshed and ready for anything that might be on the cards. There were no definite plans for him in the forenoon, except that, if he was so inclined, he and his mother might accompany the President and Mrs. Coolidge to the eleven o'clock church service. When this was suggested to him he readily acquiesced. He had somewhere come into possession of a very light-colored suit of clothes and this he donned on Sunday morning instead of the traditional blue suit that had become associated with him. When the President noticed this, he inquired if it would not be better for Lindbergh to wear a dark suit. This was diplomatically communicated to him, but he did not readily see the necessity for it and it was only after considerable indirect persuasion that he agreed to make the change. Both on their way to church and on their return the Colonel and his mother were attended by the plaudits of the crowd.

Lunch was served soon after, having been moved forward to permit Lindbergh to fill the afternoon engagements planned by the local committee. At this lunch, in addition to the Lindberghs, there were Mr. and Mrs. Henry Cabot Lodge, whom the President invited at the very last minute.

A FULL DAY

After lunch the local committee took him in charge. Their plans included a visit to the tomb of the Unknown Soldier in Arlington Cemetery, a return to Washington through the Fort Myer Reservation, and a trip to the Walter Reed Hospital, which is many miles distant on the outskirts of the city, and Flag Day exercises at the Capitol. Between these engagements Lindbergh found time to go over to Bolling Field, to inspect the *Spirit of St. Louis*. After further ceremonies, the party returned through the heart of the city to the President's house, just in time to make ready for dinner. This was served very informally, there being no guests.

Tentative arrangements had been made for the evening. Among other things they were trying to get him to be present at a reception by the Missouri State Society of Washington. There was quite a mix-up over this. The boy wished to make an early start in the morning for New York, to fill the program arranged for him there. He at first decided to go to the reception, then upon further consultation he changed his mind. This evidently made hard feelings all along the line, for of course the reception without Lindbergh, for whom it was arranged, fell far short of being a success.

The evening was spent as quietly as could be under the circumstances. Lindbergh was especially solicitous about having his plane at Bolling Field ready in the morning for his hasty departure. Twice did he telephone there to give instructions as to the handling of it. The officers wanted permission to start the engine and tune it up, so that there would be no question of its being ready, but he objected to this and told them not to attempt to do so until his arrival. Unfortunately, the next morning he could not get his engine to function properly and had to drive another plane to New York. Lindbergh took all the blame himself like a man and went out of his way to make it understood that it was entirely his fault that he could not fly his own plane to New York.

'COME ON OUT, LINDY, IT'S RAINING'

It was planned for Mrs. Lindbergh to leave at half-past nine in the evening to catch a train for New York, there to meet her son when he arrived the next morning. The Colonel went to the station with his mother, but did not get out of the automobile on account of the excitement he would cause. The crowd assembled outside the President's house, seizing the opportunity to see him as he left for the station and as he returned. But this did not satisfy them and they remained long after he had retired, calling for him incessantly. A rainstorm came up during part of the time, but it did not seem to diminish the crowd. One girl sent in her card with this written on it: 'Come on out, Lindy, it's raining!' Of course he did not see this, neither did he go out. Willing to the last to be obliging, he felt, however, that he had shown himself as often as he could with dignity.

Morning came and he was up bright and early. Arrangements had been made for his departure; the White House cars were ordered and a time set for his leaving. But everyone seemed nervous and when the committee arrived fifteen minutes early they persuaded him to go at once, thus for the first time breaking in on the scheduled plans. So, while he had arrived in the official White House automobile, he left in a hired car that was furnished by the committee on arrangements. He went to the Mayflower Hotel to attend a breakfast given by the National Aeronautical Association, and then on to Bolling Field, where after several attempts to start his own plane, he finally gave it up and proceeded in an Army plane on his journey to New York.

He left behind a splendid impression. He was always anxious to please and yet never pushed himself to the fore. There was no fault to be found with any part of his entire visit. His carriage and conduct were perfect.

19

'I DO NOT CHOOSE'

THE BOLT FROM THE BLUE

APRIL 30, 1928. 'I do not choose': simple words, but what a world of misunderstanding they have aroused! It is necessary to go back a few months in order to understand how these words came to be a national jest. President Coolidge had been elected in his own right. He had served more than half of his term and from all indications was looking forward to being the choice of his party to succeed himself. To us who saw him every day his intentions seemed perfectly clear. The summer of 1927 to be spent in the Black Hills of South Dakota was a part of his program. It had a definite object which was approved by all the supporters of the President's candidacy.

Of course there were rumblings of discontent, in the newspapers and elsewhere, at the thought of the President succeeding himself. But to no avail. Tentative preparations went on, apparently with the sanction and approval of the President.

The 'third term' tradition was the one thing that worried the President, but as time went on even this was relegated to the background. Thus the start was made for the Black Hills with I believed every intention of making political capital out of the stay. Every detail of this trip was so different from Coolidge's accustomed ways that it could have but one object. Mixing with Indians and cowboys and wild horses was never cut out for Coolidge. Living miles from nowhere and traveling eighty miles a day, back and forth to a little old shack called his office, was not like him. We who know him best realized that it must have been down-right punishment to him. Instances could be related of those who felt his wrath, aroused by the uncomfortable experiences through which he was passing. But from the political angle all was going well, when, suddenly, like a clap of thunder out of a clear sky, came the announcement, 'I do not choose to run for President in 1928.'

To Mrs. Coolidge and to the President's closest friends and advisers this came, I believe, as a complete surprise. Certainly the employees, both at the White House and at the Black Hills camp, were astonished. They immediately began to watch carefully for any change in the President's attitude or in his relations with his political advisers. Seeing none, they were forced to conclude that his hopes for the future remained unshaken. The only difference was that the nomination, instead of being sought, must now do the seeking.

AN HONOR TO BE SPANKED BY THE PRESIDENT

So the summer went on and all of the original plans were carried out. On every hand the papers and the public were discussing the meaning of the ambiguous phrase and asking why, if a definite declination was intended, it was not worded in a definite manner. The older among us at the White House remembered vividly a similar circumstance when Mr. Roosevelt issued his statement in regard to an-other term, beginning, 'I will not under any circumstances,' and recalled the positiveness with which it was uttered and acted upon later. We remembered how he was implored to change his attitude and how firmly he adhered to his original statement. The fact that in later years he did be-come a candidate again did not detract from the force of that statement as it applied at the time.

Thus we looked with interest upon the return of the President from the summer sojourn in the West. We wanted

PRESIDENT COOLIDGE REFUSES POINT-BLANK TO VACATE THE
WHITE HOUSE UNTIL HIS OTHER RUBBER IS FOUND

Gluyas Williams in *Life*

to see if he was really out of the race. It was no secret that everyone had his doubts, for we knew that he could and did express himself perfectly clearly when he wished to be understood. He had always said just what he meant, leaving no room for misinterpretation. Then, too, we realized that he knew at all times the various constructions that were being placed on his utterance and that he took no steps to clarify it.

With the President back from his vacation, life at the White House resumed its normal course, though there was particular attention shown to the 'right people.' Influential men who had before been passed over with the mere privilege of paying their respects were now asked to stay overnight. Newspaper publishers especially were not neglected during these days. It was interesting to notice the attitude of those who came. They would sit down and tell the President, for hours at a time, how, in spite of his announcement, the people were determined to have him. They would declare that this or that section of the country where they had been was enthusiastic for his candidacy. They would tell of the plans of others to back him. They would have liked to hear him say, either that he would or he would not run for another term. But their hints bore no fruit; they could get nothing out of him. A smile at their praise, a nod of the head at their solicitude, a simple remark that there were 'plenty of other good men,' or that 'I've been here about long enough,' was the limit of his comment. Still he obviously enjoyed hearing the matter discussed.

Naturally those visitors who had personal conferences with the President were interviewed by the press to obtain their opinions on the all-absorbing topic. It was amusing to see how these opinions, as published from day to day, affected the standing of the individual at the White House. Those who went away predicting his nomination, a deadlock, a 'draft Coolidge' program, or something of the kind, were always invited again. The 'spanking' of Fess was a good joke; he came back many times, both at his own solicitation and at the urgent request of the President, to be spanked again. He liked that kind of spanking, for never before had his prestige stood so high within the portals of the White House.

On the other hand, those who proclaimed they were satisfied that the President would not be a candidate, came back but seldom. Nicholas Murray Butler and George Harvey, for example, had been constant visitors until they made statements to the press that the President would not run again.

PLAYING A DEEP GAME

Then came the meeting of the Republican National Committee in Washington. The members were to be received and addressed by the President at the White House. As is the custom, these remarks were prepared in advance and copies given to the press for publication when released. Those who expected a definite statement of his position were disappointed. Word was even passed on to some of the members of the Committee that he was going to say nothing on the subject. However, at the last minute there was a sudden stir. Chairman Butler was sent for and the newspaper men were summoned in a hurry to get an important piece of news. The President had prepared a little paragraph to be inserted at the end of the address. When the speech was delivered with this last-minute addition, it caused a surprise to some, satisfaction to others, but bewilderment to most of the audience. They had heard, at least thought they had heard, and yet the situation was no clearer to them than it had been before he spoke. They simply could not understand what he meant and wondered why he did not declare his position, once for all.

The situation seemed destined to last indefinitely. Then candidates began one by one to appear. It was interesting to watch the President as he read about them in the daily papers. This was almost his only source of information, for he was discussing the situation with no one. The procession began: Hughes, Mellon, Hoover, Lowden, Curtis, Watson,

Willis, Goff — not to mention Borah, Dawes, Norris, and perhaps lesser lights. But not one word from the President as to whom he might favor. In truth he favored none of them. He was playing no favorites, apparently permitting the whole matter to drift aimlessly. He did not, however, permit a point to pass unnoticed. He read all the stories of the leading candidates published in the newspapers, followed returns from all the States where test ballots were held, and studied every forecast made by the promoters of the different candidates. It was common gossip in the household and in the Executive Offices that the President was hoping that the nomination would come to him. He certainly was making no plans for leaving, as is customary along about this time on the part of those who do not expect another term. He watched the chances of a likely candidate as a dog watches a rat-hole. When there was a boom for the Secretary of Commerce, the President refused, in spite of the entreaties of Mr. Hoover's friends, to say a word in favor of his candidacy. The situation was embarrassing to those close to the President. There was no question that he would accept the draft, if it came to him without having to be openly solicited.

All this while the 'I do not choose' statement was kept in the foreground by those interested in other candidates. The Hoover boom continued to grow by leaps and bounds; the others barely kept alive. The Hoover support from Ohio occasioned surprise and alarm in the White House, but there was no regret expressed that the Secretary of Commerce had not been more successful in Indiana.

COOLIDGE BECOMES THE GRACIOUS HOST

So the days pass and the time for the Convention in Kansas City is fast approaching. At the White House certain people continue to be welcome guests, principally those who have not allied themselves openly with any other candidate. Take, for instance, the invitation to John T. Adams, his wife, and his daughter. They are just back from Europe and he was on his way home and to the Convention at Kansas City. They are singled out to be invited to stay at the White House over a period of two or three days, although they are not intimates of the Coolidge family; in fact, they are practically strangers. But it is well known that Mr. Adams has been one of the 'draft Coolidge' advocates. Mrs. Coolidge's absence in Massachusetts gives him ample opportunity to act the part of the gracious host, so contrary to his custom when there is no political issue at stake.

The pot is boiling now. The McNary-Haugen Bill has been vetoed according to expectation and all of those who wish to put the 'I do not choose' in the discard seem pleased, feeling that it is a straw in the wind. The accompanying message, however, has caused a riot. It seems to put a little different aspect on the nomination question. But the 'I do not choose' does not change. It is the same bewildering enigma. The ones who are still trying to fathom it find themselves groping around in the dark. You hear so many interpretations that it makes you dizzy.

The President is taking particular notice of the effect of the veto on the farmers of the West. So are the Hoover promoters. They are busy. The largest wheat-grower in the West, Campbell of Montana, is sent for by the Hoover forces. He reports to Secretary Work and is passed on to Secretary Hoover, all unknown to the White House. Then the Secretary of Agriculture learns of his presence in Washington, immediately communicates this information to the White House, and the President asks Mr. Campbell to lunch. I have seldom seen so much scurrying around. We had practically to take our guest from the arms of the Secretary of Commerce and place him within the portals of the White House to be fed and petted for an entire afternoon. The President saw fit to forgo his afternoon nap to bask in the sunshine of the information Mr. Campbell brought. All the while there is an attempt to lay the blame for the veto of the Farm Bill at the door of Secretary Hoover. If we suppose that the President is interested in Hoover's candidacy, why does he not come out and say that he alone is responsible for the veto? Why permit the odium, if such there be, to be placed on the Secretary? A word from the President would have made everything clear, but that word is not spoken. There can be only one conclusion.

Now comes the choice of a place for the summer vacation. The choice is unlimited, for there are offers from all points of the compass. The foremost consideration, of course, would be the President's own comfort and peace of mind, if 'I do not choose' really meant anything. He selects Brule, Wisconsin, hardly the most advantageous place for the comfort of himself and his family. Mrs. Coolidge especially is disappointed. Her mother is critically ill in Massachusetts and she does not wish to go so far away. There must have been other important reasons for the President's decision. He says not a word in explanation. It is significant, however, that he is planning to take along a larger office force than ever, evidently anticipating extra work and an unusually heavy correspondence.

A SITUATION NEW TO AMERICAN POLITICS

Ambassadors are coming home. Morrow and Houghton come to Washington direct. The former is being mentioned as a possible choice of the President for the nomination. But there are no signs of it at the White House. Morrow is vainly endeavoring to find out himself if the 'I do not choose' has come to mean anything. He is quite as much in the dark as the rest. He dares not ask the President for countless reasons, but he is anxious to know, for others are looking to him for enlightenment. He has conferences with Dawes, Hoover, Mellon — the first two rather formal, but the third long and significant. The Secretary of the Treasury bluntly inquires of him, 'Will the President accept?' Morrow replies, 'The only way to find out is to nominate him.' This, in substance, is the feeling of all who have his nomination at heart. But they do not know. They guess and guess and are simply running around in circles. They fear lest there may be another blast of 'I do not choose' that will blow them off their feet. I am asked over and over, 'What do you know?' 'Will he accept?' I can only answer that every sign seems to indicate 'Yes.' Hitherto Ambassador Houghton had always been a guest at the White House on his visits to Washington. It is different now. He has been mentioned as a possible candidate, so he is left to cool his heels in the office of the Secretary until the President can find a few spare minutes to see him.

So it goes. The more guesses there are, the more bewildering everything becomes. What will develop? It is now a few days to the time of the assembling of the Convention. There are all kinds of rumors — rumors of messages being carried to the Convention, of letters having been written. We are getting ready for the journey to Wisconsin. What may be in the back of the President's mind, he alone can know. 'I do not choose' remains just as much a mystery as ever.

Then comes the last cabinet meeting before the departure for Wisconsin. It is just four days before the Convention will open. The papers are full of all kinds of stories of what is going to happen. Present at this last cabinet meeting were: Kellogg, Mellon, Sargent, New, Wilbur, Hoover. Mellon, New, and Wilbur will all be in Kansas City in a few hours. There sat Hoover, heralded in all the papers as the most likely choice of the Convention, provided the President was not to be considered. There sat Mellon to whom everybody seemed looking for a word that would either nominate the President and give him a chance to decline or throw the strength of his influence to Hoover and end the ordeal. And the others, how they would have liked a word to clarify the situation! No doubt they wished to ask the fatal question. But did they? No. Not a word passed at this meeting on the subject of the Convention nor was there any mention of the candidates to be paraded before it. All this I know on the highest authority. They left this meeting just as much in the dark as ever. It is reasonable to believe that no such situation has ever before presented itself in American politics. Those in the center of the stage knew no more of the real intentions of the principal actor than the man in the street. It is no secret that Mellon delayed his departure several days, hoping to have some word. Again and again he asked those who might be in a position to know if the President would accept the nomination. No satisfactory answer came; none could come except from the President.

MR. HOOVER IS ANNOYED

On Tuesday, June 12, the clans gathered at Kansas City. At the White House there was little interest in the opening ceremonies. Mrs. Coolidge was ill in bed. The President went to his office this morning as usual. Arriving there he remembered it was Tuesday, the day of the week on which cabinet meetings are held. None was scheduled for this day, as the President had planned to be on his way to Wisconsin and most of the members were at the Convention in Kansas City. However, he immediately gave orders that all cabinet members in the city be summoned at the regular time of meeting, knowing full well that most of them had gone. In response to his call there came only the Attorney General, Mr. Sargent, and the Secretary of Commerce, Mr. Hoover. The meeting of these two members with the President lasted less than half an hour, nothing really of importance having been discussed, as I was told at the end of the meeting by one of those present.

The morning papers were full of the doings, plans, and interests of the delegates out in Kansas City. All the various candidates were being groomed and a concentrated effort was being made to 'stop Hoover.' The President was still mentioned as a possible candidate, regardless of what interpretation might be put on 'I do not choose.' The story went that he was to be drafted. It was an interesting ordeal for those of us who honestly believed, from all that we had heard and seen, that the President, in the midst of all his silence, wished for just such a situation. We firmly believed, and when asked did not hesitate to say, that he would accept.

Later in the morning came the news that the idea of drafting had been abandoned and that those who were foremost in the cause had decided to support Mr. Hoover. This came to the President's knowledge just before lunch-time and the effect it created was shocking. It seemed to fall like a bomb on his wishes, his hopes, his aspirations.

At this moment 'I do not choose' became a living ghost to haunt the mind of the originator and spell gloom for all who had supported him.

We heard principally from the newspapers that Mellon and Butler were definitely going over to the cause of Hoover. There was dismay at the White House, there was sadness, disappointment, regret. Word came that Butler inferred the President favored the candidacy of his Secretary of Commerce to any other. A short, snappy telegram to Butler was promptly dispatched, saying that he had no right to make such an announcement. A denial was promptly received that any announcement had been made. But by now it was apparently settled that Mr. Hoover was to be the nominee.

The President came back to the White House visibly distressed. He was a changed man. It was evident to all, especially to the keen eye of his physician who was present at the very time, being in attendance upon Mrs. Coolidge. So plain was it that the doctor made sympathetic comments and did what he could to restore his chief's peace of mind.

On the same floor with the President's room, to which he retired immediately, there was a radio going full blast. There was also one in Mrs. Coolidge's room reporting the preliminary proceedings of the Convention. The President took no notice of either of them, forgetting even to stop in Mrs. Coolidge's room, which was his invariable custom when he came over to the house from the office. He threw himself across the bed and lay there a long time. He had no lunch and only when the physician came out a couple of times to inquire, at the suggestion of the President, for word of the Convention doings, did we know the drift of his thoughts. He remained in his room the rest of the day and night, not emerging until nearly eleven o'clock the next morning. Even then it was a different President from the one we knew. There came up immediately the question whether or not he would attend the luncheon that was to be given in honor of the Mexican flyers at the Pan-American Building. So much was this in doubt that word was passed along to be prepared for his absence. In the end he attended, but his disappointment remained as evident as before. That night he left for Wisconsin.

Thus the story of 'I do not choose' comes to an end, so far as these pages are concerned, but the phrase will live on for years as one of the most remarkable political utterances in the history of our country. In my opinion, and in the opinion of others close to the President, it was never meant to bring about the results it did. Rather it was an utterance made on the spur of the moment for a certain political effect, intended to feel out the situation. In plain words the President hoped to be the nominee, expected to be the nominee, and was disappointed and distressed when he was not chosen by the Convention.

'TRAITORS IN THE WHITE HOUSE'

In his disappointment his closest friends shared and it was only after the prize had passed beyond recall that they realized the true situation. It was humiliating to them that, with all their hopes, he had been so little considered at the Convention. They looked for someone on whom to place the blame. Naturally they turned first on the President himself, saying that he had played the game of silence in this instance far beyond the reasonable bounds and for once had made a failure of it. They figured he was always in a more or less receptive mood, but having issued the original statement of 'I do not choose' and having failed to clarify it, he had found himself in an awkward position from which he could not with propriety get himself out, and permitted his friends to become just as much enmeshed as he was himself. This they felt very keenly and believed that history would record that the President had failed them when he should have stood up and saved the country from the menace of the opposition party. They truly believed that this menace existed and that he alone was the one sure force to counteract it. They were all sad, disappointed, distressed, and it is no wonder they were slow to rally around.

One of those close friends brought back from the Convention what I believe to be the real story. He told how, even with the chances apparently against them, with no word from the President to help, they yet had hopes of stampeding the Convention. One of their leaders who had been faithful until the last had been ill in bed since coming to Kansas City. As he lay there still scheming and figuring how it could be done, there appeared in his room a man, very close to the President. This person boldly advanced the suggestion that Coolidge would not accept the nomination if it were tendered him and that for the good of the party it must not be done. He pictured how humiliating it would be to have to offer it to another, especially to the foremost candidate, the Secretary of Commerce. This suggestion, coming from this source, threw consternation into the camp of those who had intended to nominate the President, regardless of 'I do not choose.'

This word was passed around. First the man sick in bed sent for certain friends who had been affiliated with him and who stood close to the President. They in turn passed the word along until even the most optimistic realized that it would be out of place to continue to hope for the President's nomination in the atmosphere that had grown up. Thus it came to be a scramble to get on the bandwagon of the Secretary of Commerce. Feeling was bitter; on his return from the Convention a man close to the President was heard to remark, 'There were traitors right in the White House,' referring to the individual who had originally passed out the word to the sick man in Kansas City. Every sign during and after the Convention pointed to the fact that the President's friends who wished to nominate him regardless, were right in their conclusion that he would accept.

After the nomination of Secretary Hoover, Coolidge lost all interest in the Convention. He was a sick man. When told that Senator Curtis had been nominated for the Vice-Presidency he replied that he did not care who was nominated, and said it with a show of anger, as if he did not wish to be bothered. At another time when told of the proceedings he said he didn't wish to hear anything about it. So the Convention went on and adjourned with as little interest for him as could be possibly imagined.

Upon his arrival in the West he became a nervous wreck. He could neither eat nor sleep normally for at least ten or twelve days after his arrival. The employees who came in contact with him were concerned lest his condition prove serious. It was no secret that the physician in attendance was worried. But time is a great healer, and when at the end of his vacation he returned to Washington, the President was to all outward appearance quite his normal self again.

But he never recovered fully from the shock, and a shock it was. He has never been able to enter whole-heartedly into the campaign for the nominee who was named at Kansas City. The situation at the White House is very different from what it usually is at such a time. The candidate's name is seldom mentioned and then more with indifference than with any word or thought for his success. We who are in a position to observe are convinced that the President would not shed a tear if Mr. Hoover were defeated. On one occasion I heard him remark, 'The people have been so prosperous for eight years and have made so much money, they may wish to go on a spree and elect Governor Smith.'

THE SCAFFOLD

March, 1929. The building of the reviewing stand for
Hoover had no interest for Coolidge. During the whole time
that it was being erected, he never let on that he even saw it.
This was significant in view of the fact that Coolidge, above
all others, noticed every little thing that went on around the
place. The men remarked that he acted like a prisoner who
had to witness the noise and bustle attendant on the building
of a scaffold for his execution.

20

WORKING WITH THE HOOVERS

THE HOUSEHOLD IS DISRUPTED

THE Hoovers came in and upset the whole private part of the house. They evidently pictured their own private household and proceeded to arrange accordingly. Never was the place so changed, so torn up, so twisted around. There was not a room coming over to them from the Coolidge time that was not changed in some way. Most of them lost all resemblance to their former selves. The alterations started right in from the beginning. The President had no sooner landed in his study on the evening of March 4, right after reviewing the inaugural parade and before dinner, than he gave orders for this, that, and the other to be removed. A big piece of California redwood log that Coolidge had purposely left from among his own belongings was ordered out. A large clock on the mantel and a globe which had stood in this room for years suffered a like fate. The high bookcases that Coolidge had built to hold his large collection had to be removed. These were all built-in cases and it was no small job to take them down. The plan was to build lower ones, but after getting the higher ones out and the room painted, the President decided he would not use the room for the same purpose, but instead make the adjoining bedroom into his study and have bookcases built there. This was the old office used by all Presidents up to the time of Roosevelt; in earlier years it had been the cabinet room as well, and it was the room in which President Lincoln signed the Emancipation Proclamation. This evidently appealed to Hoover and formed a subject of conversation with his guests for months thereafter. An effort was made to associate the furniture in the household with this room and with Lincoln. Among other things the President brought with him from his own home a picture of the 'First Reading of the Emancipation Proclamation.' From this picture, four chairs in the White House were traced to the Lincoln period. They show plainly and were not known before the coming of the Hoovers and the picture. They were added to the furnishings of the room, together with the old *Resolute* desk, made from the timbers of the ship by that name. It was on this desk, so it is said, that Lincoln signed all the war papers and the famous Proclamation.

This move deprived the household of one of its two suites of guest-rooms. The old Jackson bed from this room, a four-poster that reached nearly to the ceiling, was placed in one of the small bedrooms. The old study that was vacated was now turned into a drawing-room and furnished with private effects. The oval room next to it was stripped of its furniture and used for moving pictures in the evening and as a sort of catch-all for furniture that had no other place to rest.

The bedrooms of the Coolidges were twisted out of all recognition. The old Lincoln bed was sent to the attic for storage and a bed belonging to the family took its place. The President took possession of the large room and the dressing-room used by Mrs. Coolidge. The latter became a room for massage, for it was here that the President underwent this daily ritual. Mrs. Hoover was shifted to the room formerly used by President Coolidge for all purposes; sleeping, eating, and exercising. Here Mrs. Hoover had her office in the daytime, her dressing-room in between times, and her bedroom at night. Fairly bespattered with papers of all kinds, it resembled a newspaper office after a windstorm.

The northwest room, which had always been used as a bedroom, became another sitting-room for a time. But it did not last long, for now with four sitting-rooms on the floor bedroom space was at a premium. So the old Lincoln bed was again dragged from the attic and placed in this room and it became the 'Lincoln Bedroom.'

The most radical alteration, however, was in the west sitting-room. This for five administrations had been the main sitting-room on the second floor, with easy-chairs, pictures on the walls, and ornaments, personal and otherwise, adorning every nook and corner. Mrs. Coolidge took delight in arranging everything to have it most attractive on her leaving. Two days after Mrs. Hoover's arrival all furniture, rugs, pictures, and everything were ordered moved. In their place came palms, ferns, flowers, pans, and pots. Vines trailed about the doors and windows. It became a complete miniature conservatory right in the living part of the house. Wicker furniture and grass rugs were brought in to take the place of mahogany pieces and Oriental rugs. The transformation was startling.

An arrangement for talking movies was installed. This necessitated tearing up the entire second floor, for it was here they were to be exhibited. One of the leading companies, without cost to either the President or the Government, agreed to install the apparatus. It was said to have cost the contributors twenty-five thousand dollars.

These are but a few of the changes that were made and contemplated. Three months after this Administration had been in existence, there was not a room on the entire second floor that had not been completely altered, and not one of them was finished. This and that was tried out to see how it would look here or there. The massive paintings of Lincoln, Washington, and Martha Washington were moved from their places and placed temporarily elsewhere. The blue plush furniture from several places on the second floor was sent to the dyeing establishment to be changed to black to adorn the old library. The beautiful gray rug from this room was sent to be dyed brown and the floor was to be stained nearly black to match with the furniture.

One of the colored employees was heard to remark that the

elevator and grand staircase at either end of the house were to be changed one for the other to see how they would look. Also that the two porticoes, North and South, were to be swapped for the same purpose. Changing seemed to become a game.

NEVER A KIND WORD

When Coolidge reigned, we thought he was an odd person, but with the coming of Hoover we changed our minds by comparison. Coolidge was quiet and did queer little things, but Hoover was even more peculiar. He would go about, never speaking to any of the help. Never a good-morning or even a nod of the head. Never a Merry Christmas or a Happy New Year. All days were alike to him. Sunday was no exception, for he worked just as hard on that day if not harder than on any of the others. There was always a frown on his face and a look of worry.

HARD PEOPLE TO WORK FOR

Of all the administrations, the hardest one to work for was that of President Hoover. Not that the hours were longer, for I have put in many more hours under previous administrations. But the Hoovers were dictatorial, attempted to do more than any of the rest, were extensive entertainers, stayed closer to the White House, were much easier of access to the outside world, seemed to know more people, felt they must entertain them, and generally were up and doing all the time. When one adds to this a certain indefiniteness in their ways, one can realize how difficult it was to give satisfactory service.

The Hoovers were great believers in lots of help, domestic and otherwise. Servants simply fell over each other around the White House. Every department was the same, from the kitchen to the attic.

CHARGE IT TO THE PRESIDENT

I am told by a newspaper man that the reason things seemed so different around the White House during the Hoover Administration was because he was the first very rich President I had served under. That may be true, but I do not believe it. They were both very plain people. The President was apparently very modest in his ideas. It was only in his liberality toward Mrs. Hoover that led one to believe he had a great deal of money. Personal finances did not seem to worry Hoover as it has other Presidents. He seemed to handle but little money. He left it all to others with implicit confidence. Mrs. Hoover spent a great deal. She was very liberal with her family and with supplies for the household and never seemed to question the amount or cost of the food consumed. In the way of furnishings for the White House, she was positively extravagant. In the first two years of her occupancy there was practically no limit to anything or any idea that struck her fancy.

The question of having enough Government money for her purpose did not enter into the question in so far as she was concerned. When the Government officials who had charge of the disbursement protested, their ruffled feathers were always smoothed and they were told not to worry; it was known there would be a deficit and it would be paid out of the President's pocket. And it was. Thousands of dollars were paid by the President for things that became Government property.

All of this was done without any excitement on the President's part. Mrs. Hoover, however, was kept so busy making decisions and selections that she worked like a day laborer.

FRIENDS VS. 'YES-MEN'

The Hoovers had a wide acquaintance. They were always entertaining, apparently feeling that was the way to make people happy and keep their friendship. On the other hand, they had few close friends. They seemed to prefer people who agreed with them about everything, so-called 'Yes-Men.' These got into the inner circle, but the greater number seemed merely passing acquaintances — more so even with the President than with Mrs. Hoover. There was no one of real consequence close to him. One here and there seemed to stand out, but as a whole he seemed to keep them all at a distance. Mrs. Hoover was particularly interested in the Girl Scouts and it was in this group that most of her friends were to be found.

MRS. HOOVER ENTERTAINS

Ideas for entertaining differ among the various ladies of the White House. Mrs. Hoover's ideas were on a generous scale, not so much in the way of large official affairs as in semi-official entertainments. What for other ladies would have been mere greetings, she turned into afternoon tea-parties. One or two extra people invited to dinner by the President would mean an additional dozen invited by her to make a party. When a guest came there had to be people in to meet him. There was no end to such affairs. A large lunch, a tea or two, possibly one at four-thirty and another at five-thirty, a dinner of from eighteen to twenty-six covers in the evening, was a normal day's schedule. This was not the exception, but the rule. The attendants, cooks, butlers, others who had the arrangements to make, were worn out. On this account more help was employed than ever before in the history of the White House.

A SIGNAL SYSTEM FOR THE HELP

Mrs. Hoover was an interesting and intelligent talker, and spoke very rapidly, especially when she seemed to be a little more intent than usual. She loved to give signals to the help,

At the turn of the century

Clinedinst Studio

As it is today

THE EAST ROOM

Photograph by Horydczak

all sorts of signals for all sorts of purposes. Signs to the waiters to change the service and to vacate the room. Signs to her secretaries and signs to the ushers. These consisted of dropping her handkerchief or her pocketbook, tossing her eyeglasses around her fingers; or perhaps, holding her glasses or her pocketbook in her hand, she would let the hand drop to her side and to the rear a little.

At an afternoon tea-party, for instance, Mrs. Hoover would take her position in the Green Room, the guests having previously assembled in the East Room, and the word would be given to me to begin showing the people in. The aides, generally two or three in number, would pick out someone to start the performance. While she would be talking to this first party, I would have to stand in the doorway and watch for the signal to inform the aide to bring in the next one. Never until he got the sign did he presume to introduce another visitor. If the party was not agreeable, the sign would come quickly, but more often it was postponed until we became quite embarrassed at keeping others waiting.

THE FIRST LADY'S WORKING HABITS

When the President went to camp alone with a few men on several occasions, Mrs. Hoover would lock herself in her room and be out to everybody, including the household.

She spent a great many hours in bed. She retired early, arose about eight o'clock in the morning, and all day long either lounged on the bed or sat up on it working. She had a bed in what she called her 'workroom' and it was on this she spent at least half of her waking hours.

THE HOOVERS WERE WELCOME NOWHERE

The Hoovers went to camp over week-ends during their four years. All of the employees at the White House were glad when they were gone; likewise when they left camp to return to the White House, all of the people there, from the commanding officer of the Marines who was in charge down to the lowest employee, were glad to see them leave.

In other words, they were welcome at neither place. My thought is that this feeling was the result of the President staying so close on the job. Four straight summers in Washington. That is a record so far as I know.

Hoover seemed to feel that he would be unfavorably criticized if he took a vacation. He reminded one of a fellow who was always afraid of losing his job and must hang around in an effort to hold on.

ALL WORK AND NO PLAY

President Hoover was unusually sensitive to newspaper criticism. He did not like the publishing of news about his fishing trips, and this consideration kept him at home many times. He felt that the people would think he was neglecting his duty. In this he differed greatly from some of his predecessors who felt that they could do as they pleased when they were President. His devotion to duty made it hard, of course, on the employees about the place, who got but little chance to relax. They worked Sundays, holidays, and many extra hours. The Hoovers worked hard themselves and thought everybody else should do the same.

THE PRESIDENT DOES RIGHT BY DOLLY GANN

The social position of Mrs. Gann was the occasion of an amusing incident at the Hoover's first New Year's Reception. Mrs. Gann's social status had been discussed when the Vice-President, the members of the cabinet, and their ladies assembled in the library on the second floor of the White House for the grand march down to the receiving-room. As is the custom, they were all arranged in a semi-circle about the room. The President and Mrs. Hoover entered and made

the rounds. Then, instead of taking Mrs. Hoover and leading the way downstairs, the President left her and walked over
and offered his arm to Mrs. Gann. There was bewilderment
for a moment, for everybody knew he was wrong. Was he
inaugurating a new scheme to give Mrs. Gann more prestige?

It was Hoover's first big social affair as President, and no
doubt he wished to be sure and give Mrs. Gann all the honor
due her. This prompted him to think he should take her as
his partner and lead the way. To relieve the embarrassment
that was evident on the part of all, Mrs. Gann included, I
quickly stepped over to the side of the President and whispered, 'You take Mrs. Hoover down, Sir.' The President
turned quickly and walked to the side of Mrs. Hoover. The
march then started.

SECRETARY ADAMS'S MUSICAL LIMITATIONS

Mrs. Hoover suggested that the band play a certain piece
of music when the receptions were near an end, that the cabinet might gather in the Red Room and be ready to march
to the second floor. This music was to be known to the cabinet members and their wives only.

When this was discussed at a meeting of the cabinet ladies
and an effort was made to decide on a tune, Mrs. Adams,
wife of the Secretary of the Navy, said her husband was familiar with only two tunes: 'The Star-Spangled Banner' and
'The Blue Danube Waltz.' With this handicap accepted by all
as serious, the latter tune had to be agreed upon, for it never
would have done to play the former. Instead of rushing to
the Red Room as planned, they would have had to come to
attention and stand in their tracks!

A VISIT TO HOOVER'S CAMP

I had been invited many times by both the President and
Mrs. Hoover to visit their camp in Virginia. They suggested

that I ought to go up there to familiarize myself with the surroundings, especially in view of the fact that I had played an important part in furnishing the camp. From the very beginning I had been sending loads and loads of all kinds of things every week and often wondered where in the world it was all going. I had heard the camp talked about by the hour and had arranged to send hundreds of other people up there. It had also been suggested at times that I might go up on special occasions to take care of the guests and make arrangements, as I was privileged to do at the White House.

I had made an honest attempt to forgo all of these privileges, for I felt if I went it would make a crossfire in regard to the running of the place. If I went with any authority at all, I feared this would be in conflict with what I understood was the usual custom at the camp, since from my point of view a President is a President, whether in the White House, in a Virginia camp, or in Timbuctoo. So I found it convenient to put off the date of my visit from time to time.

However, the time came in the fall of 1931 when Mrs. Hoover practically ordered me to go up and look the place over. Accordingly, I chose a time when the President and Mrs. Hoover were away from Washington, asked permission to use a White House car, took my wife and daughter, and went to the camp. The ride from Washington is most picturesque, but it is long and naturally tiresome. At the base of the mountain the regular road disappears and you begin to wind your way up a long incline by a circuitous route that measures perhaps two miles. Looking around, it seems very desperate and dangerous for these big White House cars to be making this climb. The thought came to me as we ascended, suppose this car starts backward and the brakes fail to hold! There would be nothing left but a crumbling mass of machinery and human remains to tell the tale.

We arrived safely at the camp. My first impression was one of bewilderment and, after inspection, of completeness. Even with all the money I knew had been spent and all the planning that had been done, I had no idea such a place could possibly exist up in those wilds. It cannot be described, it must be seen to be understood. As a camp it is just as complete as the White House is as a place of residence. There is not a detail lacking. I do not know what more money could do, except enlarge it. It is like a small village in itself, built on the side of the mountain near the top, bathed by the cool waters of two streams. Two hundred or more Marines must have been on the job to attain such results.

I had lunch at the camp and left soon after on the return trip, reaching Washington about nine o'clock in the evening. The trip had taken twelve hours of which two had been spent at the camp.

21

THE YOUNG HERO FROM COLORADO

APRIL 29, 1931. At the White House we knew about Bryan Untiedt, the boy hero of Colorado who had saved his schoolmates from death in a blizzard. We knew from the daily press that he had been invited to visit the President, but we did not know exactly when he was to come. Meanwhile, we were making extensive preparations for the arrival of the King and Queen of Siam, who were expected on the very same day that the son and daughter-in-law of the President were to return to the White House after a six months' sojourn in Asheville, North Carolina. These two events were quite enough to prepare for in any one day. So you can imagine how amazed I was when Mrs. Hoover came back from the Executive Offices the day before the arrival of these two parties and told me that the Colorado boy would be here the next morning, at practically the same hour as the King and Queen. She was obviously much surprised herself. The arrangement had been made unknown to her or to anyone else who would have the responsibility of caring for the young guest.

She immediately called together several of the staff and laid the matter before us. We decided there would be lots to do on the morrow, with the three different parties all arriving at the same time. There would be a shortage of bedroom space and one of the lady guests was asked to double up with the other and give the boy her room. The two ladies were told to get their heads together and plan for Bryan's entertainment.

At eight the next day, the young Hoovers appeared, at nine the boy hero arrived, and at ten-fifteen the King and Queen drove up at the front door. This was a busy morning.

THE HERO COMES AND CONQUERS

Young Bryan came unheralded and unannounced except that a White House car had been sent to the station with a secret service man to meet him. His arrival was uneventful. I was upstairs in conference with Mrs. Hoover about the reception of the King and Queen when he arrived, and I sent word to hold him in the Usher's Room for a few minutes.

Upon his entrance at the front door, he looked around inquiringly and walked to the room as he was directed. Several secret service men and employees immediately surrounded him, but he was quite composed in the midst of this audience. I took him in hand, introduced him to everyone, and tried to put him at his ease. I asked him how to pronounce his name and if he had enjoyed his trip East. The little fellow looked sad, yet composed. He had that unruffled calm that seems to city folks so characteristic of people from the country. His baggage consisted of a little paper suitcase, a flat pasteboard box tied with string — that had got quite crushed on the way — and a little Brownie camera, one of the kind that costs but a few dollars. What a contrast to the luggage of most visitors to the White House, which requires a baggage-wagon to fetch it from the station! This boy needed no baggage-wagon, and yet everyone was most interested in him. He was taken to the elevator and up to the second floor, where Mrs. Hoover awaited him. Introduced to her in formal fashion, he was unaffected enough to do nothing, and so acted his part well. Mrs. Hoover was lovely to him and took him to a hammock in the west palm room to sit beside her. Here she talked and laughed with him and made him comfortable and happy.

After a little while Bryan was shown to his room, where stood a big four-poster bed, large chairs, and other furniture. There was a private bath and a valet had been assigned to him. He was left alone for a few moments to get his bearings, although it hardly seemed necessary. Likewise he scarcely required a valet, but all the formality was gone through with. He had just enough clothes to get along, and no overcoat, though the weather was quite cool. He had two little caps, but very seldom wore them.

In a half-hour or so he was taken over to the Executive Offices to see the President. No royal prince or potentate was ever escorted with more courtesy. He joined the President in his private office and remained alone with him for some time.

Upon returning to the house, he was permitted to go to his room and await lunch. In the meantime, however, the two ladies of the household who had charge of him decided they would take him out for a ride. When the time came to leave, he could not be found. He had wandered out alone in the south grounds to take some pictures with his little camera. This showed his self-confidence, for only the man who was taking care of his clothes knew that he had gone.

Off for a ride he went to get a first view of the city before lunch. Upon his return, the photographers, who had learned in some way of his being out, waited around and nearly mobbed him and the lady with him.

A PICTURE LONG TO BE REMEMBERED

Word had gone forth that he must not be subjected to being interviewed or photographed; in fact, that for his own sake he should not be given too much publicity. He was not permitted to see any of the daily papers that were carrying such big headlines about him during all the time of his stay in the White House.

At lunch there was quite a large gathering, although it

contained no one outside the household. All came down to the Red Room, and when the President arrived they arose according to the custom. Not Bryan, however. Presidents coming into the room meant nothing in his young life, and he just watched from his seat on the big red sofa. It was amusing to see this little fellow, entirely composed, hold his chair when everyone else arose as if by magic. I walked over to him and with a soft word put the little fellow right. There was a smile on the faces of the President and Mrs. Hoover as the latter walked over to him and led him to the dining-room, seating him next to the President. It was a picture long to be remembered.

His innocence was beautiful, so different from anything that had ever been known at the White House before. No wonder the interest in him increased and multiplied as time went on! We originally thought that he was to spend only one night and wondered when he was to leave. It was up to the President to make the decision. The boy seemed indifferent. He had just placed himself in the hands of the President and he was quite contented.

During his stay, which lasted four days and nights, he was taken care of by everybody around the White House. He was made comfortable and looked after in every way. He was given no great amount of entertaining, but taken around to all the Government buildings, to Mount Vernon, to the parks, and got about as good a view of everything in Washington as could possibly be had in that length of time.

He always occupied the same room with all its big furniture and four-poster bed. He ate with the President and Mrs. Hoover when there was nothing special going on. When not with them, he ate with the secretaries or some of the ladies in the household. The papers had him eating and hobnobbing with the King and Queen of Siam, but of course this never happened. The chances are he never saw either of them unless he peeped out of the window of his room, which was just over the main entrance. This was exactly the sort of thing the President was particular to keep him away from.

BRYAN TALKS WHILE THE PRESIDENT LISTENS

To me the most interesting moments of his stay were when the President would take him off to his study all alone and talk to him, or rather listen to him talk. On one occasion I sat near-by and watched them for a full half-hour. The President said just enough to keep the boy going. The little fellow sat in a big armchair talking, telling the President all about his experience with an air of indifference and a calmness that was sublime. He would throw his leg over the chair, twist around calmly as he proceeded, pat the arm of the chair affectionately, and tell his story fluently.

During the stay the boy became fast friends with the little Hoover grandchildren. He seemed very happy in their company. They, the dogs, and his camera formed his principal amusements. He made several visits to the shopping district to buy souvenirs to take home to his family. Many were the interesting stories told of these exploits. His particular object was to get something for his mother. He thought perhaps it should be a dressing-gown, but she had told him that she did not want a very expensive one, for she had to have the kitchen painted.

During all his stay his wardrobe was being added to, so much so that when the time came to leave his little paper suitcase and pasteboard box would hold but a small portion of his belongings. A large leather suitcase, almost the size of a trunk, was purchased, and it managed to hold what he took back with him. This was in addition to two overcoats, a gun-case, and numerous other articles presented to him by the President and Mrs. Hoover. It is also probable that his pockets and the little pocketbook he carried contained more than they had ever been blessed with before. So he left, as he had come, in the company of one of the secret service men.

MRS. HOOVER GIVES A MOTHER'S ADVICE

He departed in the early afternoon, the President having said an affectionate good-bye to him after lunch. Just before he left, Mrs. Hoover took him off to a room and they sat together on a couch. I went for him when it was time to go and heard Mrs. Hoover's last words to him. They were such words as only a mother could say to one in whom she was interested. They must have impressed this simple little boy, coming from one in her position. There were tears in her eyes when she advised him as to his future.

But he was stoical, solid, unconsciously understanding. He was appreciative, but not demonstrative. When he had gone, he left a beautiful atmosphere behind him. Everyone was sorry and had a kind and affectionate word for him. May all that is best in the world be his, for he has shown the quality that goes to make American manhood.

22

THE KING AND QUEEN OF SIAM

APRIL 29, 1931, marks the first visit of an absolute monarch to the White House in so far as I know. There have been Presidents and Presidents-elect, Crown Princes, and even the King and Queen of the Belgians — but the latter were not entertained, since they were merely paying a short visit to Wilson during his illness.

The arrangements for entertaining the King and Queen of Siam were put in the hands of the State Department. The original intention was to do something different and grander than had ever been done before. Most of the State Department officials had observed the procedure in foreign courts in the entertainment of heads of states and it was to these formalities their minds seemed to turn. The President manifested no special interest, Mrs. Hoover very much.

The program was drawn up. It included a formal presentation on the morning of their arrival, the return of this call by the President and Mrs. Hoover, a formal dinner on the evening of the same day and a tea the following day, when the President and Mrs. Hoover were to join the King and Queen to say good-bye. The procedure at the White House, especially the reception for the King and Queen upon their arrival and the dinner, was so different from custom that it was alarming to the older employees. We feared lest the President be accused of 'aping European royalty,' and brought pressure to bear to have the plans changed.

Among other things, the State Department proposed that bowing should take the place of the good old American custom of handshaking. It would have been laughable to see the President, Hoover especially, with his natural disinclination toward social form generally, trying to bow in graceful fashion. I could see him nodding his head, but nothing beyond that. And backing out of the presence of the royal visitors — that would have been a fine situation for the President of the United States in the White House! Well, these were the plans, and it was no easy job to have them changed. The only one that went through was the seating arrangement at table. Buckingham Palace usage prevailed here in spite of our protests that the good old American way should be followed.

The regular custom is, of course, to seat the wife of the President opposite him at the table and the guest of honor on her right. The Queen would have been on the President's right. On this occasion, the President and the King were seated next to each other with the Queen on the President's left. Mrs. Hoover sat on the King's right. That Mrs. Hoover should be so subordinated was resented keenly by the so-called 'jingoes' of the White House, of which I am pleased to be classed as one.

Never before in my forty years' experience had such a seating arrangement been observed. During that time all kinds of notables had been entertained. Presidents of sister republics, premiers from countries all over the world, princes and princesses and other royalty, including Queen Marie, but always the seating had been the American way. No one ever thought to have it otherwise until now the State Department did so at the coming of this little Monarch and his Queen from far-off Siam.

FORMALITY AT ITS HEIGHT

Three White House cars, with the United States seal on their doors, were placed at the disposal of the royal party while they were in Washington. At least one of the Presi-

dent's aides escorted them to and from the White House on
each visit.

At ten-thirty the President and Mrs. Hoover came down
to the Red Room in advance of the visitors' arrival. The
Secretary of State, Mr. Stimson, awaited them there. The
President was here told for the first time what he was expected to do. The seats which they were to occupy in the
Blue Room were pointed out to him and several suggestions
made as to procedure.

Notice having come that the King and Queen were entering the grounds, the President and Mrs. Hoover and Secretary Stimson walked out in the hall purposely to appear as
if greeting them upon their entrance to the household. The
King and Queen had no wraps to leave other than the King's
tall hat, so the delay at the entrance was but momentary.
They walked across the front corridor, preceded by the two
chief aides of the President, to the rug where the President
and the others stood. Other aides formed an aisle for their
passage. They were presented by a State Department official
who had accompanied them.

All shook hands, the President first with the King and
Queen, and then Mrs. Hoover. The President suggested
without delay that they enter the Blue Room where the
chairs had been arranged. The President pointed out to the
King where he was to sit and Mrs. Hoover did likewise for the
Queen. The Secretary of State occupied the remaining chair.
It had been originally planned for the Minister of Siam to be
at this audience, but he was ill and had to be absent from all
the ceremonies in connection with the visit. This audience
lasted for ten minutes, with no others present except the
principals, all aides having retreated as soon as they were
seated. At the end of that time the doors were opened and in
response to a nod from Mrs. Hoover, the audience was
brought to a close. The Prince and Princess Svasti, the
father and mother of the Queen, were ushered in and presented by the State Department official. They had arrived a

little behind the King and Queen and had been shown to the Green Room to await their time. Upon their entrance the President and party arose and engaged in conversation for several minutes.

The suite of the King, consisting of seven persons, had come to the White House following the Prince and Princess and had been shown to the Red Room. After these few minutes of conversation, the President suggested, as previously planned, that he would be pleased to meet the suite. He led the way to the Red Room, where the suite had been lined up according to rank, and the King made the presentations as they passed along. They did not stop for conversation, but continued on through the door to the main hall where they said good-bye. The first act in the play was ended.

The President's car that took the King and Queen to their residence returned immediately to the White House for the President and Mrs. Hoover. (The President only returns visits of rulers of foreign countries.) Accompanied by a Military and Naval Aide, they were driven to the Larz Anderson house on Massachusetts Avenue where the Siamese were quartered. The President asked how many were to be present at the audience and how long it was to be. When told only the King and Queen would be present and that it would last only about ten minutes, he remarked, 'That's easy!' and off they went. Upon his return he was told that he was 'through with Royalty until dinner-time,' and again he manifested great satisfaction.

MR. GANN IS SHOVED ABOUT

The dinner was arranged for eight o'clock. The King's party were to enter by the north or private entrance, other guests by the south. The list was strictly official. When the royal party arrived, the King and Queen were shown to the Red Room where the President and Mrs. Hoover were in waiting. Prince and Princess Svasti were shown to the Green

Room. The suite were shown to the East Room, where the other guests were assembling. Each was announced as he entered. When all had assembled and were in their places, the Prince and Princess were brought in and 'made the circle.' They were then placed at the head of the line, the Vice-President and Mrs. Gann being the only ones who were supposed to be ahead of them. But here came a problem. With the Vice-President and Mrs. Gann was Mr. Gann. Naturally he went and stood beside his wife. One of the chief aides seeing him there quietly suggested to him that he should be at the end of the line and escorted him to that position. Another aide came along and noticing Mr. Gann at the end of the line, when his name appeared on the list beside that of Mrs. Gann, proceeded to inform him that he was out of place and escorted him back to the head of the line. There he remained, the innocent object of smiles from everyone in the room. Several remarked later that the problem of Mr. Gann is quite as complicated as the Gann-Longworth problem. As a matter of fact, he should have been at the end of the line, for he had no official status.

Finally the circle was arranged and the President and Mrs. Hoover and the King and Queen were announced, as 'The President of the United States and Mrs. Hoover, Their Majesties the King and Queen of Siam.' Quite a royal announcement! The only difference from the usual arrangement was the simultaneous announcement of the two titles and the addition of the words 'of the United States' after 'the President.'

The circle was made in the usual manner, the President setting the example of shaking hands and the King and Queen following in this style until they came to the other Siamese present, who did not shake hands, but bowed or curtsied instead. As they entered the room, the two men walked together, followed by the two ladies. Leaving the room, the order was changed, the President escorting the Queen and the King escorting Mrs. Hoover.

A GREAT SHOW

The march to the dining-room was very spectacular. Six aides led the procession through a lane formed by other aides, and the two American officers assigned to the King and Queen came directly behind them in the line of march. The other guests in all their brilliance followed to the strains of a march by the Marine Band, seated in the front corridor arrayed in their scarlet uniforms. What a beautiful motion picture this would have made!

When the party arrived in the dining-room there was some confusion about the seating arrangement, since most of the Americans present had dined at the same table many times and were accustomed to seeing a high-back chair at either side of the table, to be occupied by the President and his wife. Seeing four high-back chairs on the one side of the table, they were just a little nonplussed. The seating was slow, but finally all found their places.

During the dinner, for which the menu was elaborate, the guests concentrated their gaze on the four occupants of the high-back chairs. The most conversation was indulged in by Mrs. Hoover and Prince Svasti, who was seated on her right. The Queen on the President's left, with the Vice-President on the other side, had rather a lonesome evening, although both gentlemen did their best. The King divided up his time between his neighbors in an effort to be affable, and altogether it was quite evident that all hands were more than relieved when this part of the ceremony came to an end. After dinner the party marched to the Blue Room, where the men left the ladies and continued on to the Oval Room, just above the Blue Room, for coffee and cigars. For the men this was a treat, for now they had an opportunity to sound out the King, so to speak. Upon entering the room, the President turned him loose and it was not long before he was the center of a group and doing all the talking. A little fellow, but active and loquacious, he held his own with all of them. He made a good impression, I am sure. Especially interesting was his conversation with men like Senators Borah and Moses. Each took his turn and the time passed rapidly. The President seemed to be the only one in the room in the least bored. It was with a look of satisfaction that he walked over and suggested to the King that it was time to join the ladies.

THE QUEEN'S MOTHER KEEPS AN EYE ON HER DAUGHTER

When the ladies were left alone in the Blue Room, Mrs. Hoover took the Queen, the Princess, Mrs. Hughes, and Mrs. Stimson and retired to the Green Room adjoining. Here they had coffee and, in accordance with previous arrangement, others were brought in from time to time and those first present were escorted out. This was done by two of the social secretaries, the wife of the naval aide and Mrs. Fletcher, who had been appointed a sort of hostess for the occasion in view of the fact that the Minister of Siam had no wife. Mrs. Fletcher's position was a peculiar one and no one seemed to know what she was to do, but she got through with it tactfully.

The scheme of bringing in the various groups of ladies to Mrs. Hoover and the Queen worked well except in the case of the Princess Svasti, the mother of the Queen. When it came time to get her out, it was not so easy. Instead of taking her leave, she but moved to a convenient couch, no doubt to keep a watchful eye on her daughter. All the secretaries, aides' wives and hostesses could not move her. She stayed on to the end, when all except Mrs. Hoover and the Queen were pointedly asked to retire at the coming of the President and the King from the smoking-room above. These two joined their ladies in the Green Room and waited until the other men had gone to the Blue Room, found their dinner partners, and escorted them to the East Room, where there was to be a musical program.

When all had left the Blue Room, the President with the King and Mrs. Hoover with the Queen moved into the Blue Room themselves preparatory to receiving about one hundred official guests. The four leading lights arranged themselves diagonally across the room and, as the guests approached, they were taken in hand by the aides and escorted along the line, being presented to each of the four individually. It was a very pleasant feature of the evening and originated in the mind of Mrs. Hoover herself, not with the State Department.

MR. CURTIS SAYS GOOD-NIGHT

Concluding this ceremony, the four principals proceeded to the East Room. Their being seated was the signal for the music to begin. Miss Dilhing, a friend of Mrs. Hoover, played the harp. The harp was a happy choice, for the Queen told Mrs. Hoover that she was an admirer of the instrument and at times played one herself. When the program was ended and one encore had been played, the President arose and escorted the Queen to the entrance, followed by the King and Mrs. Hoover. 'Good-nights' were said and the party was over.

It was planned that the four principals should be alone at this parting, but the Vice-President, Mr. Curtis, followed out closely on the heels of the King, saying, as they halted, 'I want to say good-night to the King and Queen.' A little embarrassment ensued upon the part of the aides, but the situation was accepted with good grace. The Vice-President was permitted to say his 'good-night!'

MRS. HOOVER'S PRIVATE PARTY

There was not much more to the visit of the King and Queen in so far as the White House was concerned. Mrs. Hoover had arranged a little trip for the Queen while the

King went off to Baltimore to have his eyes examined.

First the tea was postponed from five to six o'clock, when it was discovered the trip that Mrs. Hoover planned could not be made between lunch and five o'clock. She planned to take the Queen for a ride by boat to Mount Vernon and back by motor. Very little preparation was made. A small Department of Commerce boat was secured, most inadequate for any social purpose, but the only one available, since the *Mayflower* went out of commission at the beginning of the Hoover Administration.

The Queen and her party went direct from their house to the Navy Yard where the boat was anchored. Mrs. Hoover, her daughter-in-law, and one secretary went from the White House to arrive aboard the boat ahead of the Queen. Lots of salutes and honors were indulged in by the Navy Yard officials.

The trip down was uneventful. Arriving at Mount Vernon, the party were shown about the place and were hurried into the waiting motors for the return to Washington. When the motors went to Mount Vernon one of them carried two ladies from the White House and the boy hero, Bryan Untiedt. They waited around at the Mount Vernon wharf and watched the party come ashore. This was the only time when the hero had a chance to see the royal visitor. As they left the boat, Bryan and the two ladies went aboard and returned to Washington by water. The motors bearing Mrs. Hoover and the Queen made a quick trip to Washington, over the usual route through old Alexandria City, left the Queen at the house the royal party was occupying, and Mrs. Hoover returned to the White House just in time to join the President for the visit to the King and Queen for tea and the parting word of farewell.

This did not last long. As on the previous visit, the President was told there would be only the two royal visitors present and that the audience would be terminated by himself at his pleasure. This must have come very soon, for it was just one half-hour from the time the White House car left the portico until it returned. Thus ended the visit of the King and Queen of Siam to the White House. With all the ceremony that could be devised, the State Department saw that they got off on an early train the next morning and everybody breathed easier.

MAY THE PRESIDENT ACCEPT GIFTS?

In their wake they left many favors. Presents were handed out rather liberally to all the Americans who were attached to their suite. Rumor was that all would be labeled with some honorary order of the Kingdom of Siam. Whether this ever materialized, I do not know. The six chauffeurs and footmen who handled the White House cars during the visit were left two hundred dollars, fifty for the chief chauffeur and thirty for the others.

The King presented the President with a large and handsome bowl made in Siam and brought all the way from the other side of the world. It is fifteen inches high and stands on a black wood base, in which is a gold plate engraved as follows:

PRESENTED

TO

HERBERT HOOVER

BY

PRAJADHIPOK

30th April 1931

It is unusual for a President to accept gifts from distinguished visitors or from foreign governments. The custom has been to present such things to the wife of the President, as when Prince Henry of Prussia brought handsome presents to President and Mrs. Roosevelt. Among other things was the handsome bronze bust of the Emperor which Mr. Roosevelt would accept only for the Government and immediately turned over to the Corcoran Gallery of Art. Likewise, when the French Government wished to present President Wilson with a famous Gobelins tapestry, they were told he could not accept it. Since it was already on its way, it was presented to Mrs. Wilson and hung in the East Room during the rest of their term.

All that is left to note is the criticism afterward of the manner in which the King was entertained at the White House. Some said the entertainment was not sufficiently elaborate, others publicly criticized the menu that was served. Whether it was proper to serve cold fish in the first course as an appetizer and afterward to serve hot fish on the same menu must be left to future generations to decide. Or whether cucumbers and tomatoes were proper to serve with the hot fish and a salad later on, I shall not pretend to say. It only goes to show that whatever might be served would be liable to criticism, so no one at the White House was bothered about a little thing like that.

The King and Queen made a very good impression at the White House, and they left with the best wishes of all. They conducted themselves just like any other human beings and seemed always appreciative of every effort and every courtesy that was being shown them.

23

LITTLE FACTS THAT SPEAK LOUDER THAN WORDS

MARK SULLIVAN MEETS HENRY FORD

DECEMBER 15, 1930. Mr. Henry Ford comes to the White House for dinner and to spend the night. All day the newspaper men have been inquiring for him. Upon his arrival he is met by a group of perhaps a dozen. He jumps from his car and with a wave of the hand cries, 'Nothing to say!' The representatives of the Detroit papers are especially anxious to see him. He refuses all reporters and is kept isolated from them in the White House. The entire evening is spent with the President. In the morning Mr. Mark Sullivan, who is a member of the 'medicine-ball cabinet,' is asked to come to breakfast and to have the privilege of being with Mr. Ford, to the exclusion of all other newspaper men in Washington.

HOW NOT TO HANDLE THE PRESS

This is written while the Hoover-Roosevelt campaign is on. A thought: if Hoover is defeated, a large share of his unpopularity can be attributed to Mark Sullivan. Every newspaper man in Washington is jealous of him. The President has taken him into his fold and he is given every opportunity to get the news and the inside information as no other man is privileged to do. He is at the White House so much he is considered as one of the household by the employees. It is interesting to note how the President has him for breakfast when someone has been in for conference the night before. The feelings of the other newspaper men pre-

vent them from writing many things that would be of benefit
to the President and often prompt them to write just the
something that hurts.

There is no doubt President Hoover has treated the newspaper men, especially those on duty at the White House, with
scant consideration. He has seemed suspicious of them always. Other Presidents have had them eating out of their
hands, as it were, and Hoover could have done so if he had
taken the trouble. Coolidge was a past-master at it, and I
honestly believe a very large part of his popularity was the
result of the way he handled the press. Roosevelt, McKinley,
Taft, Harding, and Wilson all played the game successfully,
and there is no reason why any President cannot do so. He
just has to put forth a little effort. But when antagonism
is experienced there is no end to the unfavorable criticism
from the newspaper men. And they are very clannish. They
stick together, representatives of all kinds of papers making
common cause.

I know them and their ways after many years of association, and I have got along with them very well. They seem
to feel that I have treated them all right, and yet I can
honestly say, I have never given them a hint of news that they
were not honestly entitled to — and I have given them news
on thousands of occasions. It is just that I have given them
fair consideration.

SHADES OF BUCKINGHAM PALACE

The experience of the Hoovers abroad had evidently made
a lasting impression on them, especially in matters of social
entertaining. From the very beginning it was noticeable that
Mrs. Hoover wanted people announced as it was done in
England. Then a segregation of the guests must be made 'as
is done in Buckingham Palace.' The goats must be separated
from the sheep, as it were. An effort was made to dissuade
her and all kinds of arguments advanced why the old Amer-

ican custom should go on. The social secretary and others about the place, fearful of criticism, managed to avoid any change during the first social season. But with the coming of the garden parties in the summer and fall, the new ideas were put into effect.

Those who attended the International Law Association party wondered at the new arrangement. There were ten or twelve groups of delegates arranged according to rank and one large group of everyday Americans who had no rank. The newspaper women, especially, could not quite comprehend what was going on. They remarked that the idea was a poor one and let it go at that. The same group arrangement prevailed at the F.I.D.A.C. party a little later, the only difference being there were not so many groups.

RAMSAY MACDONALD RECEIVED IN STYLE

Ramsay MacDonald was a very pleasing character. His daughter was even more pleasing.

Their coming to the White House was looked forward to and prepared for many days in advance. The Prime Minister upon his arrival was hustled off to the Virginia camp. Mrs. Hoover, who had previously left with Miss MacDonald, was there when the party arrived. Great preparations had been made at the camp for the party. There was more fixing up both at the White House and the camp for this visit than I had ever seen before. A great deal of furniture, etc., was bought. It was surprising, for everything was in such good shape it seemed nothing additional was necessary. It only went to demonstrate the importance placed on the visit by the President and Mrs. Hoover. The Prime Minister was not idle a minute during his stay and practically all was work, because the President did not know how to play. Conferences were held right up to the last minute. It was from one of these the final adieu was said. Leaving the President's study the two men walked down the stairs to the front door,

preceded by an usher. The Prime Minister was most profuse in his thanks for the courtesies that had been extended
to him and with many bows and salutations he took his leave
of the President.

The President in return merely waved his hand and said,
'So long!' Very characteristic of him, for he never goes out
of his way in manifestations of this kind.

THREE VISITORS COMPARED

In comparing the impressions made by the visits of three
noted foreigners during Hoover's time, those of us about the
White House observed that MacDonald came with lots of
confidence, full of importance, and with a very positive disposition generally. Laval gave the impression of one scheming, looking for something he was afraid he would not find.
He was rather hesitant as to when and how he should proceed, never, however, appearing to be open or anxious in
discussion. He was like a prize-fighter sparring for an opening. Grandi left the best impression of all. He seemed open
and honest and willing to listen. He was more like a student
than a high official. His every move was one of courtesy and
respect. Yet he appeared knowing and wise and was never
lost in the conversation. An unusual sight was the greeting
at the Grandi Dinner. The Foreign Minister kissed the
hands of all the ladies present when he made the circle.
Likewise all the Italians present followed suit and kissed
Mrs. Hoover's hand. It was more of a kissing party than
had ever been seen before in the White House.

WASH-DAY IN THE EAST ROOM

Abigail Adams, the wife of the first President to occupy
the White House, wrote: 'I will use the unfinished barn-like
room on the East side of the house for a laundry.' In
these days it is perhaps the most famous room in America,

HOOVER ESCORTS MRS. DEWEY, WIDOW OF THE
ADMIRAL, DOWN THE STEPS OF THE WHITE HOUSE
She has called to congratulate Coolidge on his election, November 5, 1924

IKE HOOVER AND PREMIER LAVAL
October 23, 1931

the great East Room. Here have been held all the famous gatherings of the past century and a half. Presidents, their wives and families, and cabinet ministers have been buried from here. It has been the scene of notable weddings, the assembly room of practically all social affairs. Many conferences and the signing of different treaties have taken place there. Presidents have received millions of visitors in this room, but it remained for Mrs. Hoover to put it to its original use.

During the second year of the Administration one of her secretaries was to be married and Mrs. Hoover had arranged a party for her before leaving. She wanted to do something different. A number of guests were invited and asked to bring their remembrances along, principally in the form of linen. A linen shower in the White House!

These were all assembled in the East Room and Mrs. Hoover had the idea of hanging them all open and spread out on a line just like Abigail Adams's wash. The line was stretched across the entire length of the room; old-time rope and clothes-pins were used. The guests all assembled in the adjoining room for coffee after lunch and, afterward, moved to the East Room. The surprise was complete and there was much amusement. It really looked like a typical wash-line, full of clothes on Monday morning. It *was* Monday, by the way.

A TICKLISH MOMENT AT CHURCH

Sunday, February 8, 1931. The President and Mrs. Hoover attended the New York Avenue Presbyterian Church. They generally attended the Quaker Church, where no collection is ever taken up. When the plate was passed on this occasion, the President was caught without a cent of money. He saw what was coming and was much embarrassed. He whispered to Mrs. Hoover and she dug around in her handbag and found two one-dollar bills and slipped them to the

President, putting nothing in the plate herself. She said afterwards she felt like sending them a contribution for their failure to remember to take money with them. Five dollars is usually put in the plate by all Presidents and their wives. I have often lent them the money when they started out for church on Sunday morning.

GENERAL DAWES AND THE R.F.C.

This is written on February 5, 1932, at the time of the organization of the Reconstruction Finance Corporation. That it will be a failure is the guess of those about the White House. The reasons are these. Dawes is but a figurehead. He has gone back. Ogden Mills and Eugene Meyer are the moving spirits of the organization. They and their policies have directed all the attempts to alleviate the depression. With all the resources and facilities at their command, for two years they have tried and tried to improve the condition, but it has grown gradually worse. They have apparently failed, and yet the President has great confidence in them.

This Reconstruction Finance Corporation is the product of their minds. Dawes is being used as a shield and will have to be the goat if the organization does not make good. It is interesting to note the order of events. Mellon had to be got rid of, and quickly. Dawes was home on leave. His personal interests and the approach of the Chicago Centennial prompted him to announce that he would at some future time, months hence, relinquish his post at London. He was in no hurry to do so. But his announcement opened the way for immediate developments. He was in Chicago. 'Let's get him to check out immediately,' they said. But how? 'Create an office in the Finance Corporation, call it "President," and appoint him to it.' No such office was thought of originally. There was to be a Chairman of the Board and that was to be Mr. Meyer. A complete understanding was entered into without Dawes's knowledge. He would be the figurehead, but Meyer and Mills would be the power behind the throne. Meyer did all the organizing; Dawes just followed in his wake. I wonder when he will see the light.

Dawes was hurriedly brought back to Washington from Chicago. The proposition was laid before him in glowing terms. His patriotism was appealed to. He seemed to demur at first and mentioned the fact that Meyer was Chairman of the Board. But this was somehow explained to his satisfaction and the scheme was agreed to.

Apparently two birds had been killed with one stone. Dawes was now safe within the breastworks. He would no longer be a political menace, as the papers were trying to make him out to be. He was tucked safely away in the Reconstruction Finance Corporation which would be run by Meyer and Mills; and Mr. Mellon would be given the London job, thereby getting rid of him for all time and placing Mills in the important position.

It is fair to say that neither Dawes nor Mellon desired the places assigned to them, but the manipulating had been so well done that neither of them had a chance to refuse. Mellon was sad. In his own words, 'It is hard to break away from a position held for eleven years.' He liked the atmosphere, he liked the life, the prestige, especially the social affairs, at the White House. He never missed one of them. It was home to him. London will be different. I predict he will shortly tire of it and be back home. As for Dawes, he just doesn't understand. Owing to the fact that he is slowing up, he may go on and let the others do what they wish; but if he does wake up, look out!

HEARST GETS THE COLD SHOULDER

How little things can count is illustrated by a point that came to my notice in connection with Hoover's renomination. No doubt from the beginning of his term he and his friends looked forward to the second term and planned accordingly. In the spring of 1932, Mr. Louis Mayer, of moving-picture fame, came to the White House as a guest. He was a close friend of the President and likewise of William Randolph Hearst. He came evidently for the sole purpose of arranging for a meeting between the President and Mr. Hearst. He pleaded with the President to permit him to bring the publisher to the White House, to talk over the matter of the coming nomination. Mr. Hearst had supported the President in the previous campaign and Mr. Mayer's belief was that he could be brought around to support him again. But Hearst had been advocating some policies in his papers contrary to what the President believed best for the country and the President had taken sufficient notice of it to refuse Mr. Mayer's request. He would not listen to argument. Mr. Mayer went away much depressed. It was only a short time thereafter when Mr. Hearst came out in his papers supporting Speaker Garner as the nominee of the Democratic Party, with the result that Garner was nominated for Vice-President by the Democratic Convention.

I saw Mr. Mayer later and he said, 'You see what the refusal to see Hearst has brought about. The President might just as well have had his support.'

HIRAM JOHNSON IS SNUBBED

The omission of Hiram Johnson from a dinner list while Hoover was President returned to haunt. When the list was made up, attention was called to the fact that all members of the Foreign Relations Committee save the Californian had been invited. Trouble was predicted. Then, when notice was taken of the slight, it was blamed on a clerk's oversight. Some of us were much embarrassed, for nothing like it had happened within memory. Certainly never had such a feeble excuse been offered.

Johnson was a hater of four Presidents — Wilson, Harding, Coolidge, and Hoover. He hated Wilson least and Hoover most. Borah hated both Coolidge and Hoover. This was known personally to the writer. Borah hated Hoover as much as Johnson did, and concealed it poorly on his calls at the White House. Once when he was lunching with Hoover, their argument became so loud and pointed that it attracted the attention of all. At the end of the lunch, Borah just got up and walked out without a word of leave-taking on the part of either.

HOOVER FAVORS REPEAL

The notification ceremony in the summer of 1932 seemed to worry President Hoover a good deal. He seemed greatly concerned about his address. No doubt the prohibition question was the cause. It is interesting to note that, if the President had conformed to his own ideas of expediency, he would have gone much farther toward the repeal of the Eighteenth Amendment. He felt it was what the people wanted and he had an open mind on the whole matter. I believe that his closest advisers persuaded him to take the position he did, and that it was the so-called liberal dry people who wrote the prohibition paragraphs in his address. No wonder they backed it up.

THE STRAIN OF THE 1932 CAMPAIGN

When President Hoover started on his trip to Des Moines there was great solicitude as to how he would be received *en route*. As the train rolled along through town after town, during the early part of the journey, the President would make his appearance on the platform; but there was little applause, little enthusiasm. As he came in on one occasion he remarked that it reminded him of the 'Harding funeral train,' on which you recall he traveled. To be sure, this condition changed as his journey progressed; the greetings grew in size and were all that the most optimistic expected or desired.

It is remarkable how Hoover got through the campaign addresses of 1932 without a breakdown. He was so nervous he actually shivered and trembled. I observed it personally at his notification speeches. They said that at Cleveland they thought he would not be able to go through with the ordeal.

EVERETT SANDERS KEEPS ON TRYING

Autumn, 1932. Everett Sanders continued on with Coolidge until the end and those of Coolidge's friends who were peeved at him just looked on to see what would happen. They thought Sanders would be given a cabinet office, or something equally good, in the Hoover Administration. I believe even Sanders himself stayed around Washington waiting for something like that to happen. But nothing did happen. Four years passed and another campaign came along. Hoover had been cool during all that time. He had asked no favors or received none. He now realized, however, that he needed someone to manage the coming campaign — and who could do it better than Sanders? The result was that after much deliberation Sanders was offered the job of National Chairman. He jumped at the opportunity, for it offered another chance to win a seat in the cabinet.

As I write this the campaign is on. If Hoover wins, let's see what will happen.

NOTES ON THE HOOVER RÉGIME

One day during Ramsay MacDonald's visit to the White House, Secretary Stimson was on his way to the President's study, where the two men were in conference. Someone suggested to him that these were 'hectic days,' and he replied, 'When two electric sparks come together, it is hard for a mere mortal to go between them.'

Young Allan Hoover remarked one day that if he did not get away from the White House pretty soon, it would give him the 'willies.'

Hoover always appeared to be unhappy at musicales. He remarked to Rosa Ponselle, 'I didn't think I cared for singing, but you have converted me.'

Mr. Root during a lunch engagement with Hoover asked me if I remembered a slogan of the Harrison times:

> Wanamaker runs the Sunday School,
> Morton runs the bar,
> Baby McKee runs the White House,
> And by God, here we are!

As the President and Mrs. Hoover entered the state parlor for a cabinet dinner during the second year of their first term, the Naval Aide announced, 'The President and Mrs. Coolidge.' All had a good laugh, including the President, who seldom laughed at anything.

The influence of New York bankers was evident at the 'moratorium' conference in July, 1931. We had understood that there was to be a long-time loan to Germany, but Mr. Lamont of Morgan and Company called at the White House one night and the next day it was decided to renew the short-time loans. Right-about-face overnight.

The conclusions of the Wickersham Report were, I believe, influenced by President Hoover. He had various members of the Commission in to see him separately, at the White House proper. Assistant Secretary Hope drew up the message accompanying the report.

Mrs. Hoover told the help to call me 'Mr. Usher,' thinking that 'Mr. Hoover' might be taken to mean the President.
It was useless to tell her no one ever referred to the President
as 'Mr. Hoover.' It was always 'the President' or 'Mr.
President.'

24

FRANKLIN D. ROOSEVELT PAYS A CALL

AN UNPRECEDENTED SITUATION

THE visit of President-elect Roosevelt to President Hoover was most interesting and unusual. It was the only time in my years of service that any President-elect came to call on the incumbent in advance of the inauguration. The visit was looked forward to with considerable nervousness on the part of all hands.

There was a good deal of doubt as to where Mr. Roosevelt would be received and who would be present at the conference. After much agitation in the newspapers and elsewhere, it was decided that the President-elect should be received in the Red Room of the White House proper and that each principal should have one man with him, like a trainer in a boxing or wrestling match.

GARNER IS NOT WANTED

Upon arriving at the south entrance the President-elect greeted those standing around. To me he waved his hand and said 'Hello, Ike!' just as his car stopped. He was escorted to the waiting elevator. He engaged in conversation as he walked, but it was very evident that he was nervous and passing through an unusual ordeal. He was especially concerned because his hair was disheveled, but he declined an invitation to go to one of the retiring-rooms. The President had come over from the Executive Offices a few minutes before and had been joined by Secretary Mills. It was apparent that both were nervous at the prospect of meeting face to face the man whom for months each had been trying to induce the American electorate to disavow. As the President came from the

Executive Offices, word was sent to him that Mr. Roosevelt would bring with him not only Professor Moley, as he had in advance suggested, but Vice-President-elect Garner also. The President did not relish this, in view of the original under-standing, and showed it plainly. Word was given that if Garner did come, Secretary Stimson should be immediately advised and summoned to the audience. But the Vice-President-elect did not appear, so there was no reason for the Secretary of State to be called.

'THE GOVERNOR OF NEW YORK'

Upon entering the room, the President-elect was announced as the 'Governor of New York,' with an idea of carrying out the supposed informality of the meeting and lessening the reminders of the recent campaign. At the announcement the President stepped forward and shook hands, remarking, 'I am glad to see you, Governor, and thank you for coming.' The President then shook hands with Professor Moley and both the President-elect and Professor Moley greeted Secretary Mills.

The President immediately invited Mr. Roosevelt to be seated. A bantering sort of conversation began between Mr. Roosevelt and Secretary Mills. They spoke of their estates up on the Hudson and made some observations, rather in jest, about the campaign.

In the meantime cigars and cigarettes were being brought in and passed, the President and Secretary Mills indulging in cigars, the President-elect and Professor Moley in cigarettes. Pitchers of orangeade and of water were also brought in and placed on a convenient table. The preliminary conversation, while these things were being done, had to do with the recent illness of the President-elect, when, according to the papers of the day, he had been confined to his bed for a week with grippe. He remarked that it gave him an opportunity to rest up a little, one that the President had not enjoyed since the election. With these arrangements made, it now became the duty of all outsiders to retire, the doors were closed, and this quartet of men were left to themselves.

A STRAIN ON THE ICE WATER

They remained thus for exactly one hour, at the end of which time the door to the corridor opened and out walked Secretary Mills and Professor Moley. The President and Mr. Roosevelt remained alone for seventeen minutes longer. At the end of this time the President rang the bell to the Usher's Office, which was a prearranged signal that the conference was over. Attendants entered the room, the President was already standing, the President-elect got to his feet, and with a rather formal good-bye the President left the room first. It was clearly evident that the audience had been a strain on them. I noticed that most of the cigars and cigarettes left in the room had been consumed and likewise all of the ice water!

BE SEEING YOU AGAIN

The President-elect went directly to his car at the south entrance and with a wave of his hand and a rather pertinent remark that he would be seeing us again, he rolled off into the darkness.

To the White House employees it was clearly evident, even before any publicity had come out, that the conference had been a disappointment. The President was heard to remark, referring to the President-elect, that 'He did not get it at all.' Of Professor Moley he suggested that the professor 'had been reading some magazine articles and that seemed to be his principal source of knowledge.' I do not recall quite so much tension in regard to any other conference. Perhaps the nearest approach was when Harriman came to see President Roosevelt after they had been calling each other liars, or when ex-President Roosevelt came to demand that he be given a command in the A.E.F.

25

DOMESTIC REVOLUTION, MARCH, 1933

ALARMING RUMORS

THE election of Franklin D. Roosevelt made every-body around the White House sit up and take notice. The very atmosphere seemed changed. The Democrats had been out of power for twelve years and those of us who had been through the mill knew what that meant. Then the papers and magazines had been full of all kinds of stories about what was going to happen if Roosevelt was elected.

It had been a custom heretofore for the Administration in office to make the first move in regard to the coming change. The Hoovers were reluctant to do this. There was not a little feeling, which tended to discourage any contact. True, the President-elect was invited to the White House for official purposes on two different occasions, but never a word was uttered in connection with any change in domestic arrangements.

On that occasion of the second visit, the papers published the story that Mrs. Roosevelt would accompany her husband. Mrs. Hoover courteously took advantage of this opportunity to invite her to look the place over and make plans for the future. Mrs. Roosevelt replied that the papers were wrong about her accompanying the President, but that she would be in Washington some days later and would be glad to call on Mrs. Hoover at that time.

LOUIS HOWE COMES DOWN 'IN SEARCH OF JOBS'

In the meantime Mr. Louis Howe, one of the President-elect's secretaries, came down to Washington and made his

appearance at the White House, unheralded and unannounced. This was most unusual, for, as it turned out, he
came solely to look the situation over. He met Mr. Lawrence
Richey, one of the Hoover secretaries, and they discussed
the question of White House upkeep, from the official
angle, 'in search of jobs,' as Mr. Richey afterward remarked.
All kinds of rumors flew around after his visit, ranging from
the opinion that few personal employees would be brought
to Washington, to the opposite suggestion that there would
be a complete new staff. Mr. Howe took no notice of the
residential part of the establishment, although the offer
was made to include it in his so-called preliminary survey.

MRS. ROOSEVELT KNOWS HER OWN MIND

From then on we were all looking forward to Mrs. Roosevelt's visit. She came about midday and was received by
Mrs. Hoover in one of the parlors on the main floor. She
appeared calm and composed, really quite indifferent.
The First Lady had in her mind many things to say. She
was so interested in what she had done to change things in
the White House that she wanted to tell Mrs. Roosevelt all
about it. Mrs. Roosevelt listened attentively, but it was
obvious that it was not what she wished to know. Not until
Mrs. Hoover mentioned the living-rooms and the kitchen
did her guest become interested. She readily accepted an
invitation to visit these places, and, with curious eyes and
many questions, she took everything in — to what extent
can be measured by the vigor with which changes were
made when she came to the house to live on the fourth of
March.

Mrs. Hoover had offered to have an official car call for
Mrs. Roosevelt, but she declined the courtesy and instead
walked to the White House from her hotel, about half a
mile away. A newspaper woman accompanied her as far
as the outer gate and there awaited her return. On her

departure Mrs. Roosevelt again refused a White House car and, accompanied by the newspaper woman, jumped into a passing taxi and went her way.

I had the privilege of a fifteen-minute conversation with Mrs. Roosevelt at the end of her visit, to ascertain the plans of the new family for Inauguration Day. This interview gave me a clear insight into what was going on and being contemplated for the future. Mrs. Roosevelt knew just what she wanted. She told me every detail of the social plans for the day, even to who would be the house guests and what rooms they would occupy; she gave the menus for the entertainments, told what household effects she would bring, what servants should be provided for, what the family liked for their meals and when they would be served, in fact about all that one would wish to know. She emphasized the fact that she wished little formality, but readily acquiesced in every suggestion offered for the conduct of the ceremonies.

HOT DOGS AND CHAFING-DISHES

Mrs. Roosevelt mentioned that hot dogs would be one of the items on the menu for the Inauguration Day luncheon. She inquired if there were chafing-dishes in the house, that she might scramble her own eggs at the table. This was rather new to White House custom. A day or two later, however, there appeared in the newspapers an interview with Mrs. Roosevelt in which every detail of her visit was discussed.

About this time came word that the chairman of the Inaugural Committee wanted advice and assistance. Because I had been through the mill, I was sent for and asked to help in the arrangements, particularly as they pertained to the White House. We considered every possible angle in the course of a three-hour discussion. It was evident that previous customs would not and could not prevail in this

Keystone View Co.

HERBERT HOOVER AND LOU HENRY HOOVER AT THEIR CAMP
ON THE RAPIDAN

FRANKLIN DELANO ROOSEVELT AND ELEANOR ROOSEVELT
Ike Hoover is at the extreme right

coming ceremony. Then, too, the ideas of how an inauguration should be handled, especially in so far as the White
House was concerned, were quite different from what we
had known before.

A DIFFICULT POSITION FOR AN USHER

The usual custom had been for the retiring President to
invite the President-elect and his wife to dinner on the
night of the third of March. I early discovered that this
would not be done, regardless of precedent. In fact, no
invitation was to be extended for any purpose. It was a
bad situation for those who had to plan and arrange for the
proper procedure.

By diplomatic inquiry I learned that the President-elect
had foreseen just such a situation and had passed the word
along that he desired no invitation to dine, but would like
to bring his family to tea on the afternoon of March 3.
The matter was mentioned on several occasions at the White
House. As the time approached, the President-elect having
arrived in the city and nothing having been done in the
way of an invitation of any kind, the situation became embarrassing. Finally, in sheer desperation I told the President of the necessity of giving the President-elect an opportunity to pay his respects and at the same time told him
that Mr. Roosevelt desired to come with his family for tea
on the day before inauguration. After this hint I was instructed to pass the word along that the President and Mrs.
Hoover would be pleased to have the President-elect and
Mrs. Roosevelt call at that time. The suggestion about the
family fell on deaf ears.

The event came off on schedule. The President and Mrs.
Hoover received the President-elect and Mrs. Roosevelt,
and tea was served as planned in the Red Room. It was
rather a cool affair all around. No one seemed comfortable
and everyone was glad when it was over.

THE SHARPEST BREAK OF ALL

The most extreme change in my experience at the White House took place on March 4, 1933. Republicans dropped out of sight overnight. Those that were left seemed to have changed to Democrats.

PART III
COMPARISONS AND VERDICTS

26

STRICTLY PERSONAL

AVERAGE MEN

THE nine Presidents whom I have known seem to me just about average men. Under normal conditions they are no different from other people. Theodore Roosevelt and Wilson were exceptions. One might say that the former was different from, the latter above, the common run of men. Roosevelt seemed to be forcing himself all the time; acting, as it were, and successfully. Wilson's intellect seemed to place him in a class by himself. Presidents like Harrison, McKinley, Taft, Harding, and Coolidge are to be ranked along with the thousands that came to see them; in fact, their visitors often seemed to be greater men than the Presidents themselves.

THE EFFECT OF THE OFFICE

All Presidents and their families change when they get in the White House. The limelight, the adulation, the whole atmosphere in which they are thrown, make it inevitable. Some carry it off gracefully, others let it turn their heads. It seemed to influence the earlier Presidents during my time less than those of recent years — with the exception of Hoover. He least of all seemed to be swayed by the pomp and glory of the position. He was actually shy, backward, and nervous toward it all. Cleveland, too, seemed to lean away from it. But the others enjoyed it, some more and some less. McKinley, Taft, and Harding — and even Coolidge — reveled in it. Wilson accepted it with grace, and it grew

on him almost unconsciously, especially when he took a
second wife.

PERSONALITY

Hoover has more personality over the radio than when you
meet him face to face, except when he is enthusiastic on
some particular subject.

Harding and Roosevelt had much personality. With the
former it was natural, with the latter rather forced, but
materially felt by all who came in contact with him.

From my particular point of view Roosevelt and Wilson
were the most interesting of the Presidents I have known;
Coolidge the least. Taft was good company. McKinley
was very fatherly and considerate. Harrison was cold and
distant. Cleveland was rather distant, but warmed up to
his close friends.

SELF-CONSCIOUSNESS

Egotism, self-consciousness or whatever you call it:
 Most: Coolidge.
 Then in order: Taft — Roosevelt — Wilson — Har-
 rison — McKinley — Harding — Cleveland — and
 Hoover, least of all.

SEEKING OTHER OPINIONS

Hoover sent for people who agreed with him. Others sent
for people who took the opposite view. It was strange to
note the difference between President Hoover and others
when differences would arise over policies. Hoover seemed
to wish to discuss matters with people whom he knew in
advance would agree with him, whereas often have I heard
other Presidents say, 'I do not wish to talk with So-and-So,
for he thinks just as I do.'

Especially did Roosevelt and Wilson seek the other side of the question. True, neither of them ever seemed to change very much, but they did like to argue it out. The big exception that stands out in my mind was the case of President Wilson and woman suffrage. He was bitterly opposed to it for the longest time, but argument brought him around and he became an advocate of the cause.

SELF-CONTROL

Those who saw Coolidge in a rage were simply startled. The older employees about the White House who had known Roosevelt used to think he raved at times, but in his worst temper he was calm compared with Coolidge. Harrison, Cleveland, McKinley, Wilson, no matter how angry they became, always controlled themselves, especially in so far as outward appearances went; Wilson, best of all. Many times it was evident that it was an effort for him to do so, but he did. Taft would break out occasionally, showing it more by his red face than by his expression. Harding, who could rave any old time about the least of things, really became profane, but was soon over it, and the effect was not lasting. It remained for Coolidge, the one who from his reputation would be least suspected, to startle the household with sparks from his anger. Many times, too, the cause was of but trifling importance. He would just work himself up to a real explosion.

LAUGHTER

How few Presidents laugh heartily! Taft was the exception. Harrison, Cleveland, McKinley, Wilson, Coolidge, Hoover — never more than a smile. Roosevelt forced himself into a laugh occasionally and Harding would break the rule once in a while. The extremes were Taft and Hoover. The latter never laughed aloud.

FEAR OF ASSASSINATION

Men like Roosevelt, Cleveland, and Wilson had no fear and they found the protection thrown around them obnoxious. Wilson especially was a brave man. All during the War he never once showed a sign of fear. On the contrary, he many times annoyed those assigned to protect him by unnecessarily laying himself open to attack. I remember well the first time he attended the theater after America had entered the War; how we all begged him not to occupy his usual place in the conspicuous corner of the box, openly exposed to the audience. We finally persuaded him to take a back seat, but he did so for that performance only. After that he occupied his regular seat, saying, 'I felt guilty hiding behind women's skirts, sitting in the back seat.' Secret service men were placed all about through the audience in an effort to protect him in case the emergency arose. But he went on throughout the entire period without visible fear, both in this country and during all the time he was in Europe amid the most dangerous surroundings.

Roosevelt, too, was no less fearless, although the conditions were not the same. Roosevelt liked the secret service men personally, but he hated to have it said that they were for his protection. He always said he could protect himself. Mrs. Roosevelt especially was solicitous of the President's welfare. Many times she would insist that men should follow the President when no secret service men were along. Nights, when there were no secret service men around, he would go out for long walks down by the Monument. When he got there he would often run around the base of this great shaft. I have often gone along behind him and stood at a distance, unknown to him, and watched him run around.

Taft considered the secret service men a necessary evil and accused them of disloyalty.

Harding hated to have them around, for he despised being watched.

The first President who seemed really to desire and appreciate the secret service men was Coolidge. He would often start for a walk or ride and if they were not about he would wait for them, whether for protection or just because it was a custom it might be hard to say.

Hoover relied on the secret service for protection without a doubt. He more than any of the others, except Coolidge, seemed to feel the possibilities of danger when he went out in public. To this was attributed the scarcity of his public appearances. I don't think he was afraid for himself, he just seemed to feel danger existed.

Yet how useless is the whole business of secret service men following the President! There is never a time when anyone disposed to harm a President could not find an opportunity. In quiet conversation the secret service men themselves acknowledge this fact. My own experience has been that the people generally are just as solicitous for the safety and comfort of the President as are those who are detailed for his protection. In forty years I have never seen anyone who wished to harm the President, in spite of the fact that I have handled many so-called 'cranks.'

SECRET SERVICE FOR THE WHITE HOUSE FAMILIES

Never until the time of Harding were secret service men thought to be necessary for the protection of anyone but the President himself. Mrs. Harding, however, adopted one of the men assigned to the President as her own. She had him assigned to her and he acted as messenger, special watchman, general handy man, and at times almost as a lady's-maid.

With the coming of Mrs. Coolidge, Mrs. Harding's man was replaced with another, who now became Mrs. Coolidge's man. In fact, during the Coolidge time the First Lady had two different men. The first one got in bad grace with the President and he was ignominiously thrown out after four

or five years of service. The second fared a little better and
remained until the coming of Mrs. Hoover. There was now
an altogether different situation. Mrs. Hoover really did
not care to have one with her, but the habit had grown up,
and the law had been changed in the meantime to read,
'for the protection of the family of the President.' This was
done in the Coolidges' time, that secret service men might
be assigned to the Coolidge boys without arousing undue
criticism.

FAITH IN THE PEOPLE

Wilson had the greatest faith in 'the people'; Hoover none
at all. Presidents find politicians and statesmen on all sides
of every question and often they know not which way to
turn. So they come to look to the people. Wilson banked
on their judgment. Hoover seemed to have more faith in
his own decisions than in popular opinion. With others it
depended on how the battle was going.

Wilson really had an abiding faith in the electorate, especially when his own fate was concerned. In Europe it
was always, 'Let me get to the people'; and he tried to do
so. On election night of 1916, when it was proclaimed that
Hughes was elected, he told those about him not to worry,
'We have not heard from the people.'

FONDNESS FOR THE LADIES

Harrison enjoyed the company of Mrs. Dimmick and often
went walking with her.

Cleveland had no interest in any lady other than Mrs.
Cleveland. He idolized her, thought of her as a child, was
tender and considerate with her.

McKinley acted the part of a martyr. He gave thought to
no one but his invalid wife.

Roosevelt was a man's man, through and through. Ladies
had no place in his mind.

Taft was a ladies' man, pure and simple.

Wilson was a great admirer of the ladies, but very dis-
criminating. He liked their company better than that of men.

Harding was a sporting ladies' man.

Coolidge had nothing to do with the ladies.

THE SOCIAL LIFE

The Presidents differed a great deal in their attitudes
toward the official social life of the White House. The one
who thrived on it most was Taft. Hoover seemed positively
afraid of it. Coolidge made a comedy of it. McKinley
rather liked it or at least pretended to. It meant nothing to
Wilson. He remarked, that if the earth would open and
swallow the whole crowd, they would never be missed.
Harding seemed bored by it. Roosevelt took it as a matter
of duty.

Coolidge paid less attention to high dignitaries than any
of the Presidents; Taft the most.

FORMS OF ADDRESS

Roosevelt called some by their first names, like Lodge,
whom he called 'Cabot' and who addressed him as 'Theodore.' Also he called Pinchot 'Gifford,' Garfield 'Jim,'
Murray 'Lawrence,' Wood 'Leonard,' and yet it was always 'Mr. Cortelyou' or 'Mr. Loeb.' And he seemed to
emphasize the 'Mr.'

Taft was somewhat uncertain; he seemed to attempt to
emulate Roosevelt, but with little success. Roosevelt always called him 'Will,' but he never replied in like manner.
He would call General Edwards 'Clarence,' or Major Butt
'Archie,' but addressed others by their official titles. Miss
Boardman always said 'Will,' and it sounded out of place,
although he always addressed her as 'Mabel.' Mrs. Taft
did not like her to call him 'Will' and would show it when
she was present.

Wilson was always dignified and particular to address all outside of the family circle as 'Mr.' It was always 'Mr. House,' or 'Mr. Tumulty,' or 'Mr.' somebody else. The only exceptions seemed to be among a few of his classmates, like Robert Bridges, whom he would address as 'Bob.'

Harding addressed practically everybody familiarly, to an extreme that lacked dignity. It was 'Harry' for Daugherty, 'Ned' for McLean, 'Will' for Hays, 'Fred' for Upham, 'Harry' for Sinclair, 'Albert' for Fall, 'Charlie' for Forbes, 'Doc' for Sawyer, 'Jess' for Smith. Even Mrs. Harding so addressed them. True, with them it was ever 'Mr. President,' which modified the effect to some extent. The only ones he did not address familiarly were Hughes, Hoover, and Mellon. To these it was 'Mr. Secretary.' Mrs. Harding was addressed by Daugherty as 'Ma,' by McLean as 'Boss,' by Forbes as 'Duchess.'

I do not think Coolidge ever called anyone by his first name while he was in office, not even his supposedly close friends like Butler, who was always either 'Mr.' or 'Senator.' Stearns was always 'Mr. Stearns,' and Morrow, 'Mr. Morrow.' With Mrs. Coolidge it was 'Mam-ma' — long drawn out, sort of a joking greeting. Mrs. Coolidge called a few by their first names, such as Morrow, whom she called 'Dwight,' but on the whole she followed the President's lead.

TASTE IN CLOTHES

Harrison was neat but not dressy.

Cleveland was indifferent toward dress. Mrs. Cleveland was after him all the time in an effort to help.

McKinley was rather dressy. Particular always to have on a clean white vest. Changed them sometimes two and three times a day. Wore them with all coats, even Prince Alberts.

Roosevelt was rather indifferent toward appearances, but always looked well. The ladies of the family kept watch on his clothes, especially Mrs. Roosevelt, who would have her maid regularly attend to changing his shirts.

Taft was quite dressy and had a large collection of good clothes.

Wilson was at first indifferent toward dress. He changed after the death of his wife and became more and more particular as he neared his second marriage.

Harding took some pains about his dress. He always looked well and varied his clothes more than any of the others. He was rather sporty in his tastes.

Coolidge was rather indifferent at first, but grew to be quite fastidious. He had more clothes than any President.

Hoover was quite indifferent toward dress and toward his appearance generally. How he looked seemed to be the least of his thoughts in the midst of all his deep thinking.

VALETS, BARBERS, AND HANGERS-ON

Almost every President seems to have a favorite servant whom he brings to the White House with him and who stays only during that one particular administration. Harrison brought his Negro barber from Indianapolis, and he did practically nothing during the four years of his stay except cut the President's hair and draw his salary as a messenger. Cleveland had his Negro Sinclair who replaced a white steward to act as valet for the President. He was very close to the family and a power and influence about the household.

McKinley had a Swiss, who was the husband of Mrs. McKinley's maid. Perhaps on that account he had to be taken care of on the payroll as a doorkeeper, none of whose duties he performed. His principal forte was to lie around his wife's room and keep well stoked up with liquor. Roosevelt had his Negro Pinkney, who succeeded Sinclair on the payroll as steward, yet performed none of the duties of that office. His principal occupations were seeing that the Roosevelt children got to and from school and doing a little personal messenger work.

Roosevelt always insisted on being shaved in the office

just before lunch, talking to callers many times while it was being done. Anyone familiar with his facial expressions knows what a job the barber had.

Taft came with two valets, Brooks, a Negro from the War Department, and Monico, a Filipino. Brooks finally worked Monico out of a job, for there was not enough work for the two of them. Monico was placed in one of the Executive Departments. Brooks, by the way, continued on to be a favorite child with President Wilson when he came to succeed Taft.

Wilson perhaps least of all followed this custom of bringing pet servants with him. Aside from a couple of Irish housemaids he brought along, he seemed to play no favorites. Brooks took care of his clothes. Mays, the front door man, cut his hair. He shaved himself.

Harding had all kinds of people hanging around him. Foremost perhaps was a major in the Regular Army and close on his heels came a secret service man. Perhaps it would be more correct to say Mrs. Harding, rather than the President, used and favored these individuals. For her they acted every part from escort and lady's-maid to checkers on the President's movements.

Coolidge came unaccompanied, but he adopted Brooks, left over from previous administrations. Coolidge was indifferent about appearances in the morning.

Hoover came with all kinds of human pets tagging on to him, but the most important was Boris, a Rumanian subject left over to him from the war-time days. Boris drew a salary and did but little, for Hoover certainly didn't need a valet. Boris was just in everybody's way.

JEWELRY

Presidents as a rule wear very little jewelry. Hoover wore none, not even a watch chain. He carried a watch, but not for purposes of adornment. Harding liked jewelry. He wore a diamond ring and scarf pin and a large watch chain. Coolidge wore a pearl scarf pin on Sunday and had several watch chains. Other Presidents had no particular fancy.

The wives likewise were modest compared with many of their guests. Lots of them had a fine collection of jewels, many given to them, but they never seemed to feel it appropriate to adorn themselves extensively.

Mrs. Wilson was buried with her wedding ring and a diamond ring on her hand.

THE QUICK-DRESSING GAME

In the old days most Presidents wore frock coats, the so-called Prince Alberts, and were ready at any time to receive anybody. Beginning with Roosevelt, the custom has been to work in business suits. With Roosevelt it was just about half and half, for very often he wore his frock coat all day, especially when he knew he was to receive a diplomat in the afternoon. But from Taft on, the Prince Alberts were practically abandoned at the White House and the cut-a-way came into fashion for afternoon affairs.

To meet diplomats in the early afternoon it became necessary to change after lunch from the business suit to the formal dress. How quickly this could be done was almost a gamble at the White House. Most Presidents did it very rapidly. They all seemed to pride themselves on the speed with which they could make the change. Taft was very slow, as goes without saying. Harding could change pretty quickly, and so could Coolidge, who would somewhat prepare himself in advance. Wilson was a rapid changer when it came to clothes, but it remained for Hoover to cap the climax.

HOOVER SETS AN ALL-TIME RECORD

To Hoover clothes generally seemed the least of his worries. He always looked neat and well dressed, but it was not because he ever gave a thought to it. The style of collar with formal dress never bothered the President. His changes were really so rapid as to be unbelievable. On one occasion, April 3, 1931, he had an appointment at two-fifteen to receive the new Belgian Ambassador, who was presenting his credentials. He had at lunch two members of the Farm Board and sat at the table long in conversation. The Ambassador, with his escort and staff, arrived and were waiting. The President was still at the lunch-table. I had been trying to persuade him to end the party by standing in the doorway, as was my custom. Two-fifteen, the hour of the appointment, arrived, and I moved on into the room, getting more and more nervous, knowing that it was most unusual to keep an Ambassador waiting and bad form, to tell the truth, especially when the President had set the time himself.

The President arose from his chair as I went in, looked at his watch, said good-bye to his company, and took the elevator up to his room. His clothes were ready for him and his valet in waiting. He came out, descended to the lower floor, received the Ambassador, engaged in a little less formal conversation. The Ambassador retired, the President returned to his room, changed back to his business suit, and at two-twenty-five was on his way to the Executive Offices. It had taken him just ten minutes to do what most Presidents took at least a half-hour to do — and that is a record to shoot at.

Of course in this rapid change he neither replaced his collar nor shoes that he had worn all day, but he had changed to all appearances from a working suit to a formal reception attire. Everybody was amazed and some were caught off their guard, figuring it would at least take him a normal time for the appointment.

In the instance I have cited, the addresses of both the Ambassador and the President were more brief than usual. Each consisted of about a page and a half, double-spaced typewriting on regulation size sheets of paper. Most addresses fill at least three pages of this kind.

HAVING THEIR PORTRAITS PAINTED

Artists who wish to paint the President and his wife are recommended by everybody. They resort to all kinds of ruses to get permission. With some Presidents it is easy to obtain, with others it is very hard. Taft, Harding, and Coolidge liked the idea of being painted. Wilson and Hoover had a horror of it. Most of the ladies rather enjoyed it.

About all the painters of recent years have tried their hands at one time or another. Some of these were entirely unknown. One fellow who came with elaborate credentials and who was permitted to paint the second Mrs. Wilson we found out afterwards obtained his reputation by painting the cows for the field advertisements of one of the malted milk concerns. Some of these artists are queer characters, and we had a time with them. They all have their peculiarities; they must have just the right place, the right light, they must be in the humor, and have the pose they like. To those who have to arrange for them they are a great nuisance.

Strange to say, they get but few good pictures, for they all seem nervous and excited at coming into contact with the President or the First Lady of the Land.

AUTOGRAPHS

Presidents are asked to autograph everything imaginable: cards, bills, books, photographs, spreads, pillow-covers, wooden ornaments, etc.

All liked it except Cleveland and Hoover. Hoover especially made work of it. It was a burden to him and his reluctance caused much trouble to those about him. Coolidge was best of all, for he would autograph anything. Roosevelt and Wilson were more sought after than any of the others.

All of the White House staff were privileged to ask the President for his autograph until Hoover came; then it had to be done through one of his private secretaries who was especially named for the purpose. This made it somewhat embarrassing, as this secretary did not enter into the spirit of the thing. It also hurt the President. Even the other secretaries had to go to this one for an autograph.

WE ELECT —

Prince of the Purple Chamber:	James G. Blaine
Best 'hail fellow well met':	Fred Upham
Most intelligent:	Woodrow Wilson
Funniest:	John Allen of Mississippi
Best to look at:	Warren G. Harding
Best Secretary to President:	George B. Cortelyou
Best cabinet officer:	Elihu Root
Most liberal giver around White House:	Alexander P. Moore
Closest friend to any President:	Colonel House
Most liberal, financially:	Grover Cleveland
Best dresser:	Harding
Most satisfactory to work with:	Wilson

27

THE BUSINESS OF BEING PRESIDENT

THE feelings of a President might be summarized as follows: the nominating convention over — happy; the election ended — doubly happy; inauguration day comes — trebly happy. The oath of office is taken and the inaugural parade reviewed. Then comes the return to the White House, and the crowd and excitement are left behind.

Invariably at this time the dawn appears. The new President more or less realizes his responsibilities. He is shown to the private part of the house and becomes the head of the establishment. I recall when Coolidge first came after Harding's death, he just looked around, as if in a daze. When Roosevelt came, under similar circumstances, all were amazed at the hilarity with which he entered. When the Wilsons arrived, the President was very serious, the rest of the family carefree and happy.

McKinley was the confident one upon entering. With that manly strut so characteristic of him, he acted as if he were true master of the situation. Harding came in full of life, but with a seriousness that was distressing to his friends. This seriousness continued on to the end even in the midst of all the unusual and wild happenings in the White House during his term.

The smoothness with which administrations change has always been a marvel to me. Strangely enough, no official notice of the election or inauguration is ever sent to the White House. Take the case of Coolidge when Harding died. We read about his taking the oath of office, administered by his father in the dead of night, and of his coming to Washington. We knew nothing more except that one day a week or so later word came through the newspapers that the President and Mrs. Coolidge would move from the Willard Hotel to the White House at three o'clock on a certain day. And sure enough they came. It was all right with us, for we had no contrary instructions. When McKinley died, we had no notice at all, not even from the newspapers, when a week or so later in walked Mrs. Roosevelt and her son Teddy, to take possession. The new President did not even accompany them. He came several days later. Again it was all right with us.

It is similar with Presidents who have been elected. They arrive in Washington, take the oath of office at the Capitol, come and take possession of the White House without any advance notice being sent by anybody that it is all right for them to do so. The whole transaction is very simple and democratic. It bears witness, in my opinion, to the remarkable form of government we have.

RENOMINATION AND RUNNING MATES

It has been interesting to note the state of mind with which each President faced the day when he must come up for renomination before his party convention. In most cases the nomination seems to have been a foregone conclusion, yet there was naturally some anxiety.

Under these conditions I have observed Harrison, McKinley, Roosevelt, Taft, Wilson, Coolidge, and Hoover. Always the same cry has gone up from the opposition that the Administration was using the office-holders to obtain the renomination; and indeed in many cases the accusation seemed justified by previous events. In cases like those of Harrison and Taft, where there seemed to be more opposition than in the others, this was particularly noticeable.

None of the Presidents seemed entirely free from anxiety.

Perhaps Roosevelt, Wilson, and Hoover were the most
confident — Wilson perhaps most of all. Roosevelt and
Hoover had misgivings about the Vice-Presidential candidate which caused them considerable worry. So did
Coolidge. I feel sure he did not want Dawes at all. I heard
him mention Borah or Hoover, but, when those two had let
it be known they would not accept, he turned to Governor
Hyde or Everett Sanders of Indiana, afterwards his secretary. Never for a moment would he listen to Dawes and
even after the nomination was made and the election won,
he had no patience with him. He was never taken into the
fold. This situation was aggravated when the Vice-President
absented himself from the Senate on the occasion that
Charles Beecher Warren lost by a tie vote the confirmation
of his appointment as Attorney-General. Coolidge always
seemed to think Dawes did this on purpose and never for-
gave him. Fortunately, Dawes did not know how the
President felt.

A similar situation presented itself when Curtis was nominated. Hoover would rather have come East for a running
mate in his try for a second term. No doubt Senator Morrow,
had he lived, or even Ogden Mills would have been acceptable, though he could scarcely have spared the latter
from the Treasury. He had grown to lean on the youthful
Secretary to an extent I had never seen before; never did I
know a President so dependent on a cabinet officer. Mr.
Mellon was nothing in comparison.

THE RE-ELECTION CAMPAIGN

Of the nine Presidents whom I have served under, up to
and including Hoover, eight have sought a second term; four
were successful, three lost, and the eighth one, Cleveland,
did both. While in office he was defeated by Harrison for
a successive term, but came right back four years later and
defeated the same gentleman. Harding was the only one

who did not have a chance to try for the second term.

President Harrison's mood during the re-election campaign was very serious and almost indifferent. He had just lost his wife and felt his defeat coming on. McKinley seemed confident and apparently put forth no special effort. He did not deem it necessary, being satisfied to maintain the dignity of the office of President. Roosevelt was enthusiastic all through the campaign and seemed to be looking for a scrap, very confident in himself. Taft was upset all through the campaign, apparently foreseeing his defeat on account of Roosevelt's candidacy. He was mad clean through, and some of his expressions, when returning from his speaking trips and while writing his speeches, would not look well in print.

Wilson was worried during his campaign. Yet he had an abiding faith that he would be re-elected, in the face of what appeared to be overpowering odds. He had an abiding faith in the judgment of 'the people' and they did not disappoint him. Coolidge was the sphinx. It was hard to guess just how he did feel. Even his campaign manager could not tell. Yet he seemed confident that he could not lose — a confidence which was borne out by the returns.

Hoover seemed the most worried and the most anxious of all. As it turned out, he was justified in this attitude; but as election day approached, he really had come to believe that there was going to be a Hoover landslide.

All the Presidents have hesitated to get out and do any campaigning for themselves. Without exception they felt it was beneath the dignity of the office to do so. Even Taft and Hoover, who were persuaded to do some campaigning, were rather ashamed of it. Hoover especially felt it against his every principle; only the desperate nature of the situation and the continuous urging of his friends prevailed upon him to go contrary to his sense of propriety.

EXTRA CABINETS

Harrison really had no outside cabinet. His diversions were principally with his family, in his walks and his billiards.

Cleveland had his small fishing cabinet consisting of Joseph Jefferson, E. C. Benedict, and Henry T. Thurber.

McKinley, who spent most of his spare time with his invalid wife, had little inclination for an outside cabinet.

The famous Roosevelt tennis cabinet included the French Ambassador Jusserand, the German Ambassador von Sternberg, Robert Bacon, George von L. Meyer, a Mr. Smith, Lawrence Murray, General McCawley, Archie Butt.

Taft had his golf friends, but they never exactly formed a cabinet, for he took on all comers.

Wilson had his little golf cabinet, consisting of Mrs. Wilson the second, Cary Grayson, Stockton Axson, his brother-in-law, and E. T. Brown, his cousin. He never played with anyone else, and yet played more golf than either Taft or Harding, the other famous Presidential golf players.

HARDING'S POKER CABINET

Harding had his poker cabinet, and it was large and important. The regular members included among others Secretary Weeks, Attorney-General Daugherty, Secretary Fall, Senators Cummings and Hale, Albert Lasker, Henry Fletcher, E. B. McLean, Jess Smith, George Christian, and old Doc Sawyer. There were a great many associate members who came in from time to time; the number, however, was always kept limited to eight at one sitting. Among these associate members might be mentioned Speaker Gillett, Secretary Wallace, Will Hays, Secretary Mellon, Senators Frelinghuysen, Edge, Brandegee, Knox, Curtis, Newberry, McKinley, Phipps, Kellogg, General Dawes, General Pershing, General Harbord, Representative Longworth, Assistant Secretary Roosevelt, Controller Crissinger, Scobey of the

Treasury Department, Forbes of the Veterans' Bureau, and Swager Sherley.

There were also many out-of-town or visiting members. Some of these were George Harvey, Alexander Moore, Mike Gallagher, Walter Wilson, Creager of Texas, Fred Upham, Arthur Sewell, William Wrigley, Charles Schwab, Harry Sinclair, and Walter Teagle.

There were many more, for it was a large cabinet and met very often, not only in the White House, but at the homes of the members whose names appear on the above list. These meetings easily averaged twice a week at the White House and at least once a week somewhere outside. They generally lasted at the White House from immediately after dinner, which would be held early, until twelve-thirty or one o'clock. Those on the outside generally adjourned at twelve-thirty.

Coolidge had no cabinet of any kind; he went it alone in all things.

The Hoover medicine-ball cabinet was interesting, for it was purely a 'yes-man' cabinet. Then, too, it held about the shortest meetings of any of the outside cabinets. The members would come for a twenty-minute session and then get a piece of toast and a cup of coffee before they left. Members were: Justice Stone, Secretaries Hurley, Hyde, and Wilbur, Assistant Secretaries Hope and Jahncke, Attorney-General Mitchell, Solicitor-General Thacher, Mark Sullivan, Will Hard, Larry Richey, Walter Newton, and Dr. Boone. Like all cabinets there seemed to be a favorite, and in this case it was Mark Sullivan, who more often than not stayed on for the regular breakfast with the President.

PRESIDENTS INFLUENCING CONGRESS

In the earlier years the Presidents made less noticeable effort to influence legislation. Harrison, Cleveland, and McKinley did not appear to those in the White House to do much along this line. Roosevelt seemed to be the one who started the custom as it is carried on today. Yet he was more formal about it, arranging to discuss the general aspect of a question some time in advance.

Taft continued in this practice, though apparently with less success. Especially was this noticeable in the making of the tariff bill passed during his Administration.

Wilson did less to influence Congress than either of his two predecessors. His method was to resort to the telephone rather than to send for the members of the Senate and House to come to him. He felt it to be a delicate proposition and, after making his suggestions, hardly ever conferred with the members while a bill was being debated. He seemed to feel that he had expressed his opinion and there was no further argument. At times a party leader would tell him of plans to change a measure under consideration, whereupon he would call up a Senator or a Member of the House and tell him very sharply and in a few words that no change was admissible. This generally brought about the desired results.

President Harding's methods were so varied that they are difficult to explain. He was on close terms with a great number of Senators and Congressmen and discussed official business with them on all occasions. Meals, golf, card games, travels, walks, every place was a field of action. They argued with him as they have done with no other President and generally had their way, convincing him that whatever they did was right. He never seemed to be very concerned with the fate of a measure under consideration, depending more on these so-called friends to take care of his interests.

President Coolidge was different from all the rest. He seemed always to be watching, rather suspicious lest something be 'put over' on him. He certainly kept good track of what was going on at the Capitol. He was continually sending for Congressmen to confer with them about pending legislation. He would read in the morning papers of plans for legislation and immediately have word telephoned to the

Senator or Representative chiefly concerned to stop in at the Executive Offices on his way to the Capitol. This was almost a daily occurrence.

A NEW WHITE HOUSE OFFICE: THE PROFESSIONAL SPEECH-WRITER

Until the time of Harding, all the Presidents, so far as I know, wrote their own speeches. With his coming a man was appointed to prepare whatever set and formal speeches he was called upon to make. The first man to hold this office was Judson Welliver, a widely known newspaper man. He had been with the President through the campaign, being close to the throne, so to speak, and naturally came along to the White House. No doubt he had made himself useful along this very line during the campaign and it was most natural that he should be kept on.

When Coolidge came, he found Welliver on the job and continued to employ him, no doubt finding him a very handy man. But Welliver retired after a time and Crawford was appointed in his place. I believe he had been engaged in newspaper work previously, but his principal business seemed to be to get books from the Library of Congress and hunt up data for the President's use. Coolidge really wrote most of his own speeches, whereas Harding wrote but few of his.

With the Administration of Hoover came another speech-writer. This time it was French Strother. Being a literary man of some reputation, he seemed fitted for the job. He must have been of considerable help to Hoover, not only in the way of preparing speeches, but in working on the various commissions organized by the President. The social welfare committees were in fashion at the time and Strother was made a member of each and every one of them. This occupied him when he was not writing speeches, preparing messages to Congress, etc.

As the whole scheme was a new one, there were many embarrassments for the individual holding down this job. For example, there was no legal appropriation for his salary. It was skimmed from here, there, and everywhere. At one time it was taken from the fund for the payment of chauffeurs and the upkeep of the garage.

Much jealousy was also aroused by this office. The regular secretaries seemed to resent the fact that, owing to the confidential nature of the work, the man holding this job had an entrée to the President which they themselves did not enjoy. He seemed always to be a separate part of the Executive Offices, under orders of no one but the President.

PRESIDENTS' SALARIES AND SAVINGS

I am often asked, 'How much does a President save out of his salary?' Most Presidents save a large part of what they earn. In recent years the opportunities to do so have been much better than they were during earlier administrations.

When I first came to the White House, for example, the President had to pay for all household supplies, public, private, and official. He had personally to own all his conveyances and pay for their upkeep. He had to pay the traveling expenses of his family, even though the railroads may have extended the courtesy of passes when the President was traveling himself.

With the coming of Taft the salary was increased from $50,000 to $75,000 and a traveling fund of $25,000 was established. The law originally read 'For traveling purposes,' but Harding added to it the words 'for official entertaining.'

I should guess that Hoover never saved a cent of his salary, even with all the privileges I have just mentioned. Probably he lived beyond it. On the other hand, I imagine that Coolidge saved practically all of his. Next to Hoover, Roosevelt was the most expensive liver, and I doubt if he ever had much left at the end of the year. I should say that Harrison,

Cleveland, and Taft saved at least half of theirs. Taft perhaps a little more, Cleveland a little less. Taft was a good saver owing to Mrs. Taft's thrifty ways. Harding would have saved a lot if he had lived, for he took advantage of every opportunity. Wilson was economical and no doubt took a large share of his earnings into private life when he retired.

SPENDING HABITS

The Harrisons were neither liberal nor generous, yet they were not close. The Clevelands were very liberal and generous to a fault.

The only generous thing during the McKinley time was the knitted slippers made by Mrs. McKinley and given to about everybody in the house and even to their families at home.

The Roosevelts were not liberal, but inclined to be generous.

The Tafts were liberal with their food, for it was they who fed all comers at the state receptions.

The Wilsons followed the same practice, since it was already established, but on the whole they were inclined to be close. The exception was the second Mrs. Wilson, who was perhaps the most liberal lady during my time of office.

The Hardings were about average. Mrs. Harding was close, the President inclined to be generous.

The Coolidges were good hands at receiving and took more away with them when they left the White House than any other administration with which I was associated, except the Wilsons. The latter had a large inventory of receipts on account of the visit to Europe.

The Hoovers were both open-handed, Mrs. Hoover especially. The President was generous when occasion presented itself, but he did not look for opportunities as did some of the others.

PIN-MONEY

Neither Roosevelt nor Hoover ever carried a cent in his pocket. If they went out to walk or to church, for instance, they would have to borrow carfare to ride home or a piece of money to put in the collection basket. Cleveland and Harding always carried a pocketful of money. Other Presidents were about normal in so far as cash was concerned. They always had enough 'in their clothes,' as the saying goes, to take care of incidentals. Coolidge kept money on him at all times, both bills and change. Unlike other Presidents, he paid all bills himself, instead of leaving them to his wife or one of the secretaries.

28

THE DAILY ROUTINE

THE first sign of life is when the President and his wife emerge from their rooms, generally about eight o'clock. If there be guests in the house, they meet their host and hostess in the upper corridor and all descend to the main floor, where breakfast is served either in one of the dining-rooms or, as with the Hoovers, on the South Porch. In the Harrison Administration the family and guests always retired to the library for morning prayer before coming down to the dining-room. The Coolidges are the only ones who did not have breakfast with their house guests. They always breakfasted alone in the President's dressing-room. The guests chose for themselves, either to eat in their bedrooms or go to the breakfast-room on the first floor. Most of them chose the former.

For breakfast the menu is about the same as in any normal American household. There will be fruit in season, a cereal of some kind, bacon, sausage or ham and eggs in some form, hot bread or toast, and cold bread, white or brown, depending on individual tastes. Jelly and marmalades are also extensively used. Heavy meats like steaks or chops are seldom served — hash sometimes. Chipped beef is often mixed with the eggs and the ham or bacon omitted. The one exception to these general rules was the Taft Administration. Taft always had to have his steak in addition to the other items on the menu. He ate a big breakfast, often remaining at the table after the others had left, reading the morning papers and eating toast and guava jelly or marmalade all the while.

Coffee is always served. President Coolidge used canned condensed milk in his coffee in preference to the rich cream used by the others.

Breakfast over, it is a scramble for the next half-hour. Many times there are overnight guests who are leaving after breakfast. It is a good-bye to them, and they go to their rooms to pack and are whisked away in a White House vehicle to the railroad station. The President makes his way to his office, whether it be, as in the old days, to the one in the White House or to the modern one in the Executive Offices Building. There are two routes to the latter, called by President Roosevelt, who built the new offices, 'the overland route' and 'the subway.' The first is through the State Dining-Room over the top of the West Terrace down a flight of winding steps directly into the Executive Offices. The subway leads down the elevator, through the corridor past the kitchen, and under the West Terrace. Two President's wives have made it a practice to walk over to the Executive Offices with their husbands: Mrs. Wilson the second and Mrs. Hoover — the first only in fair weather, when they used the overland route. Mrs. Wilson would always leave the President on the flight of stairs, out of sight of everybody, including even the secret service man who followed. We guessed that at this point there was a parting kiss.

Mrs. Hoover very seldom missed an opportunity to accompany the President to his office, whether he took the overland or the subway. Instead of leaving him on the stairs, she would often follow him into the office for a special conference that she would not otherwise have had an opportunity to enjoy.

THE FIRST LADY GETS DOWN TO BUSINESS

It takes a half-hour or so after breakfast for the place to get settled into the daily routine. Lunch, at one or one-thirty as the case may be, is the next objective. House guests occupy themselves in various ways, perhaps sight-seeing, shopping, or letter-writing. The First Lady invariably turns to her mail about this time. It is always quite voluminous. Most ladies have their secretaries look it over first, letters which are clearly personal being given to the First Lady unopened. The secretaries go through the rest of the mess and pick out the most important letters, taking care of the remainder themselves. There is, however, quite a bunch of it that goes direct to the waste-basket without being brought to anyone's attention. The mail has been handled in this way for years. The exception to this general rule was Mrs. Hoover. Though she employed two and sometimes three social secretaries, she went through the mail herself, distributing it around to the various secretaries as the subject-matter prompted.

During these morning hours the First Lady has many conferences with her secretaries, particularly during the social season. Mrs. Hoover held regular cabinet meetings before and after each large affair at the White House, consisting of her two or three secretaries, the Military and Naval Aides to the President, and the Chief Usher. Here they discussed plans and proceedings in advance and commented on ceremonies when they were over.

The First Ladies also find time to fill a few appointments during the morning hours. These are generally of an official character with members of the Executive Departments who seek out the wife of the President for one reason or another. They also do their shopping, and have fittings with their dressmakers during the morning hours. A number of social appointments are made along about midday, particularly with people who are visiting the city and who bear credentials from someone known to the White House family. They are asked in for five or ten minutes just to pay their respects. Mrs. Hoover received the various Girl Scout groups at this time.

During these morning hours sight-seers generally arrive in

force. Tourists who come to Washington may miss going to visit other Government buildings, but they never overlook the White House. Everybody, young and old, comes here. Most of them are admitted to the public part of the house, which includes the ground floor and the East Room on the main floor. Those who are so fortunate as to bear credentials or who have friends at Court are shown through the semi-private rooms: the State Dining-Room, the Red, Blue, and Green Rooms.

NO ESCAPE FROM FORMALITY

In the meantime the President has remained at the Executive Offices through the entire morning. It is seldom that he returns to the White House during this time unless he has an appointment that he wishes kept secret from the newspaper fraternity, which is always on watch at the Executive Offices for unusual visitors.

The President returns to the White House just in time for lunch, whether it be one, one-fifteen, or one-thirty. He is generally on time. Some Presidents, notably Roosevelt and Hoover, made a practice of having guests at lunch to 'talk shop.' The custom seems to have grown up in recent years. Wilson never entertained at lunch, and the earlier Presidents did so but seldom. The President returning from his office for lunch will meet the other members of the family, any house guests, and any outside guests in the Red Room. Generally all are assembled in advance of his coming. He will enter with his wife and greet the company, after which they will proceed to the dining-room, the President leading with the ranking lady, who is seated on his right. This rule is always observed. In a way they are just as formal at these regular daily meals as at the large state dinners. It seems quite impossible with the President and his wife present to get away from these formalities. It is often tried, but I have never seen it wholly successful. Some hate it at first, but it is interesting as time goes on to see them succumb to custom. Harding especially tried to get away from it, but he failed. There is the something about the office that demands formality. If the President does not choose the path himself, he is forced into it by his callers, his friends, and even his family. There is no getting away from it.

The menu at lunch is not elaborate except on special occasions. There is generally a little extra put on for company, just as in a private household. Lunch ordinarily consists of a soup or fruit cup, depending on the season of the year, a main course of meat and a couple of vegetables, a salad and a dessert. Cheese is served sometimes with the salad and at other times with the dessert. Candy and fruits are always passed at the end of the meal. Some have coffee after lunch, others not. Cigars and cigarettes are always passed to the men along with the coffee, but up to this writing, 1931, they have not passed cigarettes to the ladies. Ladies smoking around the White House has not become an open custom as yet. Some steal off to the seclusion of their rooms or a corner to take a puff — but they are exceptions.

Lunch over, the President returns to the Executive Offices (or, as in the case of Coolidge, takes a quiet nap). If luncheon guests are present they depart and house guests generally retire to the living-room floor. The early afternoon is spent in various ways. Some go to sleep, some go shopping, some take up their correspondence where they left off before lunch, and others just sit.

THE STRENUOUS TEA-HOUR

The late afternoon generally brings with it more appointments. The President will return to the White House about five or six o'clock to rest before joining the others for dinner. Even this time is often broken into, especially by Hoover, who has a number of special visitors at this hour — people whom the newspaper men know nothing about. All Presidents indulge to some extent in this practice of secret appointments. Personally I have arranged for private mailing-boxes under assumed names for at least two of the Presidents.

The ladies of the White House always set apart this late afternoon hour for receiving. These receptions have much variety, and are handled in different ways by different ladies. They generally last from four-thirty to six o'clock. Diplomats and their wives who have just arrived in Washington, or who are taking their leave, are received in private audience for ten minutes. Small teas are numerous at this time, especially during the social season, from about the first of December until the beginning of Lent. Some of the ladies, like Mrs. Hoover, have tea for about everybody; others limit it to special guests. Mrs. Hoover during the summer serves orangeade and cakes, in addition to the tea.

The requests for appointments are unlimited and have to be carefully weeded out. Nothing sounds so nice, according to some folks, as to be able to say, 'I have just been received at the White House,' or, 'I must hasten away, for I have an appointment at the White House.' More often than not an appointment means nothing and would never have occurred had it not been asked for by someone who wished to do a little climbing.

Lawn parties and visiting delegations are also allotted time in the late afternoon. If and when these various functions are ended, there may be time for a motor ride before dinner. A drive to Potomac Park or Rock Creek Park makes an appetizer for the evening meal. Most Presidents end their daily toil in the office by four or five o'clock. Some, as I have mentioned, come to the house for appointments of a confidential nature — with someone of peculiar political importance at the moment. Other Presidents take advantage of the chance for a little exercise after their day's work is done. Roosevelt always did so. Harrison, McKinley, Taft, and Coolidge would walk a little. Cleveland and Wilson would take their rides — one in a surrey and the other in a large Pierce-Arrow touring car. Taft and Harding played golf regularly, Wilson occasionally, although he seemed to prefer the early morning. Coolidge sometimes would walk out one gate and in at the other to call it a walk. The Hoovers did about as little along this line as anyone could possibly imagine. They never seemed to think of amusement, diversion, or exercise. The game of 'medicine ball' in the morning was a joke in so far as exercise for the President went. He 'talked shop' all the time and had people in to play who were willing and anxious to do so.

DINING, ALONE AND IN COMPANY

There is a breathing space before dinner. With some the hour is seven o'clock, with others seven-thirty or eight. Coolidge had dinner at seven, Hoover at eight. The Hoovers had been used to entertaining and eight o'clock is the fashionable hour. I doubt whether they had a dozen meals alone after they came to the White House. The Coolidges, on the other hand, had been accustomed through life to an early dinner and they brought their habits with them. Night after night they would dine alone, with only Mr. Frank Stearns present. Of course all formal dinners begin at eight o'clock under every Administration.

The procedure at dinner is very similar to that at lunch. If there be house guests only, they join the family on the second floor and all come down to the dining-room together. If there be outside guests, they are shown to the Red Room upon arrival. The house guests and members of the family are brought down to meet them previous to the arrival of the President and his wife. When they have been arranged in a semi-circle according to rank, the President and his wife enter and 'make the circle' as on the most formal occasions. At the conclusion of the presentation, the President precedes the company to the dining-room, escorting the lady who is to be seated on his right. The wife follows immediately with the ranking gentleman. The only exception I recall to this rule was Mrs. Cleveland, who always waited until all the guests had left the parlor and then with her escort brought up at the end of the line.

The seating arrangement at the table varies but little. The President and his wife always sit opposite each other. The honor position for ladies is right and left of the President; for men, right and left of his wife, and so on down to the end of the table. All followed this custom except Mrs. McKinley, who always sat next to the President on his right, although she would be escorted to the dining-room by the ranking male guest. When dinner is finished, the company retire to another room, the men leaving the ladies alone and continuing on to still another room where coffee and cigars are served. The ladies are served coffee, but if they insist on having cigarettes they must bring their own.

For large parties there is generally music of some kind after dinner. Outside guests are often invited in to share in this portion of the program. These musicales are always given in the large East Room where three or four hundred people can be comfortably seated.

Whether it be a large or a small dinner the ending is about the same, the President and his wife retiring to their private apartments while the ushers or aides see that the guests get to their cars and are on their way. The retiring hour varies with administrations. It was always ten o'clock with the Coolidges and always twelve with the Hardings. Others ranged between these two extremes. When the President and his wife retire, they give a signal, generally by ringing a bell, the lights go out, and the doors are locked for the night. This is quite necessary, for a guard makes regular rounds during the night, pushing buttons to check on his duties every half-hour, and one of these buttons is located right at the President's bedroom door.

When President Roosevelt rang the bell for lights out, he would always wait the coming of one of the ushers and call a pleasant 'Good-night!' Others just rang and disappeared. However, whichever way it happens, it is always a happy event, for it marks the end of another day for ushers, secret service men, police, butlers, and the rest. The strain is more or less relieved and perfect calm prevails for the next seven or eight hours.

In the absence of the President and his family from the White House, the routine goes on just the same. The strain, of course, is greatly relieved, but to all intents and purposes the scene does not change. The formal meals are dispensed with, but meals for the help must go on. The opportunity is always taken to make repairs, which are difficult when the family are in the house. The one really important change is that the flag does not fly from the staff when the President is out of the city.

PROTECTING THE PRESIDENT

When the President or his wife leave their private apartments practically everybody in the house knows of it. They never attempt to run the elevator alone. When the elevator car starts, the attendant immediately rings a bell connected with the Usher's Room, three times for the President, once for his wife, warning the ushers, the secret service men, and the police that they are coming to the main floor of the house. If by chance they continue on to the basement floor, the signals are repeated to the employees on that floor, and similarly if the President goes to the Executive Offices. The same signals are repeated when the President leaves the Executive Offices to return to the White House. There is always someone watching and waiting for him.

Most Presidents fall in with this system readily; others dislike it, but are gradually educated up to it. Roosevelt and Hoover submitted to it; Taft and Harding objected to their actions being so thoroughly broadcast. Coolidge made a game of trying to steal away from the secret service men by strolling down the stairway, but he seldom got away with it. Wilson least of all liked to be watched or followed by anybody. It was clearly distasteful to him, but he recognized it as part of the system and permitted it to go on. 'A necessary evil,' he described it.

PRECEDENCE

The rule is for the President to precede everybody, his wife included, on all occasions, formal and informal. It is universally observed except in one instance. When entering an automobile or other conveyance, Presidents will stand aside and insist on their wives going first. Entering a room, an elevator, and so on, they always take the lead. And strange as it may seem, it is the ladies who are most insistent on the observance of the rule.

Upon the coming of a new administration to the White House, there is always lots of argument on this subject. It always appears as if the lady had looked up the custom without the man's knowledge. The latter, having been accustomed to 'ladies first,' will appear awkward when he finds himself obliged to change this lifelong rule.

FORMALITIES

The formality of the White House is much less than that observed at European Courts. At most times it is no more than in any first-class American household. The watchword is simplicity. Of course there is more formality with some administrations than others. Some enter into the domestic life of the place and others hold aloof; some Presidents revel in the details of management, while others ignore them. Coolidge liked to know everything that was going on. Roosevelt and Hoover knew nothing of what was going on and didn't care.

Behind the scenes at the White House the conduct is just sensible. The best of order is observed and there is strict attention to business. The President and his wife come into immediate contact with the attendants incessantly and there is no form observed on such occasions. Everyone feels perfect freedom to address them in any way he likes, and it is no uncommon thing to see the President talking to the lowliest of the employees. The results are satisfactory and pleasing. This is in great contrast to what I found while living in Buckingham Palace, during Wilson's visit to Europe in 1919. The very dignified and efficient butler who served at table where three of us of the party ate was amazed when he saw the President talking with us. When we questioned him, he said he had been employed in his present capacity for six years and neither the King nor Queen had ever spoken to him during all that time. We asked him point-blank what happened when he met the King or Queen face to face in the household. He said he came to a stiff position of attention, made a low, sweeping bow, and said, 'Your Majesties.' The King or Queen would sometimes nod their heads, but more often paid no attention to him. This is so different from American custom that it was the occasion for comment from all of President Wilson's party.

29

WORK AND PLAY

HOW HARD DOES THE PRESIDENT WORK?

NEWSPAPER stories about how hard the President works are often exaggerated. It all depends upon the Administration. Hoover didn't know how to work; Wilson was a past-master at it. Wilson said, 'If a man knows his job, he does not have to work hard.' He remarked once that he was still a schoolboy and never worked on Saturday or Sunday. He took long automobile rides often lasting five or six hours, had few appointments, and always seemed to know beforehand what people wanted. Until the Great War came on, he worked but three or four hours a day and spent much of his time happily and quietly, sitting around with his family. From then on he spent more time at his desk, abandoning the practice of going to the Executive Offices except on cabinet days. He worked in his study where he could be undisturbed. He was a master of work, however you look at it, and yet in the end it was work and worry that put him out of business.

Hoover worried more than any President and really worked harder. He labored practically all his waking hours and never spent any time with his family. Dictation seemed particularly difficult for him, and he always went over it two or three times, doing much changing and correcting. Taft and Harding were a good deal the same way. Other Presidents did not change their original dictation very much; Wilson practically not at all, Roosevelt very little.

It was really a great pleasure to watch Wilson signing his mail. He did most of it at the White House, and I have blotted hundreds of letters for him. I do not recall his ever materially changing one of them.

THE EXECUTIVE OFFICES VS. THE WHITE HOUSE

Harrison, McKinley, and Taft spent but a few hours a day in their offices, Cleveland more because he wrote his messages and addresses in longhand. Taft read the papers all through in the office. Wilson, as I have said, spent practically no time there, preferring to work in his study at the White House. Harding spent a good deal of time at the office. He never rested at the White House during the day, and the afternoons were spent either on the golf course or resting at the Executive Offices. He kept the latest hours of any President and was always up early in the morning.

Coolidge would run over to the Executive Offices three or four times a day on Sundays and holidays; he even used them at night. He enjoyed reading the papers and would often lie down and take a nap on the office sofa.

SLEEPING AS A FINE ART

Coolidge slept on an average of eleven hours per day; to bed at ten, up between seven and nine o'clock. In the afternoon he would without fail take a nap lasting from two to four hours, one-thirty to three-thirty or four o'clock and sometimes four-thirty and five o'clock. No other President in my time ever slept so much. Harding slept least of all. He was never in bed before midnight and more often it was one or two o'clock. He was always up at eight, and when it was suggested to him that he should lie abed in the morning he answered, 'No, it is too much like a woman.' Sometimes he would go to his office, lie down on the couch, and sleep. President Taft kept rather late hours, but slept late in the mornings. He was noted for being able to sleep at any old time. Even in the midst of social affairs, such as musicales,

THE WHITE HOUSE SEEN FROM THE AIR

THE LINCOLN BEDROOM IN THE OLD DAYS

he always found it convenient to take a nap. He would sit in the parlor, when others were engaged in conversation, and sleep. He would nod many times in the midst of hearings given by him to special interests. Once when having his portrait painted this happened and the artist complained that it was impossible to make a good portrait of a sleeping President. Taft knew perfectly well his sleeping tendency and would at times try to avoid it. One of his schemes was to balance his eyeglasses on his finger end; when sleep overtook him, the finger became limp, the glasses would topple and wake him up. I have often sat beside or near him during parlor entertainments at the request of those who had his interests at stake, for the purpose of giving him a little push when he went to sleep. This, of course, was unknown to the President and the nudge was given in a sort of unintentional way, but served its purpose of waking him up.

President Wilson was unusual in regard to sleep. He slept an ordinary number of hours, retiring about ten-thirty or eleven o'clock and arising about seven o'clock. He was a master of sleeping. He very seldom lay down during the day except when he had large affairs to deal with. At these times he would do so and with much form. He could purposely put everything out of his mind and go to sleep in a few minutes, never tossing or rolling, but going right to sleep as soon as he lay down on the bed or couch. It was part of his plan of self-control and he must have so trained his mind that it had become a real part of him. He insisted on his rest at night and ordered that he never be disturbed.

On one occasion, when the trouble with Mexico was pending, an important message came from the Secretary of the Navy and at his urgent request the President was awakened to pass judgment on a certain plan. The message was given to him and he sent word to the Secretary that he would consider it and give the answer in the morning. The next morning he told the one in charge, who happened to be myself, that he should not be called again during the night, except in case of 'life or death.' He explained that no one could pass intelligent judgment when awakened from a sound sleep and that he was not going to try.

In obedience to this order he was never called again during the night, although sought after a number of times by officials high in authority who believed it was necessary for him to be informed of certain happenings. Never during the Great War was he called at night for any purpose. All of which, of course, applies to the days prior to his illness. When that came on, all was changed and the usual procedure was thrown into the discard.

Presidents Harrison and McKinley were very regular in their habits of sleep. Both retired at a comparatively early hour and never slept during the day. Cleveland also was rather regular. The exceptions with him were when he had work to do, such as preparing addresses, messages to Congress, etc. These he wrote in longhand instead of dictating to a stenographer and very often sat up late into the night working on them. A great chewer of tobacco, it was easy to judge in the mornings by the cuspidor how long he had worked. He chewed fine-cut tobacco and kept his coat pocket filled with it.

President Roosevelt slept well at night, but never in the day. He liked to read in the evening after all was quiet. The usual retiring hour was about ten-thirty, but it was always with difficulty that the President was persuaded to turn in at that time. He would promise to come along in a minute, but would immediately become absorbed in a book or magazine and it was generally after much effort and much persuasion that he would finally turn in for the night. Mrs. Roosevelt would call and call. The sound of her voice calling, 'The-o-dore!' is well remembered by all the older employees. She often appealed to me to go to the President and 'see if you cannot persuade him to come to bed.' No matter how late he sat up, he always arose at the same time in the morning and always appeared refreshed and hearty.

PRESIDENTS' DIVERSIONS

Harrison: walking, billiards.

Cleveland: billiards, carriage rides, fishing and hunting when possible.

McKinley: carriage rides, smoking, and having friends to call.

Roosevelt: horseback riding, walking, tennis, boxing, wrestling, fencing, medicine ball, and reading of books and magazines.

Taft: golf, walking, being massaged, reading newspapers, and motoring occasionally.

Wilson: much motoring, golf, solitaire, billiards, a little walking.

Harding: golf, poker, smoking, a little walking, and lots of company.

Coolidge: short walks, some smoking, sleep, and jigsaw picture puzzles.

DOGS

Most all Presidents have dogs, some more, some less. The habit seems to be growing as time goes on. Each administration seems to have more than the previous one. By the time the Hoovers came, a special kennel had to be built and a man detailed from the Army to look after them. At this writing there are nine members of the select dog class on the premises. They range from a small black poodle called Tar Baby to a massive wolfhound named Shamrock. Shamrock and Tar Baby are a great pair.

TASTES IN READING

Most of the Presidents of my time liked detective stories or at least mystery stories. There were exceptions, of course, like Roosevelt, who with all his reading, and he was perhaps the greatest reader of any President I knew, never read mystery stories. Current literature as published in magazines was his favorite. Wilson read the *Christian Science Monitor*, which he said was the only paper in America that told the truth. Wilson and Hoover, the former especially, were incessant detective story readers. Coolidge also enjoyed such stories; nevertheless, like Taft, he confined his reading principally to the daily papers. Taft especially seemed to read nothing else and would delve into every page of all the papers he could conveniently get hold of. Harding didn't seem to read much of anything. A game of chance or skill was more to his liking. Men like Harrison, Cleveland, and McKinley varied their reading, not confining themselves, so far as I could notice, to any particular line.

All read the yellow journal made up in the office of clippings, news items, editorials, and stock market reports. Coolidge and Harding watched these carefully. Wilson, Taft, McKinley, and Roosevelt never seemed to notice them. Hoover seemed to watch them.

CARDS

Card-playing was indulged in during the Roosevelt, Taft, and Harding times, especially in the last-named. Wilson played solitaire very often for diversion, the Canfield game being his specialty. I never saw him play any other game. Poker and Bridge were Harding's favorites.

There was never a deck of cards to be seen around the place during the Coolidge and Hoover times and about the same applies to the earlier administrations of Harrison, Cleveland, and McKinley.

THE BRIGHT LIGHTS

The President and his family used always to take a box when they attended the theater. President Wilson, who disliked the stage box at Keith's Vaudeville House, asked to be changed to one of the mezzanine boxes. Since then all

Presidents have occupied that box at Keith's, and occasionally a similar box at the Belasco. Mrs. Coolidge was the first to choose to be seated other than in the boxes. She asked for an arrangement that would permit her being seated in the orchestra about four or five rows back from the stage. Here often she would sit alone, especially at the regular afternoon performances, accompanied only by a secret service man.

Few Presidents seem to fancy the theater-going privilege. My experience suggests only two as being the exception in that regard. President Taft liked the shows more from a social standpoint and attended often. President Wilson liked them more than any of the others and viewed them in their artistic aspect.

President Coolidge cared for theaters least of all, and it was a hard job to persuade him to go. He seemed ill at ease always while in attendance and glad when it was over and he was back in the White House.

It was work to get President Roosevelt to attend. But when he did, he would enter into the spirit of the occasion. He would much prefer to sit at home in his study reading a magazine or a book while the other members of the family went to the shows and he encouraged them to go without him.

President Harding liked vaudeville, but much preferred spending the evenings in his study with his friends playing a game of cards.

Presidents Harrison and McKinley hardly ever attended the theater, the former evidently through choice and the latter on account of Mrs. McKinley's physical condition.

President Cleveland went occasionally to please Mrs. Cleveland, who was very fond of the theater.

Presidents are given choice seats free of charge by all the theaters. The only exception was during the Great War when they had to pay the war tax on amusement tickets. It was Presidents Wilson and Harding who had this unusual experience.

CHARACTER NOTES

MRS. HARRISON was a nice 'homey' person, kind and motherly.

Mrs. Cleveland was the most popular with the public.

Mrs. McKinley, being an invalid, took little active part in running the household. She was quiet and thoughtful.

Mrs. Roosevelt had the widest circle of real friends.

Mrs. Taft tried the hardest to be a success and was the most spectacular.

The first Mrs. Wilson was the sweetest and most beloved lady who had occupied the White House in my time.

The second Mrs. Wilson did not make much of an effort in a social way. What she did was very successful, but social life, at least so far as entertaining was concerned, evidently did not appeal strongly to her. She always seemed nervous and hesitant. She was a lovely character, however, to be classed right along with Mrs. Cleveland and Mrs. Roosevelt.

Mrs. Harding was wild and anxious, but so constituted that she could not be a social success. She made most progress with politicians who came to see the President. She believed in fortune-tellers and used to slip away with her spooky housekeeper to visit them.

Mrs. Coolidge played the part best. Members of the household remarked that she was ninety per cent of the Administration.

NONE ESCAPE AFFECTATION

My observation has led me to believe that no President's wife has escaped affectation. Mrs. Cleveland, perhaps, came nearest to doing so. Even sedate ladies like the two Mrs. Wilsons had this weakness. Mrs. Taft had less of it than Mrs. Harding, who purposely tried to put on 'side' and did it so clumsily that everybody noticed it.

I felt that those ladies had two personalities: one for the family circle and another for company. None of them were natural in public, and many times this affectation detracted from an otherwise sweet and pleasing personality.

PRESIDENTS' WIVES IN OFFICIAL BUSINESS

Few of the Presidents' wives pretend to share in their husband's official or political life. There are a few exceptions, of course, like Mrs. Taft and Mrs. Harding. It was Mrs. Harding's proud boast that she 'made Warren Harding President.' Through the President she tried diligently to keep in touch with public affairs and many times made suggestions about appointments. Her recommendations were frequently adopted, and many appointments that did not turn out so well afterwards were the result of her handiwork. She kept in touch also through private conversations with officials of the Administration. These conversations were generally unknown to the President and he often wondered where she came into possession of certain information. As he was once heard to remark, 'Mrs. Harding wants to be the drum major in every band that passes.'

Mrs. Taft likewise attempted to guide the hand of the President in many of the affairs of state. Until the time of her illness she attended almost every important conference that was held in the White House proper. She seemed to possess a keen discernment in such matters, and acted as if she had been accustomed to the rôle all her life. She would even walk in on private conferences, unheralded and unannounced. It was a familiar sight to see her and the President in a corner of the room with heads together talking to Uncle Joe Cannon, Senator Aldrich, or some other prominent politician.

I can think of no other ladies who played such parts, with one exception, which I shall mention later. For various reasons the others remained in the background. Illness kept Mrs. McKinley and possibly the first Mrs. Wilson in their own sphere. Mrs. Cleveland was so popular in society that she had no time for such things. Mrs. Roosevelt no doubt was a great help to her husband in an indirect manner. Her forte was to receive his friends socially and win them over to his point of view by her tact and consideration. Officials and political friends would just drop in for the evening and they were always welcome. They would generally find Mrs. Roosevelt knitting, the needles clicking faster and faster as the conversation became more animated. We could hear the jesting and laughter, especially when the President would find time to drop in for a few minutes in between his own formal appointments.

Mrs. Coolidge took least interest in the affairs of her husband. She knew simply nothing about them except what she read in the papers, and, sensibly, never pretended to know. Many times she did not hear until the very last minute whether she was to go somewhere with him or not, but she was always ready with her hat on, prepared to leave at a moment's notice. I would often ask her if she was to go with the President on one mission or another and she would reply: 'I do not know, but I am ready.'

Mrs. Hoover occupied a peculiar position in her husband's official life. She was willing and well fitted to enter into the game. The President, moreover, was quite willing to have her do so, but he simply did not have time to share his responsibilities with her. She could, however, discuss official matters with anybody. I am sure she often felt her isolation, but she was wise enough to go her own way and get some satisfaction out of the part she could play alone.

It remained for the second Mrs. Wilson to take a most remarkable rôle in the government of the country. She had come into the life of the President under unusual circumstances. Of strong character, she was ready either to do her bit or to remain in the background. The President himself believed a woman's sphere was the domestic side of the household. She early became aware of the fact and governed herself accordingly.

When the President was stricken, all this was suddenly changed. Unconscious for days, semi-conscious for weeks, he was never again more than a shadow of his former self. But the world must not know, and business must go on. Thus Mrs. Wilson was thrown into the maelstrom of officialdom and politics. Resourceful and patient, she influenced every act of the President. That she rose to the occasion cannot be denied, whether one approves of such a situation or not. To the end she played her part with confidence. Thus by accident she obtained what others may have wished for and sought out without success.

MRS. TAFT AND THE FIREMAN'S BEARD

Mrs. Taft insisted that all employees in the White House should be smooth-shaven. Some had mustaches and some even full beards. It was quite a job getting the men to shave them off. Old Strauss, the German fireman, had a heavy full beard and was made to get rid of it. He took it off, bit by bit, first trimming a little, then cutting rather close, hoping that he could get by. Finally he had to shave it all off to pass approval. It made him very sad, for he had worn it ever since he had been in America.

ON THE SUBJECT OF NAMES

First Ladies of the Land are very particular about the way they sign their names. I have noticed that they like to use on their visiting cards the simple form, 'Mrs. Roosevelt,' 'Mrs. Wilson,' 'Mrs. Coolidge,' etc., emphasizing the fact that this now means one person and one only, the First Lady of the Land.

In their signatures, they usually retain their family names. The only exception was Mrs. Coolidge. Before she became the First Lady she signed Grace Goodhue Coolidge, but coming to the White House she left out the Goodhue.

Here is the way they signed their names:

Caroline Scott Harrison
Frances Folsom Cleveland
Edith Kermit Roosevelt
Helen H. Taft
Ellen Axson Wilson
Edith Bolling Wilson
Florence Kling Harding
Grace Coolidge
Lou Henry Hoover

Particularly impressive was the signature of Alice Roosevelt. She always signed Alice Lee Roosevelt, and after marriage Alice Lee Roosevelt Longworth in full. I notice also that Mrs. Cleveland has retained the President's name in her signature. When in the White House it was Frances Folsom Cleveland. Since she has married again it is Frances F. Cleveland Preston. Very appropriate.

Presidents called their wives:

Harrison — Caroline
Cleveland — Frances
McKinley — Ida
Roosevelt — Edi
Taft — Nellie
Wilson — Ellen
           Edith
Harding — Florence — Duchess
Coolidge — Grace — Mam-ma

LADIES' CLOTHES

Old School: Mrs. Harrison, Mrs. Cleveland, Mrs. McKinley, and Mrs. Roosevelt.

Modern dress: Mrs. Taft, the two Mrs. Wilsons, Mrs. Harding, Mrs. Coolidge, and Mrs. Hoover. (Yet Mrs. Hoover went back more to the old school than any of the others.)

Of the first four, Mrs. Cleveland was the best dressed. She had many clothes and wore them becomingly. Mrs. Harrison and Mrs. McKinley always kept dressed as became one in their position. One never saw them when they were not fixed up. Mrs. Roosevelt had more trouble in appearing at her best. Her hair especially would not stay fixed. She had many dresses, but did not wear them particularly well. It was always a worry to her. Mrs. Taft never looked well in her street or house clothes, but took on an entirely different appearance when she dressed for parties. Both of the Mrs. Wilsons leaned back toward the old school of dress; they were very neat and always appeared perfectly gowned. The second Mrs. Wilson was more flashy in her style than the first, but either of them could easily be picked out as exceptionally well-dressed ladies. Mrs. Harding was very fixy — so much so that she looked artificial. She had many clothes, but inclined to certain shades, gray being her first choice. Mrs. Coolidge loved clothes, perhaps more than any lady of the White House in the past forty years. Usually she looked young and sweet.

Mrs. Hoover seemed the most indifferent toward clothes. She seemed to select unbecoming colors, and never to ask the advice of others. Yet when dressed for a party in the evening she looked the part. As a matter of fact, Mrs. Hoover had the background for an excellent show of dress — a good figure, tall and graceful for one of her years, a lovely complexion and an abundance of gray hair. It seemed too bad she did not take advantage of these natural endowments. She was perhaps the best qualified for elegant clothes since the days of Mrs. Cleveland, and yet she either did not realize this or did not care.

31

KEEPING HOUSE FOR THE PRESIDENT

CHANGE FOR CHANGE'S SAKE

WHEN it comes to housekeeping there are hardly any two things done alike from one administration to the other. The incoming lady always sees faults and shortcomings in her predecessor's management, and from the very beginning looks forward to making improvements. I generally hear the opinion expressed that the former mistress was a very poor housekeeper and did not keep the place properly cleaned.

One mistress will have a housekeeper; another will not; a third will say that she will have a steward, but be her own housekeeper — and yet, when the new household gets to running smoothly, things will be just about the same in any case.

Very seldom does one administration use the same rooms used by their immediate predecessors. When an incoming family finds the outgoing one occupied the south side of the house, they straightway choose the north side as preferable for sleeping quarters, or, *vice versa*, when they find the north side has been occupied, they prefer the south for the warmth and sunshine. Unfortunately, there are practically only two sides to choose from, north and south, since a long corridor extends the entire length of the building from east to west. Otherwise, judging from precedent, it would be at least sixteen years before any two Presidents would occupy the same apartments.

Then again some criticize the lack of dignity in the way their predecessors did things and others accuse them of too much formality. I never suggest that any other administration has done a thing a certain way, especially the immediately preceding one, for then it will never be right. I just go ahead and do it as I have done a thousand times before, but always give the impression that it is quite original with the present occupants and in line with their suggestion. Even though they may have seen it on many occasions, in the course of former visits to the White House, they readily adopt the idea as original and are content thinking they have changed and improved conditions and have done things never done before. In this respect the Presidential families are no respecters of politics, for the harshest criticism often comes from those of the same political faith as their predecessors.

Observation prompts one to believe there is very little ground for such criticism, for it is merely a difference of opinion at best, and each administration endeavors to leave the house in the best possible condition for those who are to come after. It is really wonderful how much is done in this way. For months prior to the change, even before the election, plans are made with the probable future occupant in mind. Seldom is opinion in the household split over whom they would like to succeed. A good illustration is the first candidacy of McKinley. The fact that he was of opposite political faith from the Clevelands did not prevent it from becoming a household word that things were being made ready for Mr. McKinley. Another instance occurred during the Roosevelt time, when young Quentin Roosevelt used to play with Mr. Taft's son Charlie. On one occasion at least a year before the convention which nominated Mr. Taft had met, while the newspapers were so full of conjectures as to whom the mantle of this strenuous President would adorn, the boys were roughhousing as usual and the noise became just a little more than the lady of the house could stand. When she called Quentin to task, he responded that it was all right, as Charlie Taft was in the bunch, and as it would soon be his house anyway, what difference did it make if he tore it to pieces!

THE DOMESTIC ORGANIZATION

To describe the domestic organization of the White House is a task. Eliminating the Executive Offices and confining ourselves to the White House proper, it is fair to say that the President's wife is the head of the establishment. Her orders are passed down by her social secretaries, whose duties are almost unlimited. Next might be mentioned the housekeeper, whose duties are principally of a domestic nature.

Most of the ladies of the White House up to the Taft time seemed to wish it known that they were their own housekeepers. Even now with the present arrangement these same ladies take a very large part of the management. Mrs. Coolidge and Mrs. Hoover especially were so interested in the housekeeping that nothing was done without their knowledge. The two Mrs. Wilsons were less concerned about it, but nevertheless took some interest in the daily routine of the establishment.

The name 'usher' is a misnomer. The Chief Usher is and has been called about everything: Chief Doorkeeper, Majordomo, Superintendent, Master of Ceremonies, Master of the Household, Lord Chamberlain, Chief Guide, Prompter, Secretary, Custodian, etc., etc. From these various designations may be gathered the extent of his duties. Certainly the Usher's Room is the clearing-house of the establishment.

The Chief Usher does very little ushering. His orders come principally direct from the President and his wife. He is asked at times to do about everything that can be imagined. In consultation with the President or his wife, he makes all plans for every sort of entertainment — personal, social, official, and political — and is present to see that the plans are carried out. His office is at the main entrance and he passes judgment on the eligibility of every individual who comes over the threshold. Many orders to the domestics pass through his hands, and he is on the job sixteen or eighteen hours a day, Sundays and holidays included, to be called on for every purpose under the sun. His telephone is the busiest one in the house and his office is open day and night, for it is here the secret service men and the inside detail of police make their headquarters.

Here is a list of the employees in the White House proper during the Hoover régime: the Chief Usher and two assistants, the housekeeper, Mrs. Hoover's lady's-maid and two assistants, the President's valet, four Negro doormen, one man in the storeroom, one engineer, three firemen, one electrician. There are four regular butlers. In the kitchen are one head cook, three assistants, and one dishwasher. Two men take care of the ground floor, one man the parlor floor, four men the upper floors. There are also two maids who look after these rooms and two other maids who do general work about the house. One man polishes the hardwood floors and one carpenter with one assistant does repairs. Mrs. Hoover had two secretaries at all times and three during the social season. There is one man who checks at the public entrance and one who attends to the dogs. There are about ten employees attached to the social room and their duties are concerned principally with the White House proper. In addition to these who are on the job regularly there is the garden force of about ten men. The police force consists of about fifty men of whom eight are detailed within the White House at all times. Then there are about twenty aides, two of whom have offices at the White House, where they are supposed to be found daily. A representative of the State Department also makes his headquarters here. There are about a dozen secret service men, one or two of whom are always on duty in the White House proper. Extra employees are brought in for all the social affairs: waiters for the dinners and hatbox attendants for the receptions. The latter will probably number as many as fifty.

The most respected person in the house other than the President's immediate family is the cook! All administrations seem to be in awe of her. She is greeted pleasantly and they really seem to be afraid to record complaints. Even President Coolidge, who hardly ever spoke to the employees, was seen to take his hat off to the cook when he accidentally ran into her.

HIRING AND FIRING

The domestic employees, like maids, cooks, butlers, and doormen, continue on as a rule from one administration to another. The only exception I recall was the coming of the second Cleveland Administration when practically all employees in the White House were replaced. The rule is generally to make room for just a few personal servants and let the others continue. At the present time there are a number of employees who have been here twenty years or more and one butler who has been here over a period of forty years, with the exception of the four years of the second Cleveland Administration. Three of the original doormen who came with the Tafts are still on the job. Very few of the Presidents bring more than one or two people with them. The Hoovers perhaps had more than any of the others; they brought about six. The Wilsons and Coolidges brought almost no one. These are the extremes.

Since the beginning of the Taft Administration, all White House servants have been paid by the Government. Prior to that the President had to dig down in his pocket to pay for practically all his personal servants. It was quite a drain on his salary, and President Taft, with his knowledge of White House doings prior to his coming, had it changed.

New employees at the White House are selected by different people: the true domestics generally by the housekeeper, ushers and others of that character by the Chief Usher, mechanics by the representative of the office of Public Buildings and Parks. Yet it is really the wife of the President who does the choosing. All employees are subject to her wishes, likes, and dislikes. She often has people recommended to her and

[285]

selects them herself, especially in the case of butlers or floor men who come into close contact with her. Some of the ladies are easily satisfied and willing to accept almost anyone who is recommended by those who hunt them up. Others are very critical. Mrs. Harding and Mrs. Hoover were extremely particular about the employees. Mrs. Wilson, in fact both Mrs. Wilsons and Mrs. Coolidge, were more lenient and relied on others as to their qualifications. Mrs. Hoover was always particularly anxious to interview every new person who was employed, but thereafter made few changes.

FAMILY AUTOMOBILES

The first automobiles were used by President Taft. He had a limousine and touring car for his own use and a landaulet for Mrs. Taft. These were bought outright. The Wilsons continued on with the same arrangement during their eight years of incumbency. When the Hardings came, there was one more limousine added to the list and a car provided for the Secretary to the President. This arrangement continued through the Coolidge time, but with the coming of the Hoovers further additions were made until the garage housed the following: three cars for the three Secretaries to the President, four limousines for family use, a touring car for the secret service men, Mrs. Hoover's three cars — a landaulet for a town car and two others, one open and one closed, for her own private use; one personal car that the Hoovers brought with them, and two baggage-wagons. In summer, when there are so many visits to the camp, a couple of extra cars are always borrowed for this purpose. In addition to all these there are now three Ford sedans, one used by the housekeeper and the other two for hauling the social secretaries and things of that kind.

MARKETING FOR THE WHITE HOUSE

The White House marketing is naturally done by the housekeeper. It used to be essential to visit the public market every day and there was a wagon provided for the purpose. It would come back loaded with the cream of the crop. This custom has slowly disappeared. Now the telephone is generally used and the orders are delivered. As a rule the so-called higher-class stores are patronized. Generally speaking, the best of the market is demanded for the White House and a liberal allowance provided. Especially does this apply to the so-called official entertaining which is paid for out of a Government fund.

WHAT THE PRESIDENTS EAT AND HOW

In food Presidents have their likes and dislikes the same as other mortals. Some eat anything and everything that is set before them. Harrison, Cleveland, and Taft were what we called good feeders. Harding liked fancy food. Roosevelt and Hoover just ate. Wilson evidently had never lived high and did not change when he came to the White House.

Roosevelt was partial to game, and the gamier it was the better he liked it. When he was alone he fancied plain dishes that he could not have at other times. He would, for instance, make a whole meal on pork and beans. Taft was fond of rich food such as caviar and heavy meats. Coolidge enjoyed cheese and would eat it by the slice like pie. Wilson always had his ice cream made without sugar.

The earlier Presidents demanded a high-class table at all times. Roosevelt, Taft, and Wilson lived fairly well. The Tafts, and to a greater extent the Hardings, always made special arrangements both in food and entertainment for their guests. The latter especially overdid it.

Speaking of high living — especially as pertains to the food at the table — the Hoovers were the highest livers of them all. Nothing was too good for them to order and eat and no questions were asked as to price. They undoubtedly set the 'best table,' as the saying goes, that was ever set in the White House. Everything in and out of season. Mrs. Hoover just reveled in elaborate menus, both for their private table and for company.

POLITICS AT MEALS

Most Presidents take mealtimes for relaxation. Not so with Hoover. He was actually so busy he did not have time to eat. Only when he had business guests did he stay long at the table. When he was alone with the family, he more often than otherwise hurried through and left them at the table. At times he would forgo the last two courses in his haste to get back to work. When alone, as he would be occasionally, the waiters could not bring in the food fast enough. He would not sit there over ten minutes. The men about the place would gamble on how long he would stay in the dining-room when he was alone. It was hurry, all the time. When it came to eating, no one attempted to keep up with him.

Coolidge was a rapid eater, but he loved to sit at the table. Between courses he picked at the candy and nuts. For that matter Coolidge never seemed to hurry about anything. He seemed to take pleasure in being deliberate.

The game of politics at meals is apparently a new wrinkle. The old school never so desecrated their table. Politicians, of course, came in to dine, but they were generally close friends. Since Roosevelt, talking politics at meals has developed into a fad. Roosevelt and Taft did it just a little, Wilson none, but with Harding, Coolidge, and Hoover it became general practice. Especially with Hoover. It was rather a rule during his time for orders to come that the President would breakfast or lunch alone with Mr. So-and-So, leaving the rest of the household to shift for themselves.

Coolidge would not bar the others in the house. Rather he would give his political guests a good meal and then take them to his study to talk it all over. Hoover would talk to them during the meal and dismiss them at the dining-room door when the meal was over. Many looked very much surprised when he said good-bye to them. The Usher here got in his fine work in an effort to make the poor fellows comfortable.

WHEN WINE FLOWED FREELY

During the Harrison time wine flowed like water. The Harrisons were great friends of the Stanfords of California, who saw that the wine-vault was always kept filled. It was principally sweet California wine, and it was dispensed with a lavishness that has never been known since. In those days Andrew Carnegie always attended to the matter of Scotch whiskey. He kept all administrations supplied up to the Wilson era. Wilson refused to accept it. Mr. Carnegie sent one small keg, however, which was not returned. Since the President declined to use it himself, the employees about the place took charge of this last keg ever sent by the old Scotch-man and saw to it that it was not wasted or dumped into the gutter. Mr. Carnegie took great pleasure in sending these kegs of Scotch directly from the old country — as he used to write — and until Mr. Wilson came they were always received with grateful appreciation.

At the large dinners in those days from four to six glasses would surround each plate. There was a different wine for each course and champagne all through the meal. We figured on a quart of champagne for every four people, and after being once iced up for the party, it was never returned to the wine-vault. Somebody had to consume it and those were the times when the employees were put to a test to see that none was wasted.

In those days stewards reigned over the culinary department and not a woman housekeeper as now. There was one old steward in particular who used to do a lot of worrying when the champagne he had iced up was not being used fast enough. He would pass around the table peering over the shoulders of the guests and, seeing glasses empty, would whisper in the ears of the so-called 'wine men,' 'Let the chammy fly!'

Many of the guests would not partake of the wines offered, some turning their glasses down and others asking for a different beverage. A number of the old Southern statesmen would ask for whiskey, a high glass and charged water, and drink this concoction all through the meal. All usually got to feeling very good, especially when the meal was topped off with liqueurs, brandy, etc., served with the cigars and coffee.

'HEEL-TAPS' AND PUNCH

'Heel-taps' were all the dregs left in the glasses when the guests arose from the table. Immediately the guests left the room, one of the butlers would be assigned to take a bucket and pour into it all the wine and liquor of every variety that was left in the glasses. This was a treat for the butlers. After adding a little sugar and charged water, it made a wonderful punch, with a great kick. The butlers drank it along with the dinner they ate after finishing the serving. They always felt the effects of this strong brew and many are the remembrances of jolly times enjoyed by this group of employees.

During the Taft and Wilson times, champagne punch was served at all of the receptions. It was good punch, too, one quart bottle of champagne for every two bottles of charged water. With a little lemon and sugar and a block of ice floating on the top, it was the pride of the household and the pleasure of the guests.

The only trouble was that often a certain group would get around the punch-bowl to the exclusion of all others. Many times it was only after these were the worse for wear that the others got a chance.

Those days are often referred to as 'the good old days.' I wonder, without attempting to express an opinion.

ROOSEVELT MINT JULEPS

At this writing the famous Roosevelt mint bed still grows and flourishes. In the old days when mint juleps were popular it was an important item in the White House menu.

The President used to get great sport out of it, introducing it to foreigners, especially to those in the Diplomatic Corps. Speck von Sternberg and Jules Jusserand were regular customers. The President always saw that the mint juleps made for these men were stronger than the usual run. He would say, 'Make them stiff,' to the butler when ordering for others, although his own were generally made very mild. Other administrations appreciated them also, but not to the same extent.

SMOKING HABITS

Harding was the only President I ever saw who smoked cigarettes. He also smoked pipe and cigars, and chewed tobacco moderately. Cleveland chewed tobacco, but never smoked. Harrison smoked a little. McKinley had a passion for cigars and was perhaps the most intense smoker of all the Presidents during my time. One never saw him without a cigar in his mouth except at meals or when asleep. Neither Roosevelt nor Wilson ever smoked or chewed. Taft smoked when he came to the White House, but stopped soon after and never took up the habit again. Coolidge smoked moderately, occasionally a pipe, but more often the best quality of Havana cigars, which were always given to him. He used a one-cent cigar-holder on a fifty-cent or seventy-five-cent cigar. Hoover smoked incessantly. The bigger and the stronger, the better he liked them, but they must always be a good brand. With the burdens of office he increased his smoking.

The only First Lady whom I have known to smoke was Mrs. Coolidge, and she never did so in public.

Smoking is seldom indulged in at the White House table. There are a few exceptions, when Presidents have men guests alone. Even then they are generally taken to another room. The President's study is extensively used as a smoking-room. There is never any smoking between courses. A guest may wish to smoke, but certainly would not do so unless at the President's suggestion. There is an unwritten law about such things that seems to be understood by all. Everything must be governed by a suggestion from the President or his wife, when in their presence. A mere hint as to their pleasure or displeasure is scrupulously adhered to.

32

THE SOCIAL WHIRL

STATE DINNERS — WHEN AND WHY

THE so-called 'social season,' beginning some time in December and lasting on to the beginning of Lent, includes several formal dinners. These dates are arranged at the beginning of the season. Until the Roosevelt time they consisted of a Cabinet Dinner, a Diplomatic Dinner — always the most spectacular and important — and a dinner to the Supreme Court. Toward the end of the Roosevelt Administration there was added the Speaker's Dinner. This was brought about by the stubbornness of Speaker Cannon, who would not accept an invitation to any of the other dinners because he was not given the rank and precedence in the guest list to which he thought his position was entitled. Time and time again he had been invited and always regretted, at times going so far as to make inquiry in advance as to his rating on the guest list. The custom was in those days to rate him below the cabinet and the Supreme Court. So Mr. Roosevelt decided to place on the program a Speaker's Dinner and invite no one of higher rank than the Speaker. It was, so to speak, a dinner in his honor. This is the origin of the Speaker's Dinner, which remains to this day a part of the official list.

Thus from Roosevelt to Hoover we had four state dinners. The latter decided to add a dinner to the Vice-President. There were several motives for this change. Formerly the Vice-President had been invited to the Cabinet Dinner, where he took precedence over all the cabinet members in whose honor the dinner was given. This was resented by the cabinet members, especially by the Secretary of State. Mr. Hoover had been a cabinet member himself and must have realized the situation. Another reason, no doubt, was Hoover's apparent desire to modify in some way the old social customs. Yet on the whole I am inclined to believe that the chief factor in inaugurating the Vice-President's dinner was the Dolly Gann–Alice Longworth social feud. The feud was at its height at the beginning of the first social season in the Hoover Administration. The Hoovers wished to avoid any hasty decision, and yet the whole world of society was looking to the White House for any move that might seem to favor one or the other of the participants. With a dinner being given in honor of the Speaker, the Hoovers figured out it would be showing preference for the Longworth end of the controversy unless something was done for the Vice-President. Thus, on their first program a dinner to the Vice-President — which, of course, included Mrs. Gann — was arranged for. This seemed to allay any thought that the Hoovers might decide the controversy, and yet within the walls of the White House it continued to be a problem to avoid showing any favoritism. Every list that was made up for any purpose was closely scrutinized with an eye to avoiding decision as to the respective rights of the rival ladies.

The official or formal dinner list was now increased to five, and no doubt it will remain there for many years, for it is not easy to discontinue a practice of this kind once it is established. It is much easier to add a dinner than it is to discontinue one.

There are other formal dinners from time to time, principally in honor of important visitors from abroad. The largest and most brilliant dinner at the White House was the one given by the President and Mrs. Roosevelt to Prince Henry of Prussia. It was of such proportions that it had to be held in the East Room. There were one hundred covers — the first time that number had been seated at one table in the White House.

A JOB FOR THE USHER

Formal dinners at the White House are always named for eight o'clock. When a guest arrives he is shown to a cloak-room. After leaving his wraps he is given a card in an envelope. Upon opening it he sees a formation of the dinner-table with his place approximately marked thereon. If it is a mixed company, the place of the lady he is to escort to the table is also shown and her name written in the center.

The giving-out of these cards is often amusing, as the men peek into them to see with whom they are to spend the evening. Their remarks are many times both humorous and illuminating. Take, for instance, a Diplomatic Dinner. It is known in advance just about who is to be present. There are always a few members of the Diplomatic Corps who are none too popular, and it is a sort of lottery to see who will have to escort them. It has happened that, after looking at their cards, guests have become suddenly ill and departed with their wives, leaving apologies to be passed on. Guests have also been known to telephone in advance to ascertain who were their partners and after learning to send their regrets at the last minute.

At the conclusion of these preliminaries, the men join their wives and proceed to the main floor, assembling in either the Blue Room or the East Room. On the way, however, they are shown a large plot of the table, indicating the complete seating arrangement. This feature is always satisfactory to the guests and seems to add greatly to their comfort.

Upon arrival in the assembly room, the men are presented to the ladies who have been assigned to them, if they do not know them already, and there is a world of conversation. When all are present, the company is arranged in a semi-circle according to rank, each man having his lady on his right. The President and his wife are now announced and enter, preceded by the Military and Naval Aides. They 'make the circle,' as they say in Court parlance, passing around and shaking hands with each guest. The President precedes his wife. One aide makes the presentations to the President, the other to his wife. When the last guest has been greeted, one of the aides brings the ranking lady over to the President and the ranking man is brought over to the First Lady. At a given signal the band, which is always in attendance at these large dinners, strikes up a march and the procession is on to the dining-room. Here with the aid of the little card given in the cloak-room and the view of the dining-room from the chart, the guests go directly to their places at the table. There is seldom any confusion, and if there is, an usher is always on hand to straighten it out. The President upon reaching his place is immediately seated and the dinner is on.

ARRANGING AMERICA'S GREATEST DINNER PARTIES

For most dinners the long, straight table is used. This has a seating capacity of fifty normally and can be widened out to seat up to sixty. The larger circular table will comfortably seat ninety-two. It can be crowded to ninety-four or ninety-six. In seating guests at these tables space is tabulated by inches. About twenty-six inches is the normal seating space. More often than otherwise less space is allowed at White House dinners. In the Taft times I remember one dinner where the guests had only an average of nineteen inches. They were sitting on each other's laps.

In arranging for a State Dinner, the first thing to decide on is the table to be used. Generally the fifty-covers table is large enough; the exception is the Diplomatic Dinner for which invitations must be sent to every diplomatic mission in Washington. Either the ambassador, minister, or ranking official must be recognized. This forms the nucleus of the list for this particular dinner. A similar start is made for all State Dinners. The Supreme Court Dinner, the Cabinet Dinner, the dinner to the Vice-President or the Speaker or to a visiting notable is likewise started with an original list. If the dinner is planned for fifty and there are numerous regrets, their places are filled from time to time by sending out additional invitations. In the case of the Diplomatic Dinner, this is seldom done, since the diplomats are themselves numerous enough to make up the entire company. There is not much room left for Americans to be invited to meet them. As a rule invitations for this dinner, outside of the Diplomatic Corps, can be extended only to the Secretary of State, the Chairman of the Committee on Foreign Affairs, and the ranking minority members of both houses of Congress on this committee. Sometimes, if he be present in the city, a former Secretary of State may be invited.

FEEDING THE DIPLOMATS

This Diplomatic Dinner has been the worry of the White House for the past sixty years, no dining-room being large enough to accommodate it. It must be remembered that no country represented in Washington can be left out when these invitations are sent. The smallest rate along with the largest and greatest. Down through the years, especially the last twenty-five or thirty, the Diplomatic Corps has grown larger and larger. The old State Dining-Room served its purpose up to about the beginning of the present century. During the McKinley time it became absolutely inadequate and President McKinley decided to have the table arranged in the long corridor on the first floor. Thus, when the Roosevelts came, they found themselves dining in the hallway at all large affairs. Not pleased with this, they planned for the next large dinner to be given in the East Room. Everything went along well, the table looked beautiful, there was plenty of room, an elegant opportunity for decorative display, everything that the eye could wish for. The company assembled and were seated and the food was brought in. But it had to be brought a long way. The kitchen and pantry were on the farthest end of the house from the East Room. It was early discovered

Prepared for a State Dinner in McKinley's time

Between meals, in the Hoover administration

THE STATE DINING-ROOM

that the soup was cold, the fish quite as unpalatable, and the main course even worse. The ice cream was melted by the time it reached the guests and the President and Mrs. Roosevelt were in despair at the state of affairs. This was the first and last dinner that was ever attempted in the East Room.

The cry went up, What shall we do? President Roosevelt consulted the New York architects McKim, Mead, and White. They came to look the place over and offered several suggestions. It was finally decided to enlarge the old State Dining-Room by tearing out the north wall that had stood for a hundred years and adding the adjoining hall space to the old room. This necessitated so many material changes that before the job was finished practically the whole house had undergone a change. Among other things, the main stairway had to be moved from the extreme west end to practically the extreme east end, where it now stands. As President Roosevelt used to say, 'The White House was restored to what it was originally planned to be.' As I have heard him explain that down through the years, the old house had undergone such a change from administration to administration that it had lost all semblance of its original self. There was a slab placed in the floor of the main corridor at the time of this work with the numerals in bronze 1792–1902. Visitors are told that they represent 'the laying of the original cornerstone and the date when the house was remodeled during the Roosevelt time.'

FULL REGALIA

The members of the Diplomatic Corps always dress in their full regalia when attending formal or 'state functions' at the White House. At affairs like the Diplomatic Dinner, they put on the whole show, medals, side-arms and all, and carry their headdress on into the rooms. Some of the uniforms are very elaborate, especially compared with the American diplomats or even with the American service uniforms of the

Army and Navy. Many of the diplomats wear what is called 'court dress,' and they differ as much as one could possibly imagine. Some of the coats are covered entirely with gold braid, and the trousers are of brilliant colors such as red and yellow and bright blue. Yet the tendency is to get away from these things and come more to the American way of formal dark evening clothes. There used to be a time when nations like the Chinese, Siamese, Turks, Egyptians, and even the Japanese, would not appear except in the costumes of their native country. Now all of that is changed and almost everyone wears formal evening dress — white shirt-fronts and what Mr. Coolidge used to call 'shad-belly' coats. Their medals are pinned on these coats and form about the only decoration to remind one of the old days. The only exceptions nowadays are the Turk and the Egyptian, who still come in their native regalia, red fez and all. They are over-conspicuous in any company in these times.

MUSICALES AND MUSICIANS

Musicales were occasionally held by Mrs. Roosevelt, but it was the Tafts who began the present-day practice of having a musicale after each State Dinner. The Wilsons continued the custom. These two Administrations were the most appreciative of the musicales; the Hardings, the Coolidges, and the Hoovers were less interested in them.

The artists appearing at musicales are never paid. This rule is absolute. Generally they are anxious to come; more offer their services than can be utilized. This applies especially to the vast number who wish to advertise their wares. Every sort of freak wishes to appear before the President and his wife. Members of Congress and others often make appeal for this, that, or the other prodigy from their districts.

For many years the custom has been to permit the art department of Steinway and Sons, New York, to pass judgment on these matters. All requests for a chance to sing or play at the White House are referred to them, and often they appear before a representative of that firm to try out their talents. The Steinway firm receive no compensation for this other than the advertisement of their piano, which is always used on these occasions. They not only select the artists, having submitted in advance a list of the possibilities for any musicales to the President's wife, but they pay their expenses to and from Washington and during the time they are there. Many of the most famous musicians are really anxious to be of service to the President and his wife, so there is no need to accept other than the very best. They invariably consider it a great honor to perform for the head of the nation and any company he may select.

Yet, generally speaking, these famed artists get very little consideration for the free service they render. During the Taft and Wilson Administrations they were presented with gold medals, costing about fifty dollars each. No others were so considerate. Of recent years they have been presented with an autographed photograph of the President and his wife. The privilege of singing or playing, and a little supper afterwards, has been about their only reward.

CONTRAST WITH THE OLD DAYS

The difference between the receptions and other social affairs of today and those of twenty-five or thirty years ago lies in the fact that the present ones are over-regulated, while in the old days there was the utmost freedom of action for all the guests. Also the vast increase in the staff of attendants — 'Aides to the President,' 'White House Aides,' and even private soldiers — who stand around ostensibly to manage the guests, detracts from everyone's pleasure and comfort. In every doorway there stands a figure in uniform to bar one's passage unless one is among the privileged few who can go anywhere.

In the old days the entire guard consisted of an usher or

two with a uniformed policeman here and there in case of emergency. At the receptions the guests roamed everywhere at will, and the 'behind the line' group, made up of a more cosmopolitan crowd, added immensely to the occasion.

The reason for this is that the service people are getting more and more into the limelight in White House affairs. The Army and the Navy like to shine socially and are very clannish. Each new administration bows to their suggestions and the White House families seem more impressed by a uniform than they used to be.

The Diplomatic Dinners of the old days were never complete without certain delicacies. First, there must always be orchids of the rarest type on the table. These 'Callaya' orchids were scarce and expensive, costing from a dollar to a dollar and a half apiece. Then the diplomats must have an appetizer of caviar, and none but the imported would do. Terrapin, too, must always be served, cooked with the finest sherry wine. Then the best brand of champagne must be procured, regardless of labor or expense.

Thank goodness, all that has changed. The foreign diplomats now sit down to a good old-fashioned State Dinner, the same as is served to our own officials, and they enjoy it.

CONGRESSWOMEN AND PRECEDENCE

With the coming of the first Congresswomen, a situation comparable to the Gann–Longworth feud arose. Where did they rank? It was several years before it was settled where they were to be placed in relation to the wives of members of the Senate and the House. It was easy among the members themselves, for they took their place according to length of service. But when it came to seating them at a dinner party with other women, it was another question.

In the beginning it was decided that the wives of Representatives and Senators should hold the rank of their husbands and the lady Congresswomen would be seated accordingly in relation to them. But the Congresswomen took issue with this and a new shuffle was demanded. They were backed in their contention by the Senators' wives, who felt they alone should take precedence over the Congresswomen. For a time this order prevailed. With the coming of the formal social season the Congresswomen insisted they be given their official status as elective officers and demanded rank above all women of the legislative branch of the Government with the exception of the wife of the Vice-President and of the Speaker. There was then a general mix-up and nobody knew where to seat them. Parties were disrupted in an effort to invite only those about whom there would be no argument.

It was not until the second year of the Hoover Administration that the question was definitely settled. At one of their Sunday night parties the matter presented itself. After an all-day search for precedents, the President and Mrs. Hoover finally decided to give Congresswomen precedence over the wives of all members and Senators, and Mrs. Ruth Pratt, the lady Congresswoman from New York, was the first one accorded the honor at the White House.

THE RECEPTION OF MRS. DE PRIEST

All the criticism of the reception of Mrs. De Priest, the wife of the Negro Representative from Illinois, was quite unnecessary. Mrs. Hoover had decided to invite all the Congressional ladies to a series of teas and the families of the different Senators and members of the House were allotted to four groups and invited accordingly, the cabinet ladies being asked to all the parties. The name of Mrs. De Priest was put aside for future consideration when these groups were made up. Everyone concerned realized that it was an unusual situation. Should Mrs. De Priest be included? The decision was postponed, for there was no precedent to go by.

Thus the four parties to Congressional ladies came and went and Mrs. De Priest was invited to none of them.

In the meantime the discussion as to what to do continued. The social secretary who had charge of these affairs took the position that she must be invited, since the parties were of an official nature. Precedents were sought, but none could be found that definitely applied. The nearest approach seemed to be the Booker Washington affair in the Roosevelt Administration. I was asked if I knew of any such entertaining since, but I did not. The records were searched for parallel cases among members of the Diplomatic Corps from the so-called Negro Republics of South America. The official angle was referred to the Executive Offices, one of the President's secretaries pondering over it for days and days. Mrs. Hoover seemed to have an open mind and was willing to be guided by whatever course was mapped out for her. However, when it was at last decided in the affirmative, she seemed hesitant and began to figure how it could be done.

After much discussion pro and con, she decided to give an extra party for Mrs. De Priest. A few chosen guests would be informed in advance of the situation.

According to plans, several days before the time set the social secretary who had been handling the matter went around personally to invite and explain to those who had been selected to take part. A small company had been chosen, with an idea that they would help out in an embarrassing situation.

All arrived on schedule with a look of expectancy on their faces. They were evidently prepared for almost anything and appreciated that they were taking part in a most unusual affair. The police officers on the outside and the doormen on the inside had been cautioned to be careful when a colored lady should present herself and say she had an appointment with Mrs. Hoover, lest they create a scene by refusing her admittance.

The guests assembled in the East Room. Mrs. Hoover was to receive in the Green Room and pass the guests on to the Red Room for tea. Mrs. De Priest was introduced to the others present and the reception immediately began. Being the lowest in rank of the official ladies, she had to await her turn while the others were being shown in.

After a few minutes of conversation with Mrs. Hoover, Mrs. De Priest moved on to the Red Room, where she was served a cup of tea in regular form. It can be stated that Mrs. De Priest conducted herself with perfect propriety. She really seemed the most composed one in the group. She certainly acted her part. In a short while Mrs. Hoover retired from the room, and Mrs. De Priest in perfect form made her exit, no doubt to the relief of all and yet leaving behind a feeling of admiration at the way she conducted herself.

33

GUESTS AT THE WHITE HOUSE

'MR. PRESIDENT'

GUESTS at the White House are never perfectly natural and inwardly comfortable. All are more or less thrilled and feel a certain awe at the approach to one so high in the responsibilities of the country, in fact of the world. Even those who have known the President and his wife intimately before they came into office undergo a change when they enter the White House. It is now 'Mr. President' with about everybody, and the phrase carries with it a hesitancy that is hard to understand and harder to explain. Few continue to use such salutations as 'Governor,' 'Chief,' or 'Boss,' and these few have to force themselves to do so. Even in the case of wives who have been accustomed to 'Theodore,' 'Woodrow,' 'Will,' 'Calvin,' or 'Herbert,' in referring to their husbands, now gradually change to 'The President.' It is interesting to see how those who have decided to go on in the same old way find it quite impossible in the new surroundings. Most friends and acquaintances are of course glad of the opportunity to say 'Mr. President,' but it is a long time before they do it naturally. To an usher who meets and arranges for the reception of all who come to the White House, it is clear how uncomfortable some of the guests are. Others are more composed, but they all feel a hesitancy lest they fail to do just what is right or lest something is expected from them that they do not know about. It is common for visitors to ask what to do, how to act, how to address the President and his wife, and dozens of other questions along the same line. It is a good usher who can make these guests even partly comfortable.

One of the pleasures of meeting these people is to note the exaltation in which they hold, without exception, the occupant of the office of President of the United States. The feeling of dignity when they come into his presence is always evident. Even during the Harding Administration, where familiarity was the watchword, there was always the same respectful approach to the President.

A WHITE HOUSE WELCOME

A guest upon arriving at the White House is met at the front door by one of the ushers. His coming has been made known to the Chief Usher's Office, and the type of invitation, whether just for dinner and night or for an extended visit. A room or rooms have been assigned by the wife of the President and he is shown here upon his arrival. I have an opportunity at this time to acquaint the guest with the time of meals. I do my best to make him comfortable and plan for him to put in the time when he will not be with the President and his wife.

The domestics do not know the person who is coming. They know someone is to arrive, for the word has gone forth to prepare the room the guest is to occupy. In the case of notable guests from afar almost everybody knows of their coming, for it is generally heralded in advance by the newspapers. Still they are not treated differently from the general run of guests. Once within the portals of the White House, the preliminary formalities being over, they all receive the same consideration. This treatment is very simple and very democratic.

The matter of an invitation to a woman alone is just the same as for a man. She is given the same consideration, met in the same way, advised in the same capacity as best a man can to a woman, especially in the way of dress, etc. The only difference might be that the wife of the President would perhaps try to see her sooner after her arrival than in the case of a man alone. A man is often left to shift for himself for hours after his arrival. To illustrate: He might arrive on one of the trains from New York reaching Washington at four, five, or six o'clock. The President — Hoover, for instance — always stayed at his office until six o'clock or after. Mrs. Hoover very seldom saw a guest arriving at the above times before dinner at eight o'clock. The President upon coming to the house would be told the guest had arrived and it was up to him to decide whether or not he would see him before dinner. If so he would go to his study and the guest would join him there. If not he would go direct to his private rooms and not see the guest until a few minutes before dinner-time.

In the case of guests like Queen Marie and the Prince of Wales, there is naturally special preparation made for their entertainment. The best foot is put forward. The best linen is got out, a more elaborate menu prepared, and the best clothes put on. Just as in a private household the White House occupants fix up for company, and the more important the company, the more fixing up goes on.

SPEEDING THE PARTING GUEST

Terminating a visit or an audience with a guest is easy. He is always anxious to know what to do and how to do it. He does not wish to make a mistake. There are hardly any exceptions to this rule, no matter how well the guest knows or is known to the family. We gather from suggestions, and many times diplomatically inquire of the President or his wife, how long they wish to be with a person or how long the visit of a house guest is supposed to be. If but an interview, we are generally told it will last for ten, fifteen, twenty or more minutes. At the end of that time we walk into the room, announce another appointment, whether one really exists or not, the President and his wife arise, and the audience is terminated. In the case of a house guest, it is a simple matter to inquire as to his plans and ask if you are privileged to do anything for him. This always leads around to the length of his stay and you can pin him down, almost from the beginning, as to the very hour of his departure. Often this information is conveyed to the head of the household and you find that the guest is desired to stay longer. It is one of the pleasant duties of the job to pass on this information. Guests are always flattered when they learn their continued presence is desired. It is an easy matter to arrange just as the President or his wife wish.

HOW THE PRESIDENTS TREATED THEIR GUESTS

Most families make plans to entertain their guests in the White House.

The Harrisons, Clevelands, McKinleys and Roosevelts were extremely considerate and solicitous.

The Tafts were good hosts.

The Wilsons had few guests outside the family.

The Hardings overdid it.

The Coolidges made few plans for their guests. They just let them drift, never meeting them except by chance, as it were, and at meals.

Hoover seemed indifferent toward his guests.

TIPPING

The practice of tipping at the White House is discouraged but not prohibited. Very few guests do it. Generally guests who wish to tip inquire as to its propriety. We always tell them that it is not necessary, but that if they wish to show their appreciation for any special service they may do so. There is no general tipping scheme like that in European Courts. This situation somehow makes the guests a little more comfortable in their dealings with the employees of the household. It would be easy to wring from any of the guests a substantial tip, for they are always very appreciative of what is done for them. A few insist upon leaving what they call 'a piece of money' for 'the boys.' However, I can positively state that they get no better service during their stay or on a return visit than anyone else.

Wilson's visit to Europe and MacDonald's to America provide a striking contrast between American and European customs. Wilson, as was expected, left a generous tip at every place he stopped. On the other hand, when Prime Minister MacDonald visited President Hoover at the White House, he gave not one cent to a single employee. Furthermore, he never inquired at the White House as to the practice, having apparently been advised in advance. I can picture his surprise when he learned of this American custom, so different from what he had known.

34

CLIMBERS AND CRASHERS

THE COMMONEST FORM OF GATE-CRASHING

ABOUT every visitor to Washington wants to see — and expects to see — the President and his wife. Some are more forward than others. Often they seek out the opportunity through their Representative in Congress or another official. Many write direct, saying they will be in Washington on such and such days and would like an appointment. Some tourists are satisfied to hang around the White House just for a glimpse of either the President or his wife. Sundays especially, when there is generally an excursion to Washington from one of the larger cities, the people assemble around the White House about church time. Often there are several thousand of them and their presence is generally recognized by a bow and tip of the hat from the President and a wave of the hand from his wife. Some Presidents notice these gatherings more than others. Wilson always greeted them pleasantly, but in a very dignified manner. Hoover seemed to notice them least of all. We often tried to get him to show some recognition, but a nod of the head was about his limit. Roosevelt was great at greeting them, waving his arms and showing his teeth. Harding once said, 'If these people want to see me, why should I not see them?' This disposition was a great help to those of us around the White House, since we did not have to get people out of his way when he came along.

Uninvited persons often attend White House receptions. They 'crash the gates,' not by slipping in unnoticed, but by misrepresenting themselves in some way. With each invitation there is a card of admission made out in the guest's name, to be presented at a certain entrance, each entrance having a different colored card. These cards are often presented by people to whom they have not been issued, for it is impossible for one doorman to know all of the three or four thousand persons who have been invited. Members of the House of Representatives are the worst offenders. When they find it inconvenient to attend, they pass the card on to a friend or acquaintance from back home. People seem to feel it is all right to do this, on the theory that anything to do with the President is public property. It is a difficult situation to overcome, since but a very small proportion of the four hundred and thirty-five members of the House are personally known. To illustrate: There is a list of invited guests at the entrance. An official arrives who has apparently honestly mislaid or forgotten to bring his card of admission. He presents himself and gives his name; a glance at the list confirms his claims. If he looks the part he will be admitted, and a note made of the fact. Thus, when his card is found the next day among those that have been taken up, we know that it has been presented by someone else. This can be readily understood by one who has attended a White House reception when he recalls the great rush at the entrances, with a thousand or more people trying to get in all at one time, and a line of automobiles blocks long still in waiting.

SOCIAL CLIMBERS

There are many 'social climbers' who seek entrance to the White House. They try to get in for private visits as well as for the formal social affairs. Every pretext is used in an effort to obtain this privilege. The ladies of the White House are importuned constantly to receive people for no purpose in the world except that they may say they have been received by the First Lady of the Land. These people will advertise the fact through various channels, especially through the social columns of the papers. It is no uncommon thing for

guests at dinner, for example, to call up the newspaper women and tell them they dined at the White House at such and
such a time. This gives the news-gatherers a tip and they inquire further and obtain the names of other guests and publish an entire list when it had not been given out at the White
House at all, perhaps because there was some reason for not
wishing it published.

The social secretaries and others are kept busy looking up
people who ask for appointments, to see whether their credentials are sufficient and proper and whether they rate an
audience. The privilege has been so grossly abused that it
has become absolutely necessary to find out whether the one
seeking an audience is not doing so for private advertising
purposes. It is a great help for one in quest of favors elsewhere to say, 'I have come from the White House, where I
was received by Mrs. So-and-So.' The requests for invitations
to the formal receptions and musicales are far in excess of the
capacity of the establishment, but the members of Congress
and other Government officials do not seem to realize this.
Congressmen especially make so many requests for their con-
stituents who happen to be in Washington during the social
season that it has been found necessary to close the list to further additions even before it is really opened. A refusal from
one of the staff many times prompts the Congressman to go
higher up, to the Secretary to the President or even to the
President himself. These cases are not unusual. They are
numerous beyond the thought of the lay mind. There are
many private girls' schools in and about Washington whose
pupils come from various States. They are more or less in the
social care of the Representatives of their districts, and so
many used to receive invitations that the receptions took on
the appearance of being school-girl receptions. A rule was
adopted, and is still in force, that no invitations would be issued to persons under eighteen years of age and none to pupils in schools. This caused a howl for a time and still does
occasionally. There are many subterfuges resorted to to

evade the rule. One of the most common is for some of these girls to be house guests of members of Congress and others in official life. Then a request is made for their house guests and it cannot be consistently denied when the officials themselves have invitations to a party. In some instances deliberate falsehood has been resorted to. At almost any large reception can be seen a number of young girls who range in age from fourteen to sixteen years, proving that someone has misstated the facts.

A DISSEMBLING JURIST AND A DETERMINED LADY

At times it is interesting to observe and follow through denials for invitations. One eminent jurist, for example, had requested invitations for a Mr. and Mrs. So-and-So and had been told the list was closed. That same evening the jurist appeared with his wife and said he had lost his card of admission. Being well known he was promptly admitted, but another couple who presented this very card of admission a few minutes later were held up. Upon inquiry they said the card had been given them by the jurist, and after some argument and explanation and owing to the prominence of the jurist, the couple were admitted. That particular jurist never received an invitation to any of the other parties during that Administration. The strange part of it lies in the fact that he did not, as is so often the case, lodge a complaint. His friends had evidently told him what happened to them and it served as a reminder, when other parties came along, of why he did not receive the coveted invitation.

Another interesting case was that of a lady who was a sister of a member of Congress. She had been in departmental service and had been let out. No doubt she tried all means to get back, including the influence of her brother. Finally she came to the White House in an effort to get Roosevelt to help her. She was interviewed by one of the secretaries, and, when told she could not see the President, she became quite violent and abusive—so much so that it was embarrassing to the secretary and he walked away from her, remarking on the way to a secret service man and a policeman, 'You will have to take care of her.' This they attempted to do, but without success. They tried to quiet her, but the more they tried, the more boisterous and abusive she became. They asked her to leave, and when she refused, declaring she would not leave until she had seen the President, they took hold of her and endeavored to lead her away. At first she went along, protesting, but halfway to the guard-room she refused to go farther. A number of newspaper men and others had followed when she left the Executive Offices. When she reached this halfway point, she deliberately lay down on the stone pavement and refused to get up. There was nothing to do but to pick her up and several men proceeded to assist in the operation. One of them, unfortunately, was a Negro butler. She was taken on to the guard-room, her people telephoned, and for the time being all was straightened out. But the newspapers published the story, the opposition press especially. The facts were exaggerated in more ways than one, particular emphasis being laid on the fact that she had been ejected by a Negro. The secretary who had the case was abused right and left. Continual reference to it made the poor man so miserable that he asked to be transferred, and his request was granted. He was appointed postmaster of Washington.

It was a long time before the incident died out, and to this day it forms an example of how careful one has to be when he is right under the eyes of the news writers.

WHITE HOUSE INTRUDERS WHO GOT IN

While Harrison was sitting on the South Porch one evening, a man, afterwards learned to be the son of a certain Southern Senator, jumped over the iron fence, came right up to the President, and engaged him in conversation. The guards in those times were few and far between. The man was drunk and harmless. His conversation was in regard to getting a position. The President calmly talked with him and eventually rang the bell to the Usher's Room. He stated the man had escaped the notice of the guard and suggested diplomatically that he be taken care of. No blame was placed on the guard, since it was not remarkable for such a thing to happen in those days, when less attention was paid to the protection of the President. The entire outside detail consisted of three officers and one watchman. It was a few years later, at the coming of Coxey's Army, during the Cleveland Administration, that the detail was increased, and it has since grown to the present force of practically fifty members, in addition to a dozen or more secret service men.

Another intruder came in on Roosevelt. Again it was in the evening. The President was accustomed to having many appointments along between nine and ten o'clock. Most of these would be known of in advance, but sometimes other people would appear who had been told by the President to come at a certain time. This evening a taxi drove up to the front door and out stepped a man in full evening dress, cloak, and high hat. He approached the police officer standing at the front door and said he had an appointment with the President. He was asked to leave his coat and hat and was invited to the Red Room. The usher on duty went to the second floor, where the President was reading, and advised him Mr. John Smith was in the Red Room and stated he had an appointment. The President said at first that he knew of no such man, but as the usher started to leave the room, he called him back and said he would go down and see the man, for he had a faint recollection of telling someone to come in at that time. Thus he was taken down and formally introduced. The President invited the caller to have a seat and the usher retired.

It was only a few minutes before my bell rang summoning me to the Red Parlor, and as I entered the President walked toward me, saying quietly, 'Take this crank out of here.' He

left the room through another door. Of course the man was
taken care of and, among other things, when searched, he was
found to possess a gun of large caliber tucked away in his rear
pocket. There was much excitement when the affair became
known and much investigating, which led to the usher's being relieved from duty for thirty days without pay.

The third and last happening of this kind in my experience
occurred just after Mr. Hoover came into office.

Once more it was evening. Within a week after the President came to the White House to live, a strange man walked
into the dining-room where he was seated at dinner with
eight or ten guests. It was startling and almost beyond belief, with a colored doorman and a police officer stationed at
the entrance and a secret service man and an experienced
usher seated not twenty feet away, all with responsibility to
see that no stranger entered. Nor must one forget that there
was a policeman stationed just outside the door, in the drive-
way that approaches the porch.

The circumstances as established afterwards were as follows: A man without hat or overcoat appeared in the dining-
room while all were seated at the dinner-table. The President
looked up and inquired, 'What do you want?' The man said,
'I want to see you.' The President remarked, 'I have no appointment with you.' The man said, 'You better have an appointment with me!' and walked over toward the President,
seated at the table. The intruder's hand was extended as if
to shake hands. Even the butlers were out of the room when
he entered and they returned just as he made this last move.
The President just looked, but Mrs. Hoover spoke up and
said to one of the butlers, 'Get the secret service man.' With
this the other guests became more or less excited, and all began to talk out loud, which drew the attention of the four
men who were within earshot. They all rushed for the dining-room, but in the meantime one of the butlers had walked
over to the intruder and pushed him toward the door from
which he had entered. It was here he was found when these

guardians of the President reached the spot. Of course there was consternation. How could it have happened? The possibilities were startling. The man could have done any harm he had seen fit to do.

There were all kinds of questioning, all kinds of excuses, a world of explanations, but to this day it cannot be intelligently explained how it could have occurred.

Fortunately, the man turned out to be an innocent sightseer, unarmed and harmless. One of those peculiar people who go until they are stopped and who nose around at all hours of the day and night. He had come to Washington from Philadelphia during the day and registered at one of the cheaper hotels. Starting out without hat or coat, he went to look around and wended his way to the White House, attracted no doubt by the lights. He just walked up the roadway, up to the porch unseen by the officer there, and on into the house. The doors were thrown open, for the weather was warm. A policeman and doorman were seated on a bench a little off to the side. The intruder had got in quite a distance (and here the story varies) before he was noticed. Halfway across the entrance corridor he was observed by the officer sitting on the bench, who nudged the colored doorman sitting beside him and inquired, 'Who is that fellow?' Looking up and seeing a man without either hat or overcoat, with his hands behind him, walking across the hall and on to the dining-room, he answered, 'It is one of the secret service men.' Neither of them made a move to ascertain the truth of the guess. The doorman was seemingly satisfied and the officer accepted his explanation.

The man walked in a leisurely fashion down the entire length of the hall looking here and there, until he came into the dining-room. He was seized, of course, and taken to the guard-room, afterwards being released with a warning. And yet he could not be blamed; he was just doing what thousands of others would like to do and would do if they could get away with it. The net result was the sending away of the two policemen and a censure for the secret service man. All hands were naturally more careful afterwards.

SOUVENIR HUNTERS

Relic hunters are numerous, but not so bad now as they used to be in days gone by. Objects made from the original timbers of the White House, removed from time to time in the course of improvements, are prized souvenirs. Canes, paper-cutters, etc., made from the old flooring have been given to friends of the families during several administrations. Mrs. Hoover had book-ends made from some of the heavy timbers and distributed them among her friends, including all cabinet officers, at Christmas, 1930. She also gave the President at the same time a large nut-bowl made of this wood. The people generally, the sight-seeing visitors, are always looking for relics. You can often see them pick up a withered flower or a strand from one of the rugs. Several of the old original mantels have had pieces chipped from them. It is not unusual to have tassels clipped from the draperies, and even the tapestry was cut from chairs on several occasions. Every year in the check-up of property there are always a lot of spoons missing, probably taken as souvenirs. Napkins also find their way into the hands of visitors. On one occasion, when the soldiers' lawn party was moved from the garden indoors on account of a sudden rain, about all of the silver spoons, salt spoons, etc., disappeared from the sideboard of the dining-room. The interesting thing about this incident was that the boys took them back to the several hospitals and presented them to their nurses. In this wise they were almost all returned to the White House and everything went off good-naturedly.

It is a peculiar condition of mind that people have. They feel privileged to help themselves to small articles around the White House. They feel they have a part ownership, and if they can slip a small souvenir in their pockets they do not hesitate. Cards marking the various ornaments, furniture, etc., in the so-called public part of the house disappear just about as fast as they are placed. Even a piece of the stationery is considered a great prize. Every guest who stops in the White House makes it a practice to write to about everybody he knows on White House stationery.

EMBARRASSMENT OF RICHES

Salesmen as a rule do not bother the President or his wife. Occasionally one comes along, but he does not get very far, for several reasons. First, appointments must be made in advance, especially if the person is a stranger, and the object of the appointment stated. They get stopped right there. Many things are sent with the idea of having an acknowledgment that may be used for just such a purpose, and many things are sent back for that very reason. When things are accepted, it is always with the distinct understanding that there will be no advertising of the fact. There is hardly a firm in the country that would not gladly furnish their product, gratis, just to have it used by the occupants of the White House. This is amply illustrated by the presence there now of such things as automobiles, electrical refrigerators, pianos and other articles, large and small, that have never cost the Government or the President one penny. Some administrations are more prone to accept favors of this sort than others. Wilson especially discouraged this practice, and on one occasion made the public remark that he did not wish so much as a potato given to him. The Hoovers, too, were very averse to receiving presents, and yet, in both cases, much was forced on them which they could not politely decline. On the other hand, there are administrations who encourage this practice. It seemed to be the rule during both the Taft and Coolidge times that if people wished to send presents, let them come and they will be received. Gifts for the table were very common — fruit, vegetables, nuts, turkeys, cakes, candies, and so on. Everybody who raises a big apple or potato seems to think it ought to be sent to the President. Hunters like to send the specimens of their prowess in the way of birds, ducks, and large game. Bear meat, elephant meat, deer meat, large fish, and many novelties like mushrooms, persimmons, and grapes, come from time to time. There is no end to such giving and more often than otherwise it is a burden to the household.

35

AS WE SAW THEM

RESPECT FOR THE OFFICE, NOT THE MAN

GENERALLY speaking, the respect for the President is for the office. Right or wrong, with the older employees especially it is always 'The President.' My feeling is that regardless of the personality or name of the incumbent, no matter who might occupy the office, the same feeling would exist on the part of the employees. Of course they have personal favorites, and some do stand out in memory as being more agreeable than others, but at the time of their incumbency there is always loyalty for 'The President' and it carries with it a faithfulness to the office much more than to the man. In my day I think Roosevelt has been the most popular man among the employees. Not that he was the greatest during that time, but that his way of doing things appealed to them and left with them personal memories that live down through the years.

THE SYSTEM IS THE BOSS

The real boss at the White House is the system that prevails. To illustrate: A family comes in like the Tafts or Hoovers, who are familiar with the details of White House operations. They have seen them, lived them, acted them, and disapproved of them. They would change. For a few weeks everything seems different. New ideas are tried, new ways are suggested, and an honest attempt is made to carry them out. But it must be remembered that more often than not these same ideas and ways have been tried before. Down through the years practically everything has been attempted. So the members of the new Administration gradually get away from these new ideas, many times unconsciously, and adapt themselves to the very ways that have been formerly disapproved of. They now adopt the old ideas as their own and feel happy in the thought that everything goes on so well. Thus the system is the master.

On the other hand, the McKinleys, the Wilsons, and the Coolidges came in and took just what was set before them and were equally successful and much more comfortable.

SATISFACTION WORKING WITH ADMINISTRATIONS

There is much more satisfaction working with some administrations than with others. And it is not dependent on the amount of work one does. Under one administration the daily grind may not be hard and yet the hours may be laborious; under another, one may put in much longer and fuller hours and yet the satisfaction obtained will more than make up for it. It was fine to work there during the Cleveland and the Roosevelt régimes. And even during the Wilson days one found worlds of satisfaction in accomplishment. On the other hand, a day was just a day during the Taft, Coolidge, and Hoover time. The broad contrast of the Coolidge and Hoover Administrations along that line was remarkable. In the former, generally speaking, there was nothing to do. In the latter there was everything to do and yet, at the end of a day, a month, or a year, there was the same little feeling of a lack of complete satisfaction with what had been accomplished.

TOKENS OF ESTEEM

All Presidents gave turkeys at Christmas to employees, up to the Harding time. I got turkeys for thirty Christmas seasons before the custom was given up.

When the Wilsons left, they gave everybody in the house, high and low, a United States Government bond, ranging in value from fifty dollars to five hundred dollars. Roosevelt gave presents. I received a large silver bowl engraved 'From T. R.'

RECORDS

The record for changing secretaries is held by Taft. He had four: Frank Carpenter, Charles Norton, Charles Hilles, Carmi Thompson. The reason for this frequent shifting was not unsatisfactory service, but political expediency.

The record for military aides is held by Coolidge, and the number is again four: Sherrill, Cheney, Winship, and Latrobe.

THE PRESIDENT IN DOMESTIC AFFAIRS

Not all the Presidents took an interest in domestic affairs. With Harrison, Cleveland, McKinley, one hardly knew they were in the house. Roosevelt, though one knew he was there, never worried with routine or details. Taft and Coolidge took notice of everything, butted in. Wilson took notice, but never butted in; he left details and routine for the women.

The employees in the house were afraid of some Presidents. Harrison was distant but respected. Cleveland just went about his way and was perfectly satisfied with very little; McKinley was easy-going, and just so long as Mrs. Mc-Kinley had her every wish seemed to care about nothing else. Neither meddled in domestic affairs and both were admired and loved by all. Roosevelt inspired everybody. All looked up to him and admired him. Wilson was respected, more for his apparent superior fitness for big things. He was not overliked, yet everyone looked up to him and thought of him respectfully and even tenderly while he was ill. Taft and

Coolidge were about alike in mixing up in routine domestic affairs. Taft talked more, while Coolidge just grunted about them. Coolidge was the hardest of all to please and the least thought of by the employees. He was so severe that everyone shunned him when it was possible. Many times he was positively unkind and his wishes were so peculiar he was positively impossible.

HOW THEY TREATED THE STAFF

Most Presidents at least passed the time of day upon first meeting the help, but Hoover seldom did so. Certainly he never took the initiative. If he was addressed, a low murmur would come from him that was seemingly forced or dragged out. He seldom engaged in any conversation with the employees, making his wants known in the simplest way and quite satisfied with the usual routine of doing things. Other Presidents were very different. Roosevelt made the employees' interests his own. Wilson went out of his way to get acquainted and knew everyone better than most Presidents. He took a peculiar pride in knowing them personally. Coolidge, with all his reputation for being sphinx-like, saw fit to go out of his way to find out about the people around him. It was one of his diversions to jest with them, and many is the time he saw fit to play jokes on them.

The earlier Presidents treated the employees almost as members of the family. Of course, there were not so many of them in those days and the task was not so difficult. Still the employees look forward to some recognition and appreciate it more than the heads of the household ever know. As a rule the ladies of the household are very kind to the people about the place. It would be hard to differentiate between them, but Mrs. Cleveland, Mrs. Roosevelt, the second Mrs. Wilson were unusually so. All the old employees swear by these three ladies.

THE LOYALTY OF THE WHITE HOUSE EMPLOYEES

This brings us to the question of how faithful the White House employees are. As a whole they are exceptionally so. They seem to feel and appreciate the importance and responsibility of their positions. Especially among the older employees, those who have been through several administrations, is there a loyalty born of time and experience. Administrations change from one political faith to another, but these old fellows go on serving faithfully. When you consider the importance of their positions, it is truly interesting to note how seldom the trust has ever been violated. Newspaper men are all about looking for something different and unusual, and holding up these people, as it were, in an effort to obtain something sensational to publish. It is no secret that Presidents do things and have people in to see them that they do not wish the world to know about. It is on such matters as this that you find the employees about the place most solicitous that the wishes of the President shall not be betrayed. There are many occasions — for example, during the oil investigation — when confidences and appointments at the White House would have been of great interest to many people. Again, a list of names of those who had been called to the White House in conference would tell to the wise ones the trend of happenings, and perhaps influence their action in the stock market. In such cases you will find the employees silent. Without word or suggestion from anyone, they seem to understand the importance of holding their tongues. No words of praise are too much for them. They are true patriots serving the cause of their Chief and their Government.

THE END

INDEX

INDEX

Daugherty, Harry M., Attorney-General, 87, 249
Davis, Dr., of Philadelphia, 102
Davis, James John, Secretary of Labor, 154, 162
Davis, Mrs. James John, 162
Dawes, Charles G., 140, 149, 171, 173, 214, 215, 247, 249
Dawes, Mrs. Charles G., 140, 149
De Priest, Mrs., 301-03
Dilhing, Mildred, 205
Dimmick, Mrs., niece of Mrs. Benjamin Harrison (1), later Mrs. Benjamin Harrison (2), 9, 11, 46, 236
Dogs in the White House, 271
Donovan, Mike, 31

Eating and drinking, 286-90
Edge, Walter E., Senator, 249
Edwards, Gen. Clarence, 45, 237
Executive Offices, 257

Fall, Albert Bacon, 249
Fess, Simon D., Representative, 169
Fletcher, Henry P., 249
Fletcher, Mrs., social secretary, 204
Flowers, at the White House, 16, 17
Forbes, Col. Charles, Veterans' Bureau, 250
Ford, Henry, 4, 113, 209
Formalities, 265, 266
Forster, Rudolf, Assistant Secretary, 49
Frelinghuysen, Joseph S., Senator, 249

Gallagher, Mike, 250
Galt, Mrs. Edith Bolling, 62-75. See also Wilson, Mrs. Woodrow (2)
Gann, Mr., 202
Gann, Mrs. Dolly, 188, 202
Garfield, Harry A., 30, 31, 237
Garner, John N., 216, 221, 222
'Gate-crashing,' 309, 310
Gibbons, James, Cardinal, 111
Gifts to the President, 207, 208, 318, 319
Gillett, Frederick H., Speaker, 249
Grandi, Dino, 212
Grant, Joe, wrestler, 31, 32

Grayson, Dr. Cary, 58, 62, 64, 68, 101, 102, 105, 107, 249
Guests at the White House, 304-08

Hacket, Chauncey, 52
Hale, Frederick, Senator, 127
Haley, James M., 133
Halford, Mrs. Elijah Walker, 11
Hammond, John Hays, 162
Hammond, Mrs. John Hays, 162
Hanna, Mark (Marcus Alonzo), 87
Harbord, Gen. James Guthrie, 249
Hard, Will, 250
Harding, Warren G., 87, 113, 114, 133, 155; comparisons and verdicts, 231-45, 249-55, 260-64, 267-73, 286, 287, 290, 307, 309
Harding, Mrs. Warren G., 17, 114, 235, 238, 240, 254, 274, 275, 278, 279, 285
Harrison, Benjamin, 3, 6-11, 87, 109, 133; comparisons and verdicts, 231-33, 236-39, 246-50, 253-56, 261, 268-73, 286-90, 307, 322
Harrison, Mrs. Benjamin (1), 8, 10, 11, 17, 109, 274, 278, 279
Harrison, Mrs. Benjamin (2), 11, 46, 47
Harvey, George, 170, 250
Hays, Will, 249
Hearst, William Randolph, 216
Henry, Prince of Prussia, 207, 293
Hilles, Charles, Secretary, 49, 56, 322
Hills, Mrs., of Northampton, 142
Hoover, Allan, 219
Hoover, Herbert C., American Food Administrator, 78, 87; President, 122, 188-227; Secretary of Commerce, 170-80; comparisons and verdicts, 231-34, 238-44, 248-56, 259-67, 271, 272, 286, 287, 290, 313-17, 323
Hoover, Mrs. Herbert C., 121-23, 182-213, 219, 220, 224-27, 236, 254, 257, 258, 261, 276-79, 282-86, 301-03
Hoover, Irwin H., helps install electric lights and bells at White House, 3-6; electrician at White House, 6; Chief Usher at White House, 7, 35 n.